IMAGINING SOCIETY

The Case for Sociology

Daniel Nehring and Dylan Kerrigan

BRISTOL
UNIVERSITY
PRESS

First published in Great Britain in 2020 by

Bristol University Press
1-9 Old Park Hill
Bristol
BS2 8BB
UK
t: +44 (0)117 954 5940
www.bristoluniversitypress.co.uk

North America office:
c/o The University of Chicago Press
1427 East 60th Street
Chicago, IL 60637, USA
t: +1 773 702 7700
f: +1 773-702-9756
sales@press.uchicago.edu
www.press.uchicago.edu

© Bristol University Press 2020

British Library Cataloguing in Publication Data
A catalogue record for this book is available from the British Library

Library of Congress Cataloging-in-Publication Data
A catalog record for this book has been requested

ISBN 978-1-5292-0487-2 hardcover
ISBN 978-1-5292-0490-2 paperback
ISBN 978-1-5292-0491-9 ePub
ISBN 978-1-5292-0493-3 ePdf

The right of Daniel Nehring and Dylan Kerrigan to be identified as authors of this work has been asserted by them in accordance with the Copyright, Designs and Patents Act 1988.

The statements and opinions contained within this publication are solely those of the authors and not of The University of Bristol or Bristol University Press. The University of Bristol and Bristol University Press disclaim responsibility for any injury to persons or property resulting from any material published in this publication.

Bristol University Press works to counter discrimination on grounds of gender, race, disability, age and sexuality.

Cover design by blu inc, Bristol
Front cover image: Orbon Alija
Printed and bound in Great Britain by TJ International, Padstow
Bristol University Press uses environmentally responsible print partners

Contents

About the authors

Daniel Nehring is Associate Professor of Sociology at East China University of Science and Technology in Shanghai, China. Originally from Germany, he studied sociology at the University of Essex in the UK. His research has taken him to many societies around the world, such as Mexico, Argentina, South Korea and China. He is the author of, among other books, *Transnational Popular Psychology and the Global Self-Help Industry* (with Emmanuel Alvarado, Eric Hendricks and Dylan Kerrigan; Palgrave, 2016) and *Therapeutic Worlds* (with Dylan Kerrigan; Routledge, 2019).

Dylan Kerrigan is Lecturer in Criminology at the University of Leicester, UK. He is also Visiting Lecturer in Sociology at the University of the West Indies (UWI), St Augustine Campus, Trinidad and Tobago. Previously he was Lecturer in Sociology at UWI from 2010 to 2019. He has a PhD in anthropology from American University in Washington, DC, where he was an adjunct lecturer between 2007 and 2010. From a Caribbean, Global South perspective, his research and publications explore how cultural and economic processes extend over long periods of time in the service of various systems of power.

Acknowledgements

We would like to thank Catherine Gray, Shannon Kneis and Christie Smith at Bristol University Press for their support and encouragement during our work on this book. Multiple rounds of thoughtful and detailed peer reviews made a big difference to our thinking and writing, and we would like to thank the anonymous reviewers for their comments. We would also like to thank graduate students in political sociology at the University of the West Indies, St Augustine Campus, as well as colleagues Dr Nasser Mustapha, Dr Shelene Gomes, Dr Anand Rampersad and Dr Talia Esnard in the Sociology Unit, who all provided feedback on the content of various chapters. Rhoda Reddock, Michael Deane-White and Mengwei Tu also offered important suggestions on various parts of the manuscript, and we appreciate their comments.

Preface: how to read this book

Imagining Society looks at two questions. First, it asks what sociology is all about. It surveys many of the key concepts and themes that sociologists study. In doing so, it situates these concepts and themes in current trends within sociology, within the history of the discipline, and within historical and contemporary developments in society at large. Second, this book asks what sociology is for. In other words, it considers in which ways sociology offers a distinctive perspective on human life, and it explains why this perspective is important for public life as much as for each of us individually.

Sociology is an academic discipline that studies the ways in which individuals' everyday thoughts, feelings, motivations and actions are interwoven with large-scale and impersonal social processes and structures. Sociology is thus as much concerned with exploring the reach of individual creativity as it is interested in the ways in which all our lives are organised by social forces over which we are likely to have very little control. In this context, sociology has, since its beginnings, taken a large interest in social problems and social inequalities, along the lines of social class, poverty, gender, race and ethnicity, age, sex, disability and so forth. While sociology, as an organised field of study, emerged in Western Europe in the late 18th century, it is a global discipline. There are sociologists and sociology departments at universities all around the world, and while the topics which sociologists study are equally global in scope there are always local variations and contexts such as 'decolonising sociology'. As such, in this book we speak of 'global sociologies' to acknowledge the variety, differentiation and plurality of sociology found around the world today.

This short summary gives you an initial idea of the issues which we will cover throughout the ten chapters of this book. We do not intend these chapters to give an 'all there is to know about sociology' overview of sociological knowledge, summarising key theories, methodologies and areas of enquiry in a comprehensive fashion. There are many other textbooks that have already accomplished this, and there is not really any need for another book of this kind. We do, however, refer you to such textbooks, as well as other useful readings, at the end of each chapter. Instead, what we would like to accomplish is to give you a firm understanding of the sociological imagination and its personal, social and political importance. The term 'sociological imagination' is closely associated with a book of the same title by the American sociologist C. Wright Mills (1959). Drawing on Mills for inspiration, we suggest that sociology is more than just a field of academic knowledge. It is a special quality of mind that allows us to understand the relationships between, on the one hand, the localised lives of individual people and, on the other hand, large-scale social structures, processes, problems and inequalities in ways that may be hard to appreciate through common sense. It can be an everyday outlook and a way of thinking, as much as this imagination is tied to an academic field of knowledge. As such, we argue that the sociological imagination is of personal and public, as well as academic, importance, and we explain how and why this is so.

In this book, we look at sociology as an intellectual perspective, and we examine some of the core themes of sociological enquiry. Chapters 2 and 3 look at the sociological imagination and ask what sociologists mean when they describe something as social. Chapter 4 looks at sociology's origins, looking at early sociological key thinkers and strands of thought. Sociology's contradictions are explored in Chapters 5 and 6, and we ask in what ways 21st-century sociology might be understood as a global discipline and not simply the imperial-derived Western sociology of the last hundred years. We go on to discuss some of the core themes and issues in sociological enquiry in Chapter 7, looking at sociological accounts of structure, agency, social change and social conflict. Chapter 8, meanwhile, considers the social organisation of difference, inequalities and social stratification. Taken together, Chapters 7 and 8 thus offer a macro-sociological perspective; in other words they are concerned with large-scale and in some cases society-wide social patterns and processes. Chapter 9 turns to micro-sociology, that is to say the small-scale organisation of the self and social interaction in everyday life. The chapter is concerned with the sociology of the individual, and it explores how the self and individuals' ostensibly idiosyncratic ways of thinking, feeling and acting might be described as social. Finally, Chapter 10 offers an appraisal of the current state of sociological enquiry. It argues that the sociological imagination has in recent years been powerfully challenged by the commercialisation of universities and by the rise of alternative modes of explaining human life, including, notably, psychological and sociobiological accounts. We analyse this challenge, and we build on the sociological imagination to think about ways to recover sociology for the 21st century.

Writing about sociology, we develop our arguments in a way that is meant to be approachable and not require extensive prior knowledge. This does not mean, however, that we altogether avoid complex language and complex arguments. We would like to suggest that the ability to make sense of complex writing – terms, phrases and entire arguments – is an essential element of the sociological imagination as well as, in a more general sense, an essential talent to cultivate. Sometimes, a difficult idea needs to be read and reread carefully in order to be fully appreciated; sometimes, a complex thought will only fully make sense after we have pondered it for a few days. We have written the book in this spirit.

To help you along the way, we have included discussion questions, case studies and examples along the way, and we have also developed a companion website (https://bristoluniversitypress.co.uk/imagining-society-online-resources) that we regularly update.

Daniel Nehring
Dylan Kerrigan
August 2019

Making sense of society

Sociology for uncertain times

'More haste, less speed' is an old Roman proverb attributed to the emperor Augustus (Suetonius cited in Rolfe 1979, 159). It suggests an age-old wisdom and form of consciousness developed to contemplate, reflect and mentally digest life. Yet what happens in a world where time speeds up? Where social change accelerates? What happens when there is little time for judgement? No time out, no space for reflection? What happens when the world runs away from us?

In the 21st century, new technologies have altered our perceptions of time and space (Virilio 2000; Wajcman 2015). Devices and technologies like smart phones and smart homes, Skyping, Snapchatting, artificial intelligence and much more have transformed our existence as they have both accelerated and decelerated the fabric of modern living. Speed in this sense is a paradox. On the one hand the logic of the rat-race increases speed and eliminates duration: we live in the moment, the future becomes unpredictable and the past has little to offer by way of guidance on how to lead our lives. We now live in a runaway world, with profound implications for how we live and for how we imagine society.

Just as the 20th century marked a break from the 19th century, so the 21st century has quickly and pervasively transformed human life from the 20th century. Looking at the 19th century, Paul Virilio described a time founded not on the production of speed but on the brake. There was little production of speed. Instead ramparts, the law, rules, religions and prohibitions provided brakes to how fast people lived. 'It's not by chance that ancient society was one of successive obstacles on the level of people, of morals, of territorial definition – whether it was the city walls, taxes, the fortified systems of the nation state' (Virilio 1997, 50). Judy Wajcman (2015) notes how time became a form of social control. She suggests that time itself was experienced socially in different ways, depending on who you were – man or woman, rich or poor, worker or middle-class professional – and she notes that the expansion of industrialisation transformed time from being something tied to the rhythms of the natural world to a commodity to be made efficient and standardised. The British sociologist E.P. Thompson made a similar point when he suggested that 'clock-time' is a consequence of the increases in efficiency demanded by the advance of Western industrialisation, first in the management of colonial plantations and then in the factories of north England, and that the modern state needed a standardised and synchronic form of time in order for work-discipline to take root (Thompson 1967, 92).

In the 21st century, flows and rankings of information, capital, people and ways of experiencing everyday life have both remade and moved beyond the invisible boundaries and 'successive obstacles' of the 19th century. The very idea of boundaries has mutated into interfaces and touchscreens; windows of the home looking out on the world became windows looking into a laptop or smart phone. For some, once fixed social identities have become trans-identities and are now fluid and precarious. For others, the social position into which they are born – as a woman or as a man, as a peasant or a migrant or a refugee, as an able-bodied or a disabled person, and so on – still amounts to an inescapable fate. The enclosures, boundaries and certainties that once divided the world have been shifted and remade anew. This new world – far from ushering in the utopias of science fiction – is riddled by expulsions (Sassen 2014), environmental destruction on an unprecedented scale (Milanovic 2011, 2016; Keeley 2015), violence (Gray 2006), disposable futures (Evans and Giroux 2015), and by new ways to sort humans into categories using faceless and weaponised algorithms (O'Neil 2017). At the same time, the dystopian futures of the early 21st century are being vigorously contested around the world, and challenges to rampant social and economic inequalities, new ways of environmentally sustainable human living, and creative forms of social, economic and political organisation do offer much hope for the future. Yet we live in uncertain times.

Why begin this book with such a pessimistic narrative of the state of the world today? You are likely to have read other introductions to sociology, and, if so, you will have found some of them to paint a brighter, more cheerful picture of life in the early 21st century. On the one hand, hope may be had from humanity's unprecedented access to knowledge, the rapid development of new technologies that may improve human lives and ameliorate environmental damage, the pursuit of greater social justice on the part of international organisations, governments and social movements, and many other current developments. On the other hand, as we will show in the following (see, for example, Chapter 9), sociology is as much concerned with exploring mundane, everyday features of human life as it is with large-scale social problems.

It is for two reasons that we have nonetheless chosen to strike a pessimistic tone. First, all reasons for hopefulness notwithstanding, the world today is facing an unprecedented crisis, of escalating inequalities and attendant social conflicts, of rights and liberties that were hard-won in the 19th and 20th centuries, of environmental collapse, and of our capacity to make sense to and respond to all these ominous developments. Second, we suggest that, at this time, sociology may have an important role to play in debates about these ominous developments – but this cannot be taken for granted. Making the case for sociology today is more important than ever. Therefore, in this book social conflict, power and inequalities form an important part of how we frame our discipline, even though we will also consider its many other facets. In this book we describe sociology as a discipline that is concerned with the critical analysis of social life, which is unavoidably political and seeks to give its arguments public relevance.

Thinking through the scenarios we have outlined, there is for some the sense that the world has gone mad (Scott and Bromley 2013, 124). Yet as we will show you, for the sociologist this is a time for answers to be had, sense to be made and knowledge to be created to help us understand how the world is changing. How can sociology make sense of the new conditions of human social life in the 21st century? This is the question with which this book is concerned.

Sociology as a field of knowledge

What is sociology? To begin answering this question, it seems indicated to sketch what precisely we mean when we write of 'sociology'. We would like to suggest that sociology can be usefully understood from three perspectives. To begin with, sociology is concerned with the systematic study of social life. Sociology shares its subject matter with common sense, in so far as it is concerned with making sense of the organisation of human life. However, it is also fundamentally different from common sense, and we use the term 'systematic study' to highlight this difference. When we go about our everyday lives, we both interact with other people and witness interactions between others without participating directly. We remember, however partially, these interactions and their outcomes, and we draw on these observations and memories to explain to ourselves the way the social world works. This is common sense. Common sense is necessarily partial and limited, as it does not reach far beyond our personal experience of the world. For example, if your experience of Chinese food is limited to visits to Chinese restaurants in your country (assuming that you are not Chinese yourself), you are likely to assume that this restaurant food is more or less like the cuisine that people eat in China. However, even in neighbouring countries, such as Korea, Chinese restaurant food is carefully adapted to local, for example Korean, tastes, and it often does not resemble at all what people cook at home or in restaurants in China.

Sociology, in contrast, seeks to place its portrayals of human social life on firmer footing. Common sense may be useful to guide us through our own lives. If you do not travel to China, then an understanding of the kinds of food you are likely to be served at Chinese restaurants in your country is perfectly sufficient in purely practical terms for you to be able to choose where to eat. If this is all you know, however, it would lead you to make wildly wrong claims if someone asked you what Chinese food is like in general. If you now consider how our closely limited common sense may feed into stereotypes and prejudices, then you may see why alternative, sociological explanations of social life are important (Wodak 2015). Sociological enquiry reaches beyond common sense in so far as it builds on the organised observation, description, analysis, interpretation and critique of social life. Instead of limiting themselves to drawing conclusions from their narrowly limited personal experience, sociologists draw on a wide range of methodological tools, from survey interviews to the observation of everyday social interaction, to observe social life first-hand, to record their observations, to assess their soundness, and to describe and explain the societal patterns and processes in which they are interested. Only by following such systematic observation, description and analysis may sociologists attempt to interpret what they have found; in other words, to make statements about the general social and political significance of their findings and to critique social problems. Sociology, in this sense, is an empirical field of study, in that it builds on the systematic and large-scale first-hand observation of social life.

In this context, sociology is concerned with what the French sociologist Émile Durkheim (2013b), writing at the conclusion of the 19th century in one of the earliest introductions to the discipline, has described as 'social facts'. Sociology concerns the social structures and institutional arrangements, of family, of school and university, of labour market and workplace, of temple and church and so on, that organise and constrain in powerful ways how we as individuals may conduct our everyday lives. At the same time, sociology looks at the ways in which individuals, through their everyday encounters and interactions, create and transform the social reality in which they live. Therefore, sociology is concerned with the explanation both of the everyday interactions and large-scale structures that organise society and of the processes that transform and remake it. Sociology studies, first, the social organisation of the self; second, the processes of enculturation and socialisation through which we come to form part of society, by acquiring language and locally specific ways of thinking, feeling and acting; third, the interactions through which individuals engage with each other in everyday life; and, fourth, the institutions of economy, government, culture, education and social care, which constitute society at large.

The ways in which sociology may accomplish this are contentious among sociologists themselves, and sociology has throughout its history for the most part been a heterogeneous discipline, characterised as much by common objectives along the lines set out above, as by diversity and controversy regarding the theoretical and methodological underpinnings of sociological enquiry. For example, as we will see later, in Chapter 4, there has long been much disagreement as to the question whether sociology might be, in some sense, scientific. Likewise, as Chapters 5 and 6 discuss, sociology has, since its emergence in the late 18th century, spread around the world, and today there are highly diverse forms of sociological thought and practice to be found in different parts of the globe. An important shared feature of much sociological enquiry around the world, though, has been a strong concern with social inequalities, with conflict and with the distribution and uses of power across society. On the one hand, sociologists have long shown an interest in the structures and processes that hold society together – in the origins of social solidarity, to state this in other words (Durkheim 1995, 2013a). On the other hand, from its beginnings in the late 18th and early 19th centuries, sociological enquiry has equally been driven by a preoccupation with new and potent forms of inequality and the uses of power that drive society apart (Marx and Engels 1988; Marx 2008). In this book, we argue that such a preoccupation may have an important role to play in a sociology for the 21st century.

Sociology as an outlook

The second perspective on sociology that we would like to introduce here might be called the sociological imagination. While the term was only popularised fairly recently in the 1950s by the American sociologist C. Wright Mills (1959), it might be used more broadly, we would suggest, to characterise a particular outlook on human life that characterises what sociologists do.

The sociological imagination describes a characteristic way for sociologists to look at and understand human social life. Since the late 19th century, the sociological imagination has become an important way, both in public life and in the academic world, to make sense of human life (Becker 1967; Goffman 1990; Giddens 1991; Bauman 2005). Most closely associated with the work of C. Wright Mills in the 1950s and 1960s, the sociological imagination was a proclamation that 'neither the life of an individual nor the history of a society can be understood without understanding both' (Mills 1959, 3). For Mills, the average person then, much like today, did not define their troubles in connection to 'historical change, institutional contradiction' and 'the big ups and downs of the societies in which they live' (1959, 3). As such Mills believed it was the task of sociological analysis, as 'intellectual craftsperson' to reveal how humans both produce and are products of their society and to teach this way of understanding society to others such as journalists, scientists and editors (see Chapter 2). 'The sociological imagination enables its possessor to understand the larger historical scene in terms of its meaning for the inner life and the external career of a variety of individuals' (Mills 1959, 5). Where ordinary people did not make such connections about individual troubles and public issues in the context of understanding their own lives, Mills believed the political and cultural task for sociologists must be 'to translate personal troubles into public issues, and public issues into the terms of their human meaning for a variety of individuals' (Mills 1959, 187). This of course means sociology must learn how to connect to and speak with the mainstream of life, not just to those with all the technical knowledge.

The sociological imagination as such connects personal biography to large social and historical forces. It demonstrates how social structure produces and is produced by individuals and the groups they are members of. Understanding an individual's thoughts, their feelings and assumptions, their wants and desires, and much more, through the lens of the sociological imagination can reveal the context of how individuals are socially produced, formed and limited in connection with the various social environments and conditions – economic, historical, cultural, political – in which they live. Put simply, where individuals (and *individualism*) see their issues and problems as personal and private, Mills's sociological imagination demonstrated those same issues as historical, cultural, political, economic and social (and *collective*). Or, as Heidi Rimke notes in her discussion of Mills's sociological imagination, 'we create ourselves, but not necessarily under conditions of our choosing' (Rimke 2010, 241).

In the 21st century, the importance of Mills's sociological imagination and its power to reveal what is hidden in plain sight has eroded. In its place other ways of imagining society, for instance in the form of biological, neuroscientific and psychological explanations of human life, have emerged. To a significant degree, these alternative narratives have pushed to the margins the sociological imagination and the importance of understanding the role of context and social structure in every individual's life. Without the sociological imagination individuals are no longer conscious of the international historical system that they and their personal life options are a part of.

Sociology as a way of working

The third perspective on sociology we would like to introduce concerns what might be termed the politics of sociological labour. In the previous sections, we have written about sociology as a field of knowledge or academic discipline and as an imagination. But sociology is not just a body of knowledge contained in books and journal articles and stored in libraries, or an outlook on the world. While all this is true, it is equally important to think of sociology as creative and institutionally situated labour. Sociology for many is a profession that comprises trained sociologists who conduct academic research while working in a relatively narrow band of organisations, typically in universities. Sociological labour is creative in its character, as it is fundamentally concerned with developing new and original ways to make sense of the world we live in. At the same time, sociological labour is conditioned by the institutional environment in which it takes place; the topics that sociologists may or may not study, the methods they use to go about their research, the ways in which they work with other sociologists and the pathways they have to communicate their findings are all structured by the institutional environment in which they do their work. This is also true of sociologists outside the academy, who may use a sociological understanding of the world to make sense of their everyday experiences and social relationships (Santucci 2010). Sociology is as much a profession as it is a distinctive way of making sense of human life.

To understand what sociology is and how sociologists work, it is necessary to critically interrogate the features of the institutions – of higher education, of politics, of labour markets and so forth – in which much of this sociological work takes place. Sociology is at heart a type of work, and in the main a form of academic labour. Most often found within the academy, there are many examples throughout the 20th century of sociologists working with non-academic organisations. In recent 21st-century times there has been the rise of sociologists as consultants, whose ideas in the main are often deployed in the pursuit of profits by large companies and governments looking for efficiencies, as a type of sociological labour. There are of course also public sociologists too who take sociological lessons and insights into their community work.

But what makes academic sociological work sociological? We suggest sociological research is sociological when it is grounded in the sociological imagination and when it explores and questions common sense, sociocultural systems and social hierarchies through the sociological imagination. At its heart, sociology asks questions about the taken-for-granted and about everyday life, and it is committed to revealing the interconnectedness of individuals, society and opportunities running counter to the simplifications sold by the mainstream media and politicians today. Sociology is inherently sociological when it asks how might we make a better world and what are the processes and mechanisms to encourage such social transformations to take place. Sociology has been able to uncover and challenge major forms of social inequality, exploitation and oppression throughout its history as an academic discipline – while also today understanding its own colonial role in the spread of problematic development paradigms (Connell 2007). Sociology's unique perspective on social life and its challenge to social inequalities make the sociological imagination worthwhile and sociology distinctive, not just as an academic discipline but as *the* way to imagine the world we all live in.

Outside the academy perhaps our definition of sociology is not so representative of what many traditionally understand as sociological labour. For example, in the world of sociological consultancy, working for a range of companies and non-governmental organisations, there is often little room to mobilise and engage the sociological imagination, little questioning of common sense and small room for changes to the status quo. This is because as a consultant, sociologists do not always have free reign to apply the sociological imagination in value-neutral ways. Instead they are often invited to work for organisations that already have a particular vision or 'terms of reference' and ideas of how managers should use and apply the professional sociological advice received.

Doing sociology

For Max Weber, 'Sociology … is a science which attempts the interpretive understanding of social action in order thereby to arrive at a causal explanation of its course and effects' (Weber 1978, 4). Yet how is this achieved? How is sociology done? And does sociology in practice do what Weber believed it should? Sociology is interested in how our societies are organised, how society influences our individual lives, and how social change more generally occurs. In order to pursue these interests sociological research methods are numerous and founded on the collection of empirical evidence; that is, evidence that is experienced or observed directly. Sociologists apply a variety of research designs and interpretive frameworks in the collection of empirical evidence. They also apply theoretical vistas to the evidence in order to understand and interpret it. These basic steps produce new knowledge about the world, societies and people, as well as provide social science results.

Popular sociological methods and research designs include: case study, survey research, observational research, correlational research, social statistics, socio-linguistics, mapping, social history, the functional method, digital sociology, and cross-cultural methods like the comparative method, ethnography and participant observation. Some sociologists also do secondary research, which means sociological analysis of the work and data of other sociologists.

In the main, during the late 19th and most of the 20th centuries sociologists were wedded to one of two main frameworks – positivism or constructivism. According to Marvasti (2004, 3) 'both positivism and constructionism have to do with the nature of reality or assumptions about what is real and how it should be studied'. As he points out, in everyday life most of us would assume we have some idea of how the world works and we operate accordingly each day. Many people might suggest this knowledge is common sense, or cultural, or that we just know what to do. Obviously, it is not just our individual selves who get by on this sort of auto-pilot every day, but everyone together in our communities and societies, with varying degrees of success. To return to Marvasti, he might suggest that the difference between positivistic sociology and social constructionism is in what they take for granted. The common sense of positivism took social reality to be based 'on self-evident truths that resemble physical laws of nature … [and] of the physical sciences, physics in particular, as the ideal model for exploring the social world' (Marvasti 2004, 4). While the common sense of social constructionists is 'concerned with "how" human interaction helps to create social reality … Constructionists believe that as human beings "we do not find or discover knowledge so much as we construct or make it"' (Marvasti 2004, 5). Constructionism can also be understood as a form of interpretive methodology or symbolic interactionism and as a counterweight and alternative understanding of the world. Interpretivism is most centrally concerned with induction (see Chapter 6), subjectivity and context.

Doing sociology, however, isn't simply about method, research design and frameworks. It is also about the environments, institutions and societies within which sociology is produced. As Marxist sociologists have long noted, it is the labour we put into making and sustaining our worlds and lives that contributes to shaping who and what we are and how we view that world. In general terms, as a form of labour sociologists traditionally have worked within institutions and not been independent of them, although of course there are many exceptions to this. In this sense, doing sociology is as much about methodology as it is also about the politics and institutional contexts of sociological labour.

In this book we argue that contemporary public life has to a large extent come to be organised by the common-sense notion that biographical events and processes are shaped by personal choices and character, rather than broader social forces. We note, in the context of the increasing commercialisation of universities, that this common sense has also become increasingly pervasive in academia. We then argue these developments call into question the nature and prospects of academic sociology itself, which, for the much of the 20th century, has largely been predicated on the sociological imagination and the sociologist as intellectual craftsperson.

There is also a second, more global, layer to this reality and that is the consideration of the globalisation of sociology alongside the interplay between global capitalism and the international institutional transformations in academia. In Chapters 6 and 7 on 'global sociologies', we analyse how these institutional changes and the theoretical and methodological formations that define sociology as an academic discipline combine to shape sociological ideas that are provincial, biased and limited to one dominant Euro-American perspective and language (Connell 2007; Meeks and Girvan 2010; Bhambra 2016). As Bhambra notes,

> I suggest that these conventional [sociological] understandings can be criticised on three grounds: substantive, conceptual/methodological, and epistemological. These criticisms imply that sociology, as currently constituted, is unable to engage with current global challenges, and, at worst, embeds a particular Eurocentred ideological response to those challenges … In the standard Habermasian division between the system and social, for example, race and ethnicity are taken as social, and not as aspects of the system; that is, they are not seen as integral to the market, bureaucracy, and state, but are understood as located in the lifeworld of social meanings and values. (Bhambra 2016, 961)

What happens when sociologists outside the Global Northwest produce sociological evidence contradicting postcolonialism as a developmental process, and instead demonstrate it as a process of underdevelopment (Escobar 2004)? Or when sociologists in the Global South demonstrate modernity has been anything but progressive for many and is instead a regressive form of colonialism – with murder and violence rates, inequality levels and levels of debt out of control, reflecting that the 'coloniality of power' and a logic of colonial history still echo in present violent social divisions (Wimberley 2008)? Did colonialism really end for many ex-colonies in the 1960s and 1970s as 'Independence' supposedly symbolised (Escobar 2004)? Do such nations really have political sovereignty? Or instead did they experience globalisation as systems of neocolonialism, neopatriarchy and new forms of oppression (Watson 2015)? What do sociologies that are grown and developed in such global environments and under such labour conditions tell us about the world? Is the 'Global South' a denigrating term or 'a metaphor of' human 'suffering caused by capitalism and colonialism?' (de Sousa Santos 2012, 51).

Mills's work on the sociological imagination suggested sociological labour should provide the skills and methods to answer these questions and to see what are the normally hidden and obscured lines between private lives and public issues. Mills's sociological imagination claimed that individual biographies are inextricably intertwined with larger social processes. As Rimke notes, for the sociologist then, 'what is normatively seen and represented as individual, personal, natural, normal, private, and so forth, is instead sociologically understood as historically constituted, culturally produced, politically oriented, and socially maintained/resisted' (Rimke 2010, 241). This is the type of sociology this book offers to readers.

So why sociology?

In the runaway world of the 21st century our certainties and understandings about the world no longer provide the security they once did, and meanings shift. Where once religion provided places for congregation, brotherhood and hymn-like belonging, today, for many, sport has become their 'civil religion' (Schultz and Sheffer 2015). Where once our daily commutes symbolised reliable motion and travel, a daily commute today for many is often an endless traffic jam and queue, with sometimes impromptu pop-up marketplaces and fellow commuters who separate themselves from each other either by travelling alone in a car or wearing noise-cancelling headphones or airpods on the bus, train or maxi-taxi to remind others not to speak to them (Davison 2004). Where we now make sense of the world using maladaptive schema and coping strategies, we have developed from failed schooling systems (Deosaran 2016). Where social media networks replace our traditional ideas of kinship and relationality (Horst et al 2005). Where the implicit bias in the adjudication of magistrates and judges drive judiciary systems and criminal justice systems around the world, yet sociological testimony revealing such bias is often excluded from courts (Tomaskovic-Devey 2011; Kerrigan et al 2017). Where 'champagne solutions' – the art of attending a talk by a renowned academic or politician at a fancy institution and sipping champagne at the reception, all the while engaging in chit-chat with technocrats – is the main solution on offer to deal with social problems. Where social solidarity arrives today not with unionism or political social movements but instead in the organic community solidarity of the death of icons like Princess Diana, Nelson Mandela and George Michael, or pay-to-attend music and sporting events.

Where at the same time many young people face long-term job insecurity, low wages and dulled opportunities. Where anti-establishment voting, increasing militarisation, rising poverty, transnational anti-black racism, religious fervour, homophobia, gender-based violence and an economic system based on finite fossil fuels worryingly define the daily lives of a great number of people. In such a runaway world, societies have become more complex and much more uncertain, less friendly and more hostile. For many people, their lives and the societies in which they live in are now increasingly illegible – why and how did society run away from us? How do we push back? What should the role of sociology be in such a push back?

Living in this runaway world can make many of us feel helpless. We struggle to make sense of it. Being constantly bombarded with disinformation and misrepresentations of context and history can make us loose our intellectual footing. We slip into thin simplifications, emotional responses and simplistic explanations of what is happening to us and to the world around us. This can also embolden others who imagine the world in less honest ways. Yet by recognising the importance of linking biography, history, social structures and power through the sociological imagination, sociology can return a sense of control to our lives. It can make you aware of what side you are on and why – and let you decide for yourself what side you should be on and why. Sociology isn't simply about academics, or even labour and consultancy, money and qualifications. At its heart, sociology allows both individuals and their groups to take back power by applying the analytical significance of the sociological imagination to their own lives. In the 21st century there is a distinct need for a reappraisal and renewed justification of the significance of this way of imagining society.

THINKING SOCIOLOGICALLY

'The crisis consists precisely in the fact that the old is dying and the new cannot be born; in this interregnum a great variety of morbid symptoms appear' (Gramsci 1971, 276).

Read the following short biography of Antonio Gramsci. Then consider: what might be meant by 'activist sociology'? Should sociology be activist? In which ways? Why (not)?

Antonio Gramsci is recognised as one of the most famous **activist sociologists** ever. In his biography of Gramsci, Antonio Santucci (2010) noted how Gramsci took sides in the central issues of the day about society and what society could and should be, and he hated those who didn't. Gramsci was a constant writer, and was learning to create and communicate counter hegemonic discourses and ideas from those that dominated at the time and that for him were born on the terrain of the contradictions engendered by the material forces of production. 'The material forces of production' is another way of describing how Gramsci and others experienced their everyday lives in terms of the things they need to live. Social realities like jobs, wages and everyday freedoms, which were particularly hard in 1920s and 1930s Italy, shaped how they viewed the social. Nothing happened immediately however to make Gramsci into an activist sociologist. Rather it happened through the events in his life.

He moved from the south of Italy to the Turin factory council movement and the workers in the north of Italy. Gramsci's sociology and his sociological imagination were actively produced. His worldview emerged. He was an **organic intellectual** of the times he came from and was actively shaped and made by the social and economic structures and realities around him and that structured his everyday agency. Gramsci lived the socioeconomic conditions of his time and they shaped his worldview. As Marx might have said, the economic base of the society influenced the superstructure (the ideas and culture of the society), which then fed back into the base and so on into the future. Ultimately, however, Gramsci's activist sociology and his support for the proletariat made his ideas dangerous to those in power and he was imprisoned. It is from his time in prison that he produced his most well-known piece of sociological work, the *Prison Notebooks* (1971).

MINI PROJECT

This is a sociology tedX talk on empathy. Take a look at it, here:

www.youtube.com/watch?v=kUEGHdQO7WA

Why is empathy important to sociologists, and to the sociological imagination at large?

TALKING POINTS

1. 'In the 21st century, new technologies have altered our perceptions of time and space.' [p1] Can you think of any examples of such technologies? How have they changed perceptions of time and space? What consequences have these changes had for everyday life? What consequences do they have for your own life?

2. '[W]e live in uncertain times.' [p 2] What might this mean? Do you agree? Why (not)?

3. 'In the 21st century, the importance of Mills's sociological imagination and its power to reveal what is hidden in plain sight has eroded.' [p 6] What is this statement trying to say? Do you agree with this assessment?

4. What is meant by the 'politics of sociological labour'? [p6] Why, if at all, are they important for understanding how sociology is organised?

5. In your own words, try to formulate a definition of sociology. Explain why you have chosen to define sociology in this way, and illustrate each element of your definition with relevant examples.

6. Should social inequalities and conflict be a central focus of sociological analysis today? Why (not)?

READ ON ...

We hope that this book will give you at least a good basic understanding of what sociology is and of what sociologists do. However, it will also be useful for you to read other introductions to sociology, as these will provide you with perspectives on sociology that differ from ours. C. Wright Mills's *The Sociological Imagination* (1959) might be read as an introduction to sociology. It is now somewhat dated, in that it was written for the world of the mid-20th century, but its portrayal of sociological enquiry is as important as ever. Among the more recent introductions to sociology, Ken Plummer's *Sociology: The Basics* (2016) and Zygmunt Bauman's and Tim May's *Thinking Sociologically* (2001) stand out from the crowd, in that they are at once lively and readable and challenging and thought-provoking. If you can find it, Robert Nisbet's *Sociology as an Art Form* (1976) is another sophisticated reading of sociology that goes far beyond what most introductions to sociology manage to accomplish.

Check the companion website at https://bristoluniversitypress.co.uk/imagining-society-online-resources **for a suggested project and writing task.**

2

The sociological imagination

How to become a sociologist

As you are reading this book, you are fairly likely to be a sociology student who is new to the discipline; and if not a student at university then at least someone who wants to know more about sociology. We assume the former, however, because this book was commissioned by a publisher to be an introductory textbook: it has a proposed social function in this regard to be used as set reading in classes in introductory sociology, and the publisher – notwithstanding their social endeavour – hopes to generate sales of the book to substantial numbers of students. Textbooks are different from other academic publications, such as research monographs and articles in scholarly journals, in so far as they, for the most part, do not set out to make original contributions to sociological knowledge. Instead, they are intended to provide students new to sociology with a baseline of knowledge about the concepts, theories, methods and fields of enquiry that have been agreed on by sociologists and characterise sociology as an academic discipline. In other words, textbooks mark the starting point of your socialisation as professional sociologists.

This can mean you are faced with a book that, in a rather rote manner, regurgitates bits of sociological knowledge – definitions of key terms, summaries of exemplary pieces of research and so forth – which you are meant to memorise and repeat in tests, so as to demonstrate that you have learned something. Traditionally, such books often pursue what you might think of as a kitchen-sink approach: they present you with a very wide array of facts to learn, in order for you to demonstrate you know enough to pass your class and, in the end, obtain a degree. In the US, for example, introductory sociology textbooks frequently come packaged with ready-made banks of multiple-choice questions, which lecturers may then use to quickly test the knowledge of large numbers of students on large numbers of facts. There is a case to be made for such books, as you do indeed need to develop a very thorough understanding of established sociological knowledge to be able to consider yourself a sociologist. However, in a very important sense, these books – and the textbook industry at large – miss the point, while also taking certain things – *like making the case for sociology* – for granted.

Socialisation into the body of knowledge and methods of professional practice that conform sociology as an academic discipline is essential for students. However, as we saw in Chapter 1, to be able to call yourself a sociologist, it is equally essential you develop a particular way of looking at and explaining the social world that in this book we term the sociological imagination. Our usage of this term is inspired by an introduction to sociology of the same title (Mills 1959) that we regard as very important for our discipline. You might alternatively speak of a sociological mindset or a sociological world view or a distinctive professional ethos of sociology. This does not matter that much. The point to be made, rather, is that becoming a sociologist requires a distinctive quality of mind, rather than just comprehensive knowledge of a certain body of facts (Bauman and May 2001; Plummer 2016). It means you need to do sociology and think sociologically as much as read sociology.

In this chapter, we introduce you to the sociological imagination in three ways.

- First, we look at the way in which the notion of the sociological imagination was developed by its original proponent, the US sociologist C. Wright Mills (1959), around the middle of the 20th century.
- Second, we argue that to understand the sociological mindset it is important to consider the institutional circumstances from which it emerges – namely the social world of universities, academic sociologists and academic careers – but of course this is not the only way.
- Third, we point out that the sociological imagination may take shape and find expression in diverse ways, beyond the institutional confines of professional sociology.

We use the example of C. Wright Mills's own academic biography – largely confined to the US and closely enmeshed with the features of North American society and politics of the time – to consider how sociological thinking may be shaped by the institutional arrangements in which it takes place.

Who was C. Wright Mills?

Our point of departure for all this is C. Wright Mills's *The Sociological Imagination* (1959). Since its publication nearly 60 years ago, Mills's introduction to sociology has remained prominent in Western sociology, and it is still frequently used to introduce students to the discipline (Dandaneau 2009; Hoop 2009; Storrs 2009). Numerous other starting points would have been available to us, as sociology is characterised by the pluralism of its analytical approaches and methods of enquiry as much as by its unifying concerns. We decided to build on *The Sociological Imagination*, first, because it sets out a distinctive ethos for sociological enquiry that we believe offers important insights into the discipline as it is today. In formulating it, Mills draws on a powerful assessment of intellectual trends in sociology and of the institutional contexts of sociological labour. While this assessment is rooted in the US of the mid-20th century, it can be usefully built on in a contemporary exploration of sociology's disciplinary identity.

Second, *The Sociological Imagination* and C. Wright Mills's wider work are useful in tracing the blind spots and limits of sociological enquiry. As a classical work of 20th-century sociology, *The Sociological Imagination* shares in many of the limitations of sociological knowledge and sociological labour that have characterised the discipline for much of its history. Examples of this are sociology's Eurocentrism and historically situated limitations in its attention to matters of race, ethnicity and gender. Using C. Wright Mills's work as a point of departure, it becomes possible to trace these limitations, to consider the extent to which they have been surpassed and explore new intellectual and practical boundaries that may have sprung up in their stead (see Chapters 6 and 7). In other words, while the sociology of C. Wright Mills exhibits notable analytical weaknesses and blind spots in its thematic scope, these weaknesses and blind spots can be usefully mobilised as benchmarks against which the development of the discipline can be traced. Taken together they can help us in making the case for sociology in the 21st century.

Charles Wright Mills was born in 1916 in Waco, Texas, into a middle-class family. He attended Texas A&M University and later the University of Texas at Austin, graduating with an undergraduate degree in sociology and a master's degree in philosophy. In 1942, he concluded his studies with a doctorate from the University of Wisconsin-Madison. From 1941 to 1945, he held a position as Assistant Professor of Sociology at the University of Maryland, College Park. He moved to Columbia University in 1945, where he was promoted to the rank of Associate Professor in 1950 and made Professor of Sociology in 1956. He died in 1962, having suffered from a heart condition for much of his life.

Mills's time as a professional sociologist thus remained unfortunately short, spanning little more than two decades. However, he was a prolific author and highly visible in academia and wider public life. In the words of J.E.T. Eldridge (1983, 13), at the time of his death Mills was, 'reputed to be the most widely read sociologist in the world'. His academic works were popular during his lifetime and provoked considerable – and often highly controversial – debate. At the same time, Mills acted, in contemporary language, as a public sociologist, writing for journalistic publications such as *The New Republic*, *The New York Herald Tribune* and *The New Leader*, giving public lectures, participating in debates on television and radio and testifying to a US Senate committee on problems faced by small business (Horowitz 1983; Summers 2008). Table 2.1 lists Mills's books, as well as articles published in academic journals. While this list comprises many of his key works, these are complemented by an array of other texts, including essays, journalistic writings, interviews, research reports and numerous book reviews.

Table 2.1: Selected works of C. Wright Mills

Books	Articles in academic journals
1946	**1939**
From Max Weber: Essays in Sociology, translations (with Hans Gerth), New York: Oxford University Press.	Language, logic and culture, *American Sociological Review* 4(5): 670–80.
1948	**1940**
The New Men of Power: America's Labor Leaders, New York: Harcourt, Brace and Company.	Methodological consequences of the sociology of knowledge, *American Journal of Sociology* 46(3): 316–30.
1950	Situated actions and vocabularies of motive, *American Sociological Review* 5(6): 904–13.
The Puerto Rican Journey: New York's Newest Migrants (with Clarence Senior and Rose K. Goldsen), New York: Harper & Bros.	**1943**
1951	The professional ideology of social pathologists, *American Journal of Sociology* 49(2): 165–80.
White Collar: The American Middle Classes, New York: Oxford University Press.	**1945**
1953	The powerless people: the social role of the intellectual, *Bulletin of the American Association of University Professors* 31(2): 231–43.
Character and Social Structure: The Psychology of Social Institutions (with Hans Gerth), New York: Harcourt, Brace and Company.	**1946**
1956	The middle classes in middle-sized cities: the stratification and political position of small business and white collar strata, *American Sociological Review* 11(5): 520–9.
The Power Elite, New York: Oxford University Press.	**1953**
1958	Two styles of research in current social studies, *Philosophy of Science* 20(4): 266–75.
The Causes of World War Three, New York: Simon and Schuster.	**1958**
1959	The structure of power in American society, *British Journal of Sociology* 9(1): 29–41.
The Sociological Imagination, London: Oxford University Press.	
1960	
Images of Man: The Classic Tradition in Sociological Thinking, New York: George Braziller.	
Listen, Yankee: The Revolution in Cuba, New York: McGraw-Hill.	
1962	
The Marxists, New York: Dell Publishing.	
1963	
Sociology and Pragmatism: The Higher Learning in America, New York: Oxford University Press (posthumous publication).	

Table 2.1 is useful in so far as it points to the central themes and issues that motivated Mills's work at large. His earliest publications (1939, 1940a, 1940b) make distinctive contributions to the sociology of knowledge, exploring how sociological enquiry is situated in its social context and considering the relationships between human mental life and society. His interest in the basic problems of sociological analysis is equally apparent in his later work. For example, *Character and Social Structure* (Gerth and Mills 1953) further examines the relationships between individuals and social structure and sets out a theory of social organisation. *The Sociological Imagination* (Mills 1959) offers a trenchant evaluation of prevalent modes of sociological analysis and sets out an alternative perspective.

Mills's work therefore has a significant theoretical dimension. Nonetheless, it may be most accurate to characterise him as a public sociologist committed to analysing the social and political problems of his time, speaking to both academic and, importantly, non-academic audiences and challenging their views where necessary. His theoretical work, while important in its own right, supplied him with the vocabulary necessary to do so. Mills's sociology is centrally concerned with the relationships between social structures and individual character and biography. This concern is ultimately motivated by Mills's interest in public affairs and the social organisation of power. Mills's concern with the public affairs of his time is apparent, on the one hand, in his academic works. Works such as *The New Men of Power* (1948), *White Collar* (1951) and *The Power Elite* (1956) analyse institutional transformations in US society, uncover structures of power and consider their political implications. Alongside his academic works, Mills engaged extensively with a general audience. For example, *The Causes of World War Three* (1958) and *Listen, Yankee* (1960) are both political pamphlets that look at the social and political implications of the Cold War. Mills wrote *Listen, Yankee* in the immediate aftermath of the Cuban Revolution. In it, he drew on his observations during a visit to the island, including interviews with prominent political leaders, to give voice to the revolutionaries and to challenge dominant public perceptions in the US. In turn, *The Causes of World War Three* (1958) contested the social, economic, military and political power structures that motivated conflict with the Communist bloc in the US and set out a case for a politics of peace. Alongside these longer works, numerous contributions to journalistic publications, radio and television interviews and political statements speak to Mills's involvement in public life. Against the backdrop of his concern with power, politics and social change Mills reflected on the role of the professional social scientists. In 'The Professional Ideology of Social Pathologists' (1943) and 'The Powerless People' (1945), Mills considers the role of intellectuals in the US and asks how they might influence public and political life. This theme likewise plays an important role in *The Sociological Imagination* (1959), where Mills highlights the political dimensions of sociological enquiry and considers to what extent social science might 'save the world'.

Developing his sociology, Mills built on, extended and critiqued established theoretical traditions. Early on in his intellectual biography, Mills came to hold Thorstein Veblen in high regard as a model for his own work as a social theorist and critic (Eldridge 1983). His engagement with the work of Max Weber is apparent, for instance, in *From Max Weber: Essays in Sociology* (Gerth and Mills 1946), a volume that for the first time made translations of important parts of Weber's writings available to Anglophone readers. Alongside Weber and Veblen, pragmatist social thought inspired Mills in important ways, and the influence of Dewey, Mead, Peirce and James is readily visible in many of his works (Mills 1939, 1940a, 1940b, 1963; Gerth and Mills 1953). Finally, Marxism provided another significant, albeit much more ambivalent, point of reference to Mills, culminating in an extensive analysis and critique in *The Marxists* (Mills 1962), the last book he saw published in his lifetime.

Today, Mills is perhaps most widely remembered through *The Sociological Imagination* (1959), which still frequently forms part of introductory classes in sociology around the world and is often quoted in textbooks. In his lifetime, however, Mills was both much more widely known and much more widely controversial. On the one hand, he worked closely with prominent sociologists and drew inspiration from their work. For instance, Hans H. Gerth, a German émigré, first was his teacher at the University of Wisconsin-Madison, before later collaborating with Mills on various projects and ultimately falling out. At Wisconsin, the muckraking sociology of E.A. Ross came to be a further important inspiration. Later, at Columbia University, Mills worked alongside Robert Lynd, Robert Merton and other leading sociologists of the mid-20th century. On the other hand, Mills often found himself at odds with his colleagues. Perhaps due to their vocal challenge to the status quo, his works attracted considerable controversy and criticism. Texts that are today regarded as classics of sociological thought were met with praise by some contemporaries (Vidich 1954; Highsaw 1957) and with considerable scepticism by others (Parsons 1957; Kolb 1960).

Introducing *The Sociological Imagination*

The Sociological Imagination was published in 1959. It embodies many of Mills's broader concerns. First, it evaluates central trends in sociological analysis and sets out an alternative approach. Second, in this context, it offers a critique of the institutionally situated scholarly practices that characterise sociology. Third, it formulates a distinctive ethos of sociological enquiry. In contemporary sociology, the term 'sociological imagination' has come to refer to this ethos and, to some extent, the analytical perspective underpinning it. In this sense, to consider the sociological imagination means to ask what sociology is about and how sociology might be done. These objectives are clear in the opening statements of the book:

It is my aim in this book to define the meaning of the social sciences for the cultural tasks of our time. I want to specify the kinds of effort that lie behind the development of the sociological imagination; to indicate its implications for political as well as for cultural life; and perhaps to suggest something of what is required to possess it. In these ways, I want to make clear the nature and the uses of the social sciences today, and to give a limited account of their contemporary condition in the United States. At any given moment, of course, 'social science' consists of what duly recognized social scientists are doing – but all of them are by no means doing the same thing, in fact not even the same sort of thing. Social science is also what social scientists of the past have done – but different students choose to construct and to recall different traditions in their discipline. When I speak of 'the promise of social science,' I hope it is clear that I mean the promise as I see it. (Mills 1959, 18f.)

Here, Mills acknowledges an important tension that is inherent in his task. Sociology is an academic discipline that has, throughout its history, been notably diverse in its theories, methods and objects of enquiry. Neither among the early sociologists of the 19th century nor in Mills's time nor today do sociologists engage in the same type of work. Nonetheless, for sociology to have coherence as an intellectual field and a form of scholarly practice, it must be characterised by a central ethos, ambition and set of objectives. Mills attempts to formulate this defining ethos – 'the promise of social science', while at the same time acknowledging that 'I mean the promise as I see it'. In this sense, answers to the questions 'what sociology is about?' and 'how sociology might be done?' are inherently contentious, and the extent to which they come to be widely accepted is an outcome of the politics of academic life.

At the same time, for Mills, sociology is political in terms of the ways in which it forms part of broader public life. In Mills's (1959, 18f.) words, sociology has 'implications for political as well as for cultural life'. Rendering these apparent and making them part of the public conversation beyond academia is a central task for sociologists still today, and Mills was quite clear about this, both in *The Sociological Imagination* and elsewhere in his work (1943, 1945, 1956).

At the same time, the sociological imagination is a personal quality – a mental stance allowing sociologists to become aware of, analyse and understand the relationships between individuals and broader social structures – and we hope this is the minimum you will take away by the end of this book too. This is implicit in the quoted statement above in so far as Mills suggests that the sociological imagination can be 'developed' and 'possessed'. Elsewhere, Mills makes this point quite clear:

> [The sociological imagination] is the capacity to range from the most
> impersonal and remote transformations to the most intimate features of
> the human self – and to see the relations between the two. Back of its
> use there is always the urge to know the social and historical meaning
> of the individual in the society and in the period in which he has
> his quality and his being. That, in brief, is why it is by means of the
> sociological imagination that men now hope to grasp what is going
> on in the world, and to understand what is happening in themselves
> as minute points of the intersections of biography and history within
> society. (Mills 1959, 7)

The sociological imagination is not just an ethos that defines an academic discipline. It is a distinctive mental stance that makes it possible for individuals to clearly locate themselves within society at large. Elsewhere, Mills (1959, 8) famously describes it in terms of the ability to understand how 'personal troubles of milieu' might form part of broader 'public issues of social structure'. Moreover, it seems important that Mills also describes it as an 'urge'. While he does not explain this further, it can perhaps be usefully understood as an emotional corollary of sociological knowledge – as a personal desire to understand the meaning of individual lives through their social settings. This suggests that the sociological imagination is as much a defining characteristic of sociology as an academic discipline as a distinctive mindset of the professional sociologist and, hopefully, the public at large. It is in this sense that it can be described as an ethos, rather than as the analytic objectives of an academic discipline.

At the most basic, the sociological imagination for Mills refers to the ability to understand the relationships between individual biographical trajectories and broader social structures. From this point of departure, he derives a set of central questions for sociological analysis:

> The sociological imagination enables us to grasp history and biography
> and the relations between the two within society. That is its task and
> its promise. […] No social study that does not come back to the
> problems of biography, of history and of their intersections within a
> society has completed its intellectual journey. Whatever the specific
> problems of the classic social analyst, however limited or however
> broad the features of social reality they have examined, those who
> have been imaginatively aware of the promise of their work have
> consistently asked three sorts of questions: (1) What is the structure of
> this particular society as a whole? What are its essential components,
> and how are they related to one another? How does it differ from
> other varieties of social order? Within it, what is the meaning of any
> particular feature for its continuance and for its change? (2) Where
> does this society stand in human history? What are the mechanics by

which it is changing? What is its place within and its meaning for the development of humanity as a whole? How does any particular feature we are examining affect, and how is it affected by, the historical period in which it moves? And this period – what are its essential features? How does it differ from other periods? What are its characteristic ways of history-making? (3) What varieties of men and women now prevail in this society and in this period? And what varieties are coming to prevail? In what ways are they selected and formed, liberated and repressed, made sensitive and blunted? What kinds of 'human nature' are revealed in the conduct and character we observe in this society in this period? And what is the meaning for 'human nature' of each and every feature of the society we are examining? (Mills 1959, 6f.)

Sociology thus is concerned with the analysis of social structures and institutions, with social change and institutional transformation, and with the relationships between individual behaviour and social structure. Mills develops these three concerns in the final three chapters of *The Sociological Imagination* (1959, chapters 7–10), and we consider their contemporary significance in this book.

At this point, it is useful to consider a further defining dimension of Mills's mode of sociological analysis. To characterise it, Mills develops the term, and we have used it a few times already in this book, of 'intellectual craftsmanship'. Intellectual craftsmanship furnishes him with the title and the subject matter for a much-cited appendix to *The Sociological Imagination*. Addressing students, Mills (1959, 195) intends this appendix to convey a sense of basic tasks and activities involved in doing sociology, from research design to writing strategies. His account is organised around the image of the sociologist as a craftsman:

To the individual social scientist who feels himself a part of the classic tradition, social science is the practice of a craft. A man at work on problems of substance, he is among those who are quickly made impatient and weary by elaborate discussions of method-and-theory-in-general; so much of it interrupts his proper studies. [...] Be a good craftsman: Avoid any rigid set of procedures. Above all, seek to develop and to use the sociological imagination. Avoid the fetishism of method and technique. Urge the rehabilitation of the unpretentious intellectual craftsman, and try to become such a craftsman yourself. Let every man be his own methodologist; let every man be his own theorist; let theory and method again become part of the practice of a craft. Stand for the primacy of the individual scholar; stand opposed to the ascendancy of research teams of technicians. Be one mind that is on its own confronting the problems of man and society. (Mills 1959, 195, 224)

What is important here is the contrast between the sociologist as a technician and the sociologist as an intellectual craftsman. Through it, Mills encourages sociologists to pursue intellectual autonomy and to identify with their scholarship and its contributions to 'confronting the problems of man and society'. Disparaging the 'fetishism of method and technique', Mills does not de-emphasise the need for systematic enquiry, and the remainder of the appendix sets out suggestions in this regard. Instead, he encourages sociologists to think of themselves as intellectuals whose work is motivated by the wish to engage with current social and political problems, rather than by the technical problems of their own profession. Mills's notion of intellectual craftsmanship is thus arguably closely associated with his commitment to a public sociology that is politically charged and engaged in the public debates of its time (Mjøset 2013).

Against this distinctive account of what sociology is and what sociologists should be, Mills (1959, chapters 2–6) subjects prominent trends in sociological enquiry to a trenchant and often acerbic critique. This includes direct criticism of prominent US sociologists, notably Paul Lazarsfeld and Talcott Parsons. It is this critique that drew much attention following the book's original publication and contributed significantly to its negative reception by some prominent sociologists of the time. In a lengthy review, for example, Edward Shils (1961, 601, 621) describes *The Sociological Imagination* as 'a vehement invitation to sociologists to do something much different from what the overwhelming majority of them have been doing'; claims that Mills identifies 'the ideal sociologist' with himself; suggests that 'Professor Mills will continue to play his rat-catcher's pipe' to mislead younger academics; and concludes that it 'is a great pity that what is sensible in his book is so entangled with what is wild and ridiculous'. While Shils considers the book's argument in considerable detail, it seems that his dismissal is as much a response to C. Wright Mills's style and tone as to his ideas. In our present ominous times, 'tone policing' is a familiar form of misdirection and is the least of our concerns.

Sociology in question

For our purposes, this controversy is much less important than Mills's sketch of a distinctive sociological ethos. The landscape of sociological analysis has shifted considerably since Mills's critique, and the sociologists whose work he attacked – Parsons and Lazarsfeld – have long ceased to be the defining figures they used to be (Misztal 2000). In a recent review of an anniversary edition of *The Sociological Imagination*, Barbara Misztal arrives at an ambivalent conclusion as to its contemporary significance: 'So if Mills's dismissal of his contemporary giants seems less relevant, what about his more general observations on the state and status of sociology?' (Misztal 2000, 105).

Misztal's own response to her question is ambivalent; she concludes, that more may be needed for a revitalisation of sociology than a distinctive sociological ethos:

> While we should, following Mills, encourage the doing of an 'imaginative sociology', one which requires a passion for social inquiry and a recognition of the interdependence between the realm of ideas/ theories and everyday life, we need more than relying on the talents of thinkers such as Mills. In order to rebuild sociology, we need to develop and strengthen groups, schools and networks of scholarly exchange. (Misztal 2000, 105)

This ambivalence is equally manifest in other contemporary reviews. John Brewer (2013, 220) argues that there is little substance to Mills's argument and that it is 'a bumper sticker, a flag, an icon – call it what you will – for a way of doing sociology differently'. Mills's vision of sociology, he concludes, has been surpassed by that of contemporary scholars, most notably by Michael Burawoy's public sociology. Iain Wilkinson (2012, 189) points to Mills's 'failure to produce a viable model of methodological practice' while acknowledging its significance to a contemporary sociology of social suffering. Lars Mjøset situates *The Sociological Imagination* in its historical context, maps tensions and ambiguities in its argument and points to its ultimate failure to meaningfully influence the development of sociological practice. Today, he concludes, 'it seems that many introductions to contemporary sociology rather hijack Mills's formula of the sociological imagination, uncritically selecting quotes that gloss over these tensions' (Mjøset 2013, 85). Mills's work itself *is* beset by notable blind spots and shortcomings. Beyond the vagueness of his proposals for sociological analysis in *The Sociological Imagination* (Mjøset 2013), his relative lack of attention to inequalities of race, ethnicity and gender contrasts sharply with his highly critical accounts of US capitalism. Likewise, his interest in Latin America and his collaboration with European academics notwithstanding (Mills et al 1950; Gerth and Mills 1953; Mills 1960), he was very much an American intellectual whose outlook was defined by white American intellectual life. Mills's work therefore very much forms part of a 'Northern sociology' (Connell 2007) concerned with the problems of a Western industrialised society and removed from intellectual developments in the Global South). His sociology in this sense might be understood as a product of its time that does not reflect the expansion of sociological enquiry since the 1960s and the discipline's global turn, which we will look at in detail in Chapters 5 and 6 (Bhambra 2014a).

These assessments are hard to dismiss, and we will cover their implications throughout this book in our call for a revival and development of the sociological imagination. At the same time, we argue that there is more than has been considered so far to *The Sociological Imagination* and Mills's work at large that can be mobilised to think about contemporary sociology too. The fissures and gaps in Mills's work can be turned into points of departure into the formulation of a sociological imagination for the 21st century, informed by Mills's ethos and craftsmanship, but amended to allow for an understanding of the crisis of the social in the early 21st century as we will describe in multiple and interconnected ways.

As we argued in the introduction, the world of the 21st century is just emerging from the US's 'war on terror', the economic collapse of 2008, centuries of escalating environmental degradation, large-scale population displacement, growing socioeconomic inequalities, technological developments with unpredictable consequences, the rise of new far-right nationalisms, the eroding legitimacy of democracy, and growing difficulties for states, social institutions and individuals to cope with the resulting risks. These ominous trends have been analysed, charted and critiqued in social research, and social scientists have made extensive proposals to counter them. Nonetheless, their appraisal in public life remains controversial, as shown by, for instance, the widespread denial of climate change in some societies, hostile responses to immigration in some Euro-American societies, and current concern about disinformation and 'fake news' in online social media and by politicians around the world (Marchi 2012; Dunlap 2013; Wodak 2015; Associated Press 2017). Sociology might play an important part in these public debates, through arguments grounded in systematic scholarship.

Arguably, it does not do so, having faded from public view in spite of highly visible public sociologists who are involved in media conversations, policy debates and exchanges with governmental and non-governmental organisations. Sociology today faces significant challenges, both in public life and within the academic world. In public life, sociology's role has been challenged for the past four decades by a cultural and political idiom that explains individual biographies, differences and inequalities as the outcome of purely individual attitudes, choices and responsibilities, on occasion denying the existence of society altogether (Harvey 2007; Dardot and Laval 2013). Sociological narratives that explain biographies, differences and inequalities in terms of broader social structures have lost legitimacy and perhaps even intelligibility. Nearly six decades ago, C. Wright Mills (1959, 14) argued that the 'sociological imagination is becoming … the major common denominator of our cultural life and its signal feature'. Today, this claim seems far from true. At the same time, sociology is being called into question by the contemporary transformation of universities into businesses, the precarisation of academic careers, the remaking of students as consumers and the shifts in the legitimation of scholarship towards standards of economic utility (Williams 2012; Cantwell et al 2014). A conversation about sociology's disciplinary identity, its place in academic life and its role in public life therefore seems like a timely task. *The Sociological Imagination* and the work of C. Wright Mills have much to offer in this regard.

Why dedicate a whole chapter to C. Wright Mills, though? Books such as this one often make mention of *The Sociological Imagination* (Mills 1959), but they generally do not devote detailed attention to its author, or, for that matter, to the life and work of any particular sociologist. We have taken a different approach in this book because we wish to emphasise that sociology can only be properly understood if we consider it as an institutionally situated form of labour. Sociology is, on the one hand, a set of concepts, theories and methods of systematic enquiry – a knowledge formation that offers a distinctive narrative of human life. Mills's sociological imagination brings many central features of this narrative to the fore, and it deserves attention for this reason. On the other hand, it is important to understand that in many ways the sociological imagination as has been traditionally understood is a product of scholarly labour in a particular historical period, in a specific society, in a particular type of university, and in the context of a particular kind of academic career.

We cannot fully understand the sociological imagination, and we cannot fully understand sociology at large if we do not account for their material and institutional production. C. Wright Mills's work stands for a particular type of academic career that is arguably characteristic of those of many of the sociologists from the Global Northwest) who populate the pages of English-language sociology textbooks. Therefore, in looking at Mills's career alongside his ideas, we may gain a clearer sense of the circumstances under which the sociological imagination was produced. Moreover, looking at Mills from the point of view of what made, for some time and in some societies, a successful academic career in sociology, we can trace divergent patterns in contemporary global sociology (see Chapters 3, 5 and 6), and we can delineate changes in contemporary academic labour and their consequences for sociologists and for sociology.

A few initial observations in this regard seem in to be in order. First, the dual notions of the sociological imagination and intellectual craftsmanship entail important questions about the disciplinary ethos of sociology and the professional ethos of individual sociologists and sociology students, at a time when academics, in the UK as much as elsewhere, are under intense pressure to justify their work solely in economic and numeric terms. In academia and in public policy, sociologists today are asked, as much as other academics, to demonstrate their professional standing through the income they have generated in research grants and the measurable impact their work has had on social and economic life. The careers of individual sociologists and the prospects of entire sociology departments may hinge on their performance in audits that place a heavy emphasis on the ability to instrumentalise scholarship on these terms.

The analogy to Mills's distinction between the sociologist-as-technician and the intellectual craftsman is obvious and deserves further consideration. Mills meant to criticise inward-looking obsession with theory and method, rather than the instrumentalisation of scholarship for economic ends. However, ultimately, both detract from the public commitment that Mills sees as central to sociology and the sociologist's professional identity.

At the same time, sociological labour has come to be heavily stratified, through the increasing scarcity of long-term academic employment and ever more intensely felt hierarchies between universities, academic departments and individual scholars. Mills's suggestion that sociologists should strive to become autonomous intellectual craftspersons might therefore be rather more significant than Misztal

(2000) recognises, in an age in which academics are subject to ever expanding regimes of audits and bureaucratic regulation (Alvesson 2014; Watts 2017).

Second, Mills's proposals for intellectual craftsmanship also draw attention to the professional practice and identity of individual sociologists. Discussions about sociology's history and future tend to focus on its conceptual and methodological substance (Connell 2007; Bhambra 2014a), while the ways in which sociologists' day-to-day practice – the ways in which sociologists actually work – have received much less attention. At a time in which universities are changing dramatically, it seems urgent to reconsider the practices of everyday sociological labour, to ask how these are defined by the institutional structures in which they are set, and to examine their implications for the professional identity of sociologists. We argue that the ideal of the intellectual craftsperson may serve as an analytically useful benchmark in this regard.

These concerns have structured our argument in this book, as we mobilised the sociological imagination. The image of the sociologist as an intellectual craftsperson to explore our discipline and examine how it might address the ominous social processes that are increasingly defining life in the early 21st century is also an important idea. On the one hand, this is a book about making the case for sociology once again, and as such sociology's identity and significance as an academic discipline. On the other hand, this book can still be read as an introduction to sociology. Of course, it departs notably from the format that such texts usually have, in that we are less concerned with developing a detailed account of sociological theories and methods than with considering what sociology means today, what it might mean and what it should mean. At a time of crisis and uncertainty, such fundamental concerns – and how to possess a distinctive sociological ethos towards the world – arguably deserve attention before the technical details of theory and method.

THINKING SOCIOLOGICALLY

There are two ways to think about the sociological imagination. On the one hand, sociology is a clearly bounded academic discipline, defined by its own key thinkers, concepts, theories, methods and areas of enquiry. In this sense, it is different from other areas of the social sciences, such as human geography, social and cultural anthropology, and one of your tasks as a student of sociology is to learn about the aforementioned key thinkers, ideas and practices that conform academic sociology. From this perspective, the sociological imagination is the outlook that defines academic sociology. On the other hand, it seems essential to recognise that sociology is – or at least that it might be and should be – more than a closely confined academic niche. The sociological imagination characterises the reasoning of scholars, intellectual and activists far beyond the remits of academic sociology proper, and academic sociology proper often can learn much from these thinkers.

In this light, explore the life and work of the following social thinkers and writers – pick three or four if time is limited. Document their biographies and their key ideas in writing and record your findings in a handout or a poster. In particular, consider whether they self-identified as sociologists and to what extent and in which ways their arguments may be important to sociologists today.

1. Karl Marx
2. Friedrich Engels
3. Charlotte Perkins Gilman
4. Walter Rodney
5. Jane Addams
6. George Herbert Mead
7. Antonio Gramsci
8. Bob Marley
9. Olive Schreiner
10. Ibn Khaldun
11. Henri de Saint-Simon

MINI PROJECT

C. Wright Mills was born in 1916 and died in 1962. What were the major social, economic and political developments of his lifetime, both in the US and at the international level? How, if at all, did they inform Mills's work?

For this project, you will need to do some background research, using relevant academic sources, as well as other published materials. Biographies of C. Wright Mills, such as Tom Hayden's *Radical Nomad* (2006) and Irving Lewis Horowitz's *C. Wright Mills: An American Utopian* (1983) may be useful starting points, as may overviews of Mills's work, for example A. Javier Treviño's *The Social Thought of C. Wright Mills* (2011). It is not the point of this project to engage with these sources in comprehensive details. Rather, it is meant to give you a sense how Mills's preoccupations as a sociologist were shaped by the times he lived in.

Working in groups, in so far as feasible, summarise your findings and display them in a poster presentation.

TALKING POINTS

1. 'The point to be made, rather, is that becoming a sociologist requires a distinctive quality of mind, rather than just comprehensive knowledge of a certain body of facts.' [p 16] What is this statement trying to say? In which ways is sociology a 'quality of mind'? Why?

2. 'At any given moment, of course, 'social science' consists of what duly recognized social scientists are doing – but all of them are by no means doing the same thing, in fact not even the same sort of thing' (Mills, 1959, 19). What does Mills mean by this statement?

3. What may be the significance of the sociological imagination beyond professional sociology, to social and political life at large?

4. In this section, we have referred to Mills as a 'public sociologist'. [p 17] What does this term mean? Are all sociologists public sociologists? Why (not)? Give examples of contemporary public sociologists and the issues with which they are concerned.

5. Is sociology political ? [p 21] Why (not)?

6. As a white male US sociologist with an elite academic background, C. Wright Mills's biography arguably represents some of the social inequalities inherent in Western sociology in the mid-20th century. Is sociology today more diverse? Consider how you might answer this question: What might your point of reference be – international sociology, sociology in a particular country and so on? What sources might you draw on to answer this question?

Working in groups, if feasible, summarise your findings in writing and present them for discussion.

READ ON ...

Of Mills's own works, *White Collar* (1951) and *The Power Elite* (1956) are still particularly timely and readable. There are also numerous recent summaries and appraisals of Mills's work. Among these, A. Javier Treviño's *The Social Thought of C. Wright Mills* (2011) and John Scott and Ann Nilsen's edited collection *C. Wright Mills and the Sociological Imagination* (2013) make for good starting points to learn more about Mills's work. Alternatively, two biographies – Tom Hayden's *Radical Nomad* (2006) and Irving Lewis Horowitz's *C. Wright Mills: An American Utopian* (1983) – provide important insights into Mills's life and times.

Check the companion website at https://bristoluniversitypress. co.uk/imagining-society-online-resources **for a suggested project and writing task.**

3

What is 'the social'?

Are you going through a difficult period in your life? Have you been feeling stressed, under pressure and generally out of sorts? Is your preparation for a difficult exam, essay or journal article getting to you? Have you been anxious about your career prospects? Is your workload too much? Would you like to improve your health and wellbeing? Then mindfulness might just be the right thing for you!

Mindfulness addresses central problems of contemporary human life. Jon Kabat-Zinn, one of its chief proponents, explains this clearly at the outset of *Coming to Our Senses*, an introduction to the benefits of mindfulness:

> I don't know about you, but for myself, it feels like we are at a critical juncture of life on this planet. It could go any number of different ways. It seems that the world is on fire and so are our hearts, inflamed with fear and uncertainty, lacking all conviction, and often filled with passionate but unwise intensity. How we manage to see ourselves and the world at this juncture will make a huge difference in the way things unfold. (Kabat-Zinn 2005, 1)

Note the similarities to *The Sociological Imagination* (Mills 1959). Just as C. Wright Mills does, Jon Kabat-Zinn begins his argument with a strongly worded reference to the uncertainty and anxiety that human life today entails. Moreover, in similarity to Mills, Kabat-Zinn also emphasises the importance of how 'we manage to see ourselves and the world' in addressing this sense of uncertainty. Even more, Jon Kabat-Zinn also offers his readers a new way of understanding their lives. This new way – mindfulness – may bring about fundamental change, as he explains:

> The first step on the adventure involved in coming to our senses on any and every level is the cultivation of a particular kind of awareness known as mindfulness. Mindfulness is the final common pathway of what makes us human, our capacity for awareness and for self-knowing. Mindfulness is cultivated by paying attention, and, as we shall see, this paying attention is developed and refined through a practice known as

mindfulness meditation, which has been spreading rapidly around the world and into the mainstream of Western culture in the past thirty years, thanks in part to an increasing number of scientific and medical studies of its various effects. (Kabat–Zinn 2005, 11)

And here the similarities with *The Sociological Imagination* end. As the preceding extract shows quite plainly, mindfulness is not an approach to sociological understanding and social relations that would require systematic engagement with the social world. On the contrary, mindfulness promotes a sort of emotional and cognitive inward turn on the part of those who practise it. Mindfulness is about 'coming to our senses' through meditation and careful introspection, thus realising our potential for 'awareness and for self-knowing', so as to better cope with the challenges we face in everyday life. Moreover, Jon Kabat–Zinn is not a sociologist, but rather a Professor of Medicine at the University of Massachusetts in the US.

Why does mindfulness matter in a book about sociology? Mindfulness matters because it forms part of the modes of understanding and imagining human life that in the early 21st century have arguably become more important, more publicly visible, and more commonsensical than the sociological imagination. In particular, mindfulness stands for the psychologisation of human life (Madsen 2018). By psychologisation, we refer to explanations of individuals' thoughts, feelings and actions, and of larger social processes and inequalities, through psychological processes and qualities – depression, anxiety, happiness, wellness and so on. The sociological imagination asks us to understand events in the lives of individual people and the thoughts and emotions that are associated with these events as elements of much larger, social processes and relationships – unemployment as a result of labour market constraints, marriage and divorce as society-wide arrangements of family life and so on. Mindfulness, in contrast, asks us to look at our mental life, revise it through meditative techniques, and improve our personal wellbeing as a result.

In recent years, mindfulness has become widely fashionable. Self-help books teach their readers how to meditate (Bien and Bien 2003; Kabat–Zinn 2005; Williams and Penman 2011), workshops and therapy sessions purvey training in mindfulness techniques (University of Bangor 2017a), universities found mindfulness centres and offer mindfulness degree courses (University of Aberdeen 2017; University of Bangor 2017b), and mindfulness is at the forefront of solutions to concerns about students' wellbeing (Swain 2016; Mindfulness for Students 2017). All this is underpinned by a wide range of academic and seemingly academic publications that give mindfulness an air of scientific soundness (Weick and Putnam 2006; Chrisman et al 2008; Barber and Deale 2014). The mindfulness fad, in turn, forms part of the much wider business of popular psychology. A wide range of products and services offer consumers psychological solutions to pressing everyday problems, from self-help books to motivational workshops. Hundreds of thousands of self-help books are sold every year in the UK, at annual value of at least £6 million, and the sales figures for other countries, from China to India to South Africa to the US are similar or greater (Nehring et al 2016).

This points to the deep roots that psychological, rather than sociological, explanations of human life have taken in contemporary common sense, and it raises questions about the contemporary significance of sociological thought. Nearly sixty years ago, C. Wright Mills argued that the sociological imagination was becoming 'the major common denominator of our cultural life and its signal feature' (Mills 1959, 14). The same cannot easily be assumed today (see Chapter 10), and it seems questionable to what extent sociological ideas, concepts and theories still seem plausible and meaningful to those who are not professional academic sociologists.

Therefore, in making our case for sociology in the 21st century it seems important to start with the foundations of the field and consider what sociologists might mean when we claim that something is *social* and the various adjuncts of the social in classic sociology such as social physics, social facts (structures), social action, social selves and social conflict. As a field of knowledge and scholarly practice, sociology is built on the assumption that mental life, interpersonal relationships and institutions all share the special quality of being social. To understand what this means in this chapter we turn now to the history of sociology and the enquiries of some of the earliest sociologists. Early sociologists explained in great detail the assumption that human life is social and, in so doing, justified the importance of establishing sociology as a new and distinctive academic discipline. These justifications are of considerable interest today, at a time when sociological thought seems to be fading from public life and alternative narratives, such as those of psychology and populism, have risen to prominence. But these theories of the 19th and 20th centuries may not be enough to understand the 21st century. A point to which we will return at the end of the chapter.

Imagining the social

Sociology is a result of far-reaching social, cultural, political and economic transformations in the 18th century. Throughout the previous centuries, certain countries in Western Europe had been greatly enriched by the expansion of trade, the exploitation of colonies in the Americas, Africa and Asia, and the Atlantic slave trade. As these countries – Great Britain, France, Spain, Portugal, the Dutch Republic and parts of what today is Germany – increased their wealth, cities grew and an urban middle class of well-to-do and educated traders, bankers, lawyers, artists and scholars developed. New ideas spread that contested long-held Christian religious worldviews and the divine authority of kings, and modern science, in the form of disciplines such as physics, began to emerge. Collectively labelled the Enlightenment, these ideas found expression in far-reaching philosophical and political debates. Widely revered scholarly works of Western liberalism such as John Locke's *Two Treatises of Government* (2003), Adam Smith's *An Inquiry into the Nature and Causes of the Wealth of Nations* (1999) and the *Encyclopédie* edited by Denis Diderot and Jacques le Rond d'Alembert (1954) resulted from these debates. Moreover, they played an important role in great political upheaval towards the end of the century, in the form of the Declaration of Independence of Britain's colonies in the contemporary US in 1776, the beginning of the French Revolution in 1789, the revolution of Haiti's enslaved population against French rule in 1791, and the temporary abolition of the French monarchy in 1792. At the same time, new technological developments such as the invention of the steam engine in the 1780s played a central role in the very early stages of industrialisation and the transition of some European societies to urbanised, industrial modern life.

Sociology as a discipline was thus born into a time of great upheaval and change. It emerged in Western Europe through the work of scholars such as Auguste Comte. From there, it gradually spread around the world first through colonialism and then globalisation, with sociologists in the Americas, Africa, Asia and Oceania building different and distinctive modes of sociological enquiry and conceptualisations of the social world. In the early 21st century sociology is a truly global endeavour, as witnessed, for instance, by thousands of sociologists from around the world who gather every year at the conferences of the International Sociological Association. This brief overview of the birth of sociology is discussed in decolonial terms in Chapter 6, as is the story of the Enlightenment in Chapter 7.

Comte and social physics

In sociology's early days, when 'sociologist' was a novel label for a scholar, degree courses in sociology barely existed and sociology departments were few and far between at universities. There was much work to be done to explain what the new discipline was all about and why it should occupy a place among older, well-established fields such as theology, philosophy or the natural sciences. Convincing explanations of sociology's characteristic subject matter were thus a major preoccupation among many early sociologists. Among these explanations, the one offered by Auguste Comte in France is still frequently cited today. Comte was born in 1798, during the turmoil of the French Revolution, and he died in 1857. During his lifetime, France experienced the revolution and the Napoleonic Wars, several further revolutions, and social and economic upheaval. Comte responded to this by proposing a new science, 'a science of society', which he named social physics:

> It is in deference to as much as is reasonable in this apprehension that I propose to state, first, how the institution of a science of Social Physics bears upon the principal needs and grievances of society, in its present deplorable state of anarchy. Such a representation may perhaps convince men worthy of the name of statesmen that there

is a real and eminent utility in labours of this kind, worthy of the anxious attention of men who profess to devote themselves to the task of resolving the alarming revolutionary constitution of modern societies. (Comte 2000, 117)

In Comte's usage, the terms social physics and sociology are closely related, and he explains that sociology is 'the term I may be allowed to invent to designate Social Physics' (Comte 2000, 168). His case for a new science of the social proceeds from the assumption that 'the needs and grievances of society' have reached such an alarming state that they must be urgently addressed. Sociology, in this very early formulation, is thus geared towards analysing, understanding and resolving pressing social problems. Sociology is needed, Comte goes on to argue, because long-established disciplines such as theology or philosophy are ill-suited to the task at hand (Comte 2000, 177).

Comte makes a point that is foundational to the sociology project as a whole. His case for sociology – and against theology and philosophy – rests on the distinction between speculation and empirical – that is, experience-based – observation. He is critical of the 'preponderance of imagination over observation' that characterises theology and philosophy, as this leads them 'to exercise an arbitrary and indefinite action over phenomena which are not regarded as subject to invariable natural laws' (Comte 2000, 177). In other words, theology and philosophy cannot adequately address specific social problems because their emphasis on imagination or speculation may result in arbitrary conclusions. Therefore, Comte looks to natural sciences such as physics, and he concludes that their search for laws of nature can be productively applied to the study of society. This view – that sociologists ought to view their discipline as a science and identify law-like regularities in social life – has remained influential all the way to the present day, but it also continues to spark sometimes heated controversy. More importantly for our purposes, though, Comte points to a fundamental feature of sociology on which all sociologists can agree, namely that our discipline is concerned with the empirical study of the social. The social consists of individual actions and events that can only be fully understood through direct, systematic observation.

Durkheim and social facts

This raises the question in which ways human actions and the events of human life may be social? To answer this question, we turn to the work of another early French sociologist, Émile Durkheim (1858–1917). Durkheim's lifetime spans much of the second half of the 19th century, as well as the early 20th century, up to the final years of the First World War. He contributed in very important ways to establishing academic sociology in France, founding the first French sociology journal, *L'Année Sociologique*, and teaching the first sociology course at a French university. Durkheim's academic publications were likewise meant to make a case for sociology. In *Suicide* (2005), for example, Durkheim set out a detailed sociological analysis of what might be, common sense suggests, one of the most personal and individual choices that a person can make. However, looking at data such as statistical accounts of suicide rates, Durkheim showed that individuals' decisions to take their own lives might be related in profound ways to much larger developments in society. Of equal importance is *The Rules of Sociological Method* (2013b), a programmatic statement of the new discipline and its importance. In *The Rules of Sociological Method*, Durkheim begins his case for sociology with observations that in many ways parallel those made by Auguste Comte more than half a century earlier:

> We are so little accustomed to treating social facts scientifically that certain propositions contained in this book may well surprise the reader. However, if a science of societies exists, one must certainly not expect it to consist of a mere paraphrase of traditional prejudices. It should rather cause us to see things in a different way from the ordinary man, for the purpose of any science is to make discoveries, and all such discoveries more or less upset accepted opinions. Thus unless in sociology one ascribes to common sense an authority that it has lost for a long time in the other sciences – and it is not clear whence that might be derived – the scholar must determinedly resolve not to be intimidated by the results to which his investigations may lead, provided that they have been methodically carried out. (Durkheim 2013b, 9)

In similarity to Comte, Durkheim argues for the scientific study of social life, and he emphasises that 'traditional prejudices' have no role to play in a 'science of societies'. Here we have another argument central to sociology. Sociology operates on the assumption that its insights into the social can reach much further than common sense can, whether in the form of theological speculation or traditional prejudices or the sense of being trapped that C. Wright Mills famously describes in the opening chapter of *The Sociological Imagination* (1959) or the runaway world that we described in Chapter 1. Sociologists may study common sense to gain insights into social life, but its biases should not inform sociological analysis. This privileged status of sociological knowledge derives from sociology's capability to systematically observe, record and analyse empirical social processes and relations, in difference from the unfounded assumptions inherent in common sense and personal anecdotes. This – the notion that systematic empirical enquiry must be allowed to speak for itself – is what Durkheim means when he argues that the scholar 'must determinedly resolve not to be intimidated by the results to which his investigations may lead, provided that they have been methodically carried out' (Durkheim 2013b, 9).

Durkheim then goes on to specify what he means by the social, by introducing the concept of 'social facts', in a much-quoted statement that is foundational to sociology at large. Durkheim's begins his explanation of social facts with a series of examples:

> Every individual drinks, sleeps, eats, or employs his reason, and society has every interest in seeing that these functions are regularly exercised. If therefore these facts were social ones, sociology would possess no subject matter peculiarly its own, and its domain would be confused with that of biology and psychology. However, in reality there is in every society a clearly determined group of phenomena separable, because of their distinct characteristics, from those that form the subject matter of other sciences of nature. When I perform my duties as a brother, a husband or a citizen and carry out the commitments I have entered into, I fulfil obligations which are defined in law and custom and which are external to myself and my actions. Even when they conform to my own sentiments and when I feel their reality within me, that reality does not cease to be objective, for it is not I who have prescribed these duties; I have received them through education. Moreover, how often does it happen that we are ignorant of the details of the obligations that we must assume, and that, to know them, we must consult the legal code and its authorized interpreters! Similarly the believer has discovered from birth, ready fashioned, the beliefs and practices of his religious life; if they existed before he did, it follows that they exist outside him. The system of signs that I employ to express my thoughts, the monetary system I use to pay my debts, the credit instruments I utilize in my commercial relationships, the practices I follow in my profession, etc., all function independently of the use I make of them. Considering in turn each member of society, the foregoing remarks can be repeated for each single one of them. Thus there are ways of acting, thinking and feeling which possess the remarkable property of existing outside the consciousness of the individual. (Durkheim 2013b, 20)

Through these mundane examples, on money, language, family relationships and so forth, Durkheim highlights an important quality of the social: It consists of 'ways of acting, thinking and feeling which possess the remarkable property of existing outside the consciousness of the individual'. Human life consists of the thoughts, feelings and actions of individual human beings. However, as Durkheim notes, it is possible to identify among these thoughts, feelings and actions those that are not merely individual and personal, but rather social, or, as Durkheim puts it, external to individual consciousness. If I forget that the gas inspector is due to visit my house in South Korea as I did several times last week, my frustration at my forgetfulness is, in a sense, entirely my own; in the first place, it has to do with my psychological state last week – being overworked, forgetful, absentminded and so on. If, however, I consider that I communicated with the gas inspector in Korean, using both the spoken language and letters written in the Hangeul alphabet, I realise that there is a distinctly social dimension to my interaction with her. Language, just as any social fact, is social in so far as it is widely shared among the members of a given society, acquired by individuals through a process of education or learning, and largely resistant at the efforts of particular individuals to change or reject it. Had I resisted the need to speak proper Korean in Korea, by, say, speaking German or English or saying Korean words backwards, the inspector would not have understood me, and our communication would have failed. The Korean language is a part of my mind, as I have learned it and speak it in my own idiosyncratic way, with all the mistakes a non-native speaker might make. However, Korean certainly exists outside my individual consciousness, as it is a shared feature of Korean society, where it has developed over millennia. This quality of social facts leads Durkheim to a further conclusion:

> Not only are these types of behaviour and thinking external to the individual, but they are endued with a compelling and coercive power by virtue of which, whether he wishes it or not, they impose themselves upon him. Undoubtedly when I conform to them of my own free will, this coercion is not felt or felt hardly at all, since it is unnecessary. None the less it is intrinsically a characteristic of these facts; the proof of this is that it asserts itself as soon as I try to resist. If I attempt to violate the rules of law they react against me so as to forestall my action, if there is still time. Alternatively, they annul it or make my action conform to the norm if it is already accomplished but capable of being reversed; or they cause me to pay the penalty for it if it is irreparable. If purely moral rules are at stake, the public conscience restricts any act which infringes them by the surveillance it exercises over the conduct of citizens and by the special punishments it has at its disposal. In other cases the constraint is less violent; nevertheless, it does not cease to exist. If I do not conform to ordinary conventions, if in my mode of dress I pay no heed to what is customary in my country and in my social class, the laughter I provoke, the social distance at which I am kept, produce, although in a more mitigated form, the same results as any real penalty. (Durkheim 2013b, 21)

Thus, not only are social facts widely shared, acquired by individuals through learning, and resistant to individual efforts to change them, they also possess compelling power. What is meant by this becomes obvious if we stay with the example of language and consider what happens, as it might have occurred to you, when one finds oneself in a foreign country, unable to speak the local language or to find speakers of one's own language. The need to learn the local language acquires compelling force, and efforts to resist will result in misunderstandings and missed opportunities and personal isolation. Durkheim's example of the law makes the point equally clear. The law is a social fact, as it is a shared feature of life in a particular society, learned, however, imperfectly, by individuals, largely resistant to immediate change, equipped with compulsory force and is produced by groups of humans working together over time. For example, laws that prohibit theft are a shared, widely known feature of many societies, and even though I might claim that I did not know the law when I stole that rare, out-of-print book from the library, I will still face a substantial fine or worse for taking it. Through the work of Émile Durkheim, we have therefore uncovered the first set of features of the social, in that it is external to individuals' thoughts, feelings and actions and may exert compelling force over them. In contemporary sociology, rather than speaking of social facts, the term 'social structure' is frequently used to refer to those aspects of social life that constrain, compel, direct or guide individuals' lives over prolonged periods of time. Thus the social consists of social structures also known as social facts.

Weber and social action

Émile Durkheim's account of social facts makes a strong case for sociological analysis. If sociologists only focused on the analysis of social facts or social structures, we would find it difficult to account for human creativity and social change. If we only considered how human life is regulated by the structural arrangements that exist in society, then we might come to think of individuals simply as rule-following automata. Therefore, we need to look more closely at the problem of social action and agency.

For this, we now turn to the work of Max Weber. From its early days, sociology has been an intellectually diverse discipline. It has always shared a common core of assumptions – this is what we mean when we speak of a sociological imagination – but different sociologists and groups of sociologists have emphasised different aspects of the social in their work. Max Weber, one of the most important German sociologists, was born in Erfurt in 1864 and died in Munich in 1920. Even though Weber today is often portrayed as one of the founders of sociology, in his lifetime he was equally associated with the fields of history and political economy, as sociology was only just beginning to emerge as a recognised academic discipline in Germany. Today, Weber is mainly remembered for his scholarly enquiries into topics such as religion, capitalism and politics (for example, 1965, 1968, 2001) and the methods and foundational concepts of social research (for example, 1949), even though he was equally involved in public and political debates (1994). One of Max Weber's most important works is *Economy and Society*, a lengthy programmatic statement for social research left unfinished during Weber's lifetime and published for the first time posthumously in the early 1920s. *Economy and*

Society begins with a series of definitions of foundational sociological concept. The first of these definitions concerns sociology itself:

> Sociology (in the sense in which this highly ambiguous word is used here) is a science concerning itself with the interpretive understanding of social action and thereby with a causal explanation of its course and consequences. We shall speak of 'action' insofar as the acting individual attaches a subjective meaning to his behaviour – be it overt or covert, omission or acquiescence. Action is 'social' insofar as its subjective meaning takes account of the behavior of others and is thereby oriented in its course. (Weber 1978, 4)

Weber's definition overlaps in important ways with Émile Durkheim's, in so far as both characterise sociology as a science and emphasise the social. However, Weber's definition differs from Durkheim's in its emphasis on *individual action*. Social life begins with individual people's actions. By action Weber refers specifically to conduct which holds a subjective meaning or significance for a person. Thus, giving a lecture falls under Weber's definition of action because it has specific meanings for me as lecturer – communication with my students, intellectual curiosity, boredom at repeating the same lecture year in and year out and so on. In contrast, stubbing my toe while I rush to the lecture theatre does not have a meaning – it is merely an unfortunate and in itself meaningless mishap. Weber makes the important point that action is social in so far as 'its subjective meaning takes account of the behavior of others and is thereby oriented in its course'. What Weber means by this is that, for most of our waking lives, our actions in some way take into account the behaviour of others or involve direct interaction with them, that is, the social. Stubbing my toe while rushing into the lecture theatre is a meaningless mishap, but consciously saying 'ouch', straightening myself and resuming a normal stance and pace are all social actions, as they are meant to demonstrate to others that I am a socially competent adult who is aware of the generally accepted rules for walking and stumbling through a university campus. Carefully choosing a gift according to my partner's taste and presenting it to them at the right moment are social actions, in so far as their meaning lies entirely in my partner's reaction – joy or disappointment. Therefore, the social is found in individuals' actions and the meanings they attach to them, and sociological explanations, as Weber points out, needs to begin with the interpretation of these actions and their meanings. In Anglophone countries, Weber's sociology is thus often associated with the German word *verstehen*, a verb which means 'to understand'.

Cooley and social selves

Other early sociologists took this emphasis on individuals even further and explored the social constitution of the self. In Western societies at least, it may seem difficult to think of our selves – our mental life, our thoughts and feelings, our character – as social. In the Western world, the self is commonly viewed as separate and distant from the world in which it exists. However, some early sociologists contested this notion and argued that the self is deeply connected to the social world. A particularly clear and evocative account of the social self can be found in Charles Horton Cooley's *Human Nature and the Social Order* (1983). Cooley (1864–1929) was born in Michigan in the US, studied at the University of Michigan, and spent his working life at the same institution. He was involved in the foundation of the American Sociological Association, served as its president, and played an important role in establishing a current of sociology that is today known as symbolic interactionism (Denzin 1988). In *Human Nature and the Social Order*, Cooley explains the social self as follows:

> The social self is simply any idea, or system of ideas, drawn from the communicative life, that the mind cherishes as its own. Self-feeling has its chief scope *within* the general life, not outside of it; the special endeavor or tendency of which it is the emotional aspect finds its principal field of exercise in a world of personal forces, reflected in the mind by a world of personal impressions. (Cooley 1983 179, emphasis in original)

Cooley here argues that the self is social in so far as it appropriates systems of ideas 'drawn from the communicative life', that is to say from society at large. In this sense, our self-feeling – the ways in which we think, feel and act with regard to ourselves – form part of broader social processes and are not separate from these. Cooley explains this still more clearly in his famous account of the looking-glass self:

> In a very large and interesting class of cases the social reference takes the form of a somewhat definite imagination of how one's self – that is any idea he appropriates – appears in a particular mind, and the kind of self-feeling one has is determined by the attitude toward this attributed to that other mind. A social self of this sort might be called the reflected or looking-glass self:
>
> 'Each to each a looking glass
>
> Reflects the other that doth pass.'

> As we see our face, figure, and dress in the glass, and are interested in them because they are ours, and pleased or otherwise with them according as they do or do not answer to what we should like them to be; so in imagination we perceive in another's mind some though of our appearance, manners, aims, deeds, character, friends, and so on, and are variously affected by it. (Cooley 1983, 183f.)

In important ways, we cannot see ourselves directly, and we only come to understand who we are through the ways in which others respond to our appearance and our interaction with them. As I am an academic, teaching and doing research characterise my self. Yet my understanding of my abilities as a teacher depends on my students' reactions to my lectures, explanations and class activities, and my appraisal of myself as a researcher is a result of other academics' responses to my books, articles and conference papers. The self is social, it is *relational*, and its features are a result of our interaction with others.

Social inequalities and social conflict

On the preceding pages, we have shown that the social reaches from large-scale structural arrangements, such as the language we speak or the laws we obey, all the way into our self and who we are as a person. If this is so, then it is reasonable to consider that the inequalities marking human life are likewise social. Indeed, social inequalities and the conflicts attached to them have been central to sociological enquiry from its beginnings and continue to be central today. The work of Karl Marx (1818–1883) and Friedrich Engels (1820–1895) is prominent in these beginnings. Both Marx and Engels were born and spent important parts of their lives in what today is Germany and in their lifetimes was the Kingdom of Prussia. Both Marx and Engels were born into well-to-do families that we would today describe as middle class. Life in Prussia was then characterised by a reactionary backlash against the political and civic achievements of the French Revolution and the Napoleonic era. Both men travelled within Europe, became involved in radical political activism, and had to leave Prussia after the failed revolutions of 1848 and 1849. They eventually settled in London. They published widely (for example, Marx and Engels 1998; Marx 2008; Engels 2009, 2010) and they are known as two of the foundational key theorists of socialism and capitalism. Today, they are also often identified as founders of sociology, even though in their lifetimes their work was more closely associated with philosophy and political economy.

In 1848, at the outset of a time of revolutions and violent political conflict in much of Europe, Marx and Engels published the *Manifesto of the Communist Party*. Intended as a political statement, the manifesto also outlines Marx's and Engels' understanding of the social:

The history of all hitherto existing society is the history of class struggles. Free man and slave, patrician and plebeian, lord and serf, guild master and journeyman, in a word, oppressor and oppressed, stood in constant opposition to one another, carried on an uninterrupted, now hidden, now open fight, a fight that each time ended either in a revolutionary reconstitution of society at large or in the common ruin of the contending classes. [...] The modern bourgeois society that has sprouted from the ruins of feudal society has not done away with class antagonisms. It has but established new classes, new conditions of oppression, new forms of struggle in place of the old ones. Our epoch, the epoch of the bourgeoisie, possesses, however, this distinctive feature: it has simplified the class antagonisms. Society as a whole is more and more splitting up into two great hostile camps, into two great classes directly facing each other: bourgeoisie and proletariat. (Marx and Engels 1988, 209f.)

Marx and Engels characterise the history of human societies as a history of socioeconomic inequality and conflict culminating in the modern industrial world and the struggle between two classes – the bourgeoisie (the bankers, businesspeople and merchants who own land and capital and dominate economically) and the proletariat (workers who have nothing to sell but their physical capacity to labour and who find themselves at the receiving end of escalating economic exploitation). The social is defined by inequality between socioeconomic groups or classes, and societies change and develop along the lines of the conflict between these classes. To understand this, consider, for example, the long-standing inequalities in access to elite universities in the UK, where a privileged family background seems to play a large role in admissions. In 2010, a report in *The Guardian* newspaper pointed out:

Is class still the defining feature of university education in the UK? We wanted to find out if the official data tells us if that's still the case. The following table lists the percentage of students that come from routine/ manual occupational backgrounds at universities across the UK. Using this measure, Oxford University has the lowest proportion of working-class students, with 11.5%. London Metropolitan University has the greatest proportion, with 57.2% The average for all universities in the UK is 32.3%. (*The Guardian* 2010)

This pattern seems highly resistant to change. Public criticism over the years notwithstanding, another report in *The Guardian* five years later suggested that little had changed:

The universities of Oxford and Cambridge are facing an unprecedented attack from government advisers for their failure to increase the number of state school pupils studying at Oxbridge colleges. The elite institutions' records will be criticised and individual colleges named and shamed in a hard-hitting annual report by the Social Mobility and Child Poverty Commission. [...] Written by the former Labour cabinet minister Alan Milburn and former Tory cabinet minister Gillian Shephard, his deputy on the commission, the report is expected to say that: Despite an increase of 6% in the proportion of state-educated pupils between 2003–04 and 2013–14, independently schooled pupils still make up around two-fifths of the intake at both Oxford and Cambridge. (Boffey 2015)

Considering that Oxbridge degrees play a significant role in access to many professional fields (Weale 2016), it is not difficult to see how class inequality defines contemporary British society.

Class, however, is not the only axis of social inequality that sociologists consider, and inequalities and conflicts along the lines of race and ethnicity, sex and gender, age, disability, nationality, language and others play a major role in sociological research. W.E.B. Du Bois (1868–1963) an early black American sociologist and civil rights activist, drew attention to endemic racism in the US, social divisions along racialised lines, and the personal consequences of these divisions. In *The Souls of Black Folk* (Du Bois 2007), originally published in 1903 and a seminal work of sociological analysis of the social, cultural and political dynamics of race, Du Bois explains:

> The history of the American Negro is the history of this strife, – this longing to attain self-conscious manhood, to merge his double self into a better and truer self. In this merging he wishes neither of the older selves to be lost. He would not Africanize America, for America has too much to teach the world and Africa. He would not bleach his Negro soul in a flood of white Americanism, for he knows that Negro blood has a message for the world. He simply wishes to make it possible for a man to be both a Negro and an American, without being cursed and spit upon by his fellows, without having the doors of Opportunity [sic] closed roughly in his face. (Du Bois 2007, 9)

The strife Du Bois refers to must be understood in two ways. On the one hand, the term alludes to the violent discrimination and exclusion of African Americans from social life in the US – the 'being cursed and spit upon' and the 'having the doors of Opportunity closed'. On the other hand, strife concerns the problem of African American self-identity and the sense of not belonging in a white supremacist American society in which it is not easily possible 'for a man to be both a Negro and an American'. Du Bois' analysis thus shows how social inequality and conflict may reach from the level of social structures – here in the form of the systematic exclusion and oppression of African Americans – all the way down into individuals' minds, occasioning profound questions and troubles of self-identity.

A similar argument is central to Charlotte Perkins Gilman's *The Dress of Women* (2002). Like quite a few of the other early sociologists mentioned in this chapter, Gilman (1860–1935) was not only committed to sociological research for academic purposes. Rather, she was a widely known important feminist activist in the US of the late 19th and early 20th centuries, and her writings must be understood in this context. Today, Gilman's most widely read work is *The Yellow Wallpaper* (2009), a short story that explores issues of gender inequality through a narrative of a women's encounter with mental illness. However, her sociological writings on a wide range of issues, such as the economic and cultural dimensions of gender relations (Gilman 1998), clothing (Gilman 2002) or ethics (Gilman 2004), are arguably of equal contemporary relevance. In *The Dress of Women*, originally published in 1915 as a series of magazine articles, Gilman opens her argument by characterising clothing as a social tissue that facilitates our interaction:

> Cloth is a social tissue. By means of its convenient sheathing we move among one another freely, smoothly, and in peace, when without it such association would be impossible. The more solitary we live, the less we think of clothing; the more we crowd and mingle in 'society,' the more we think of it. (Gilman 2002, 3)

Here, Gilman points out that the manufactured material objects furnishing everyday life must equally be thought of as social, in so far as they structure the ways in which we interact with each other. This point is easily illustrated by the large role which fashion and the ownership and display of certain kinds of clothing play in contemporary society. My students' reactions to me will vary greatly, depending on whether I wear a Mohamed Salah football shirt or a suit to my lectures. Importantly, however, material objects such as clothing can also be sites of social inequality, as Gilman suggests:

> So in regard to the human body, its functions and its clothing, we have obscured the simple truths of nature by a thousand extravagant notions of our own. The clothing of men is most modified by physical conditions. The clothing of women is most modified by psychic conditions. As they were restricted to a very limited field of activity, and as their personal comfort was of no importance to anyone, it was possible to maintain in their dress the influence of primitive conditions long out-grown by men. And as, while men have varied widely in the manifold relations of our later economic and political growth, women

have remained for the most part all in one relation—that of sex; we see at once why the dress of men has developed along lines of practical efficiency and general human distinction, while the dress of women is still most modified by the various phases of sex-distinction. A man may run in our streets, or row, visibly, on our rivers, in a costume—a lack of costume—which for women would be called grossly immodest. He may bathe, publicly, and in company with women, so nearly naked as to shock even himself, sometimes; while the women beside him are covered far more fully than in evening dress. (Gilman 2002, 11)

Here, Gilman explains evocatively how clothing is a function of gender inequality in the US of the early 20th century. Men's clothing is 'most modified by physical conditions', in so far as men are able to participate extensively in public, economic and political life. In contrast, women's clothing 'is still most modified by the various phases of sex-distinction', in so far as women's activities remain narrowly restricted and they are largely excluded from public life. In this sense, substantial gender difference in dress renders visible profound gender inequality in social life at large. The social is thus a site of inequalities and conflicts at multiple and intersecting levels.

Modes of social organisation

So far, we have set out a rather general set of statements about the social. Even though these statements are general and abstract, however, it is important to consider them in relation to the historical and geographical contexts to which they refer. The classical sociological texts from which we have quoted derive from social life in France, Germany and the US in the late 19th and early 20th centuries, while the contemporary account that we offer is grounded in our education at universities in the US and the UK. In other words, the concepts and theories that constitute sociological knowledge are very rarely universally valid and generalisable to human societies across historical, geographical and sociocultural distances – even though many theorists claim just that. This is an issue we will consider at length in Chapter 6 on global sociologies. However, a basic account of the social would not be complete if it did not at least briefly consider the differences in modes of social organisation that structure sociological knowledge. For example, while it seems reasonable to assume that human selves are always in some sense social, the ways in which social processes organise the self vary considerably between societies, and sociological analysis must account for such differences. Therefore, efforts to frame sociological knowledge in terms of differences in modes of social organisation have played an important role in sociology's worldwide emergence. The opening statement of Fei Xiaotong's *From the Soil* (1992) usefully illustrates this point. Fei (1910–2005) was a leading Chinese sociologist who played a central role in the development of the discipline in China. In *From the Soil*, a compilation of various shorter texts first published in 1947, Fei sets out key concepts and themes for the sociological study of Chinese society. Consider the opening statement of the book's English edition:

> Chinese society is fundamentally rural. I say that it is fundamentally rural because its foundation is rural. Several variations have arisen from this foundation, but even so, these variations retain their rural character. Moreover, in the past hundred years, a very special society has formed as a consequence of the encounter between East and West. For the time being, however, I am not going to discuss the characteristics of these variations, but instead will concentrate exclusively on rural society and on those so-called hayseeds, the people living in the countryside. They are truly the foundation of Chinese society. We often say that country people are figuratively as well as literally 'soiled' (*fuqi*). Although this label may seem disrespectful, the character meaning 'soil' (*tu*) is appropriately used here. Country people cannot do without the soil because their very livelihood is based upon it. In the earliest times, there may have been some groups of people in the Far East who did not know how to farm; but for us now, how those primitives lived is merely a matter of curiosity. Today, most people in East Asia make a living by working in the fields. To be more specific, even from early times, the tributaries of China's three large rivers were already entirely agricultural. Historically, wherever people from those agricultural regions migrated, they took with them their tradition of making a living from the soil. (Fei 1992, 1)

Here, Fei draws attention of the predominantly rural character of Chinese society in the first half of the 20th century, and he explains that the relationship between 'country people' and the land on which they live is fundamental to understanding social life at the time. Similar statements would not apply to, say, the UK or Germany in the same period, given that both societies were highly urbanised and that urban social relationships were highly significant to these societies' organisation, for instance in the forms of the class relations between bourgeoisie and industrial proletariat that are so central to European Marxist theorising. In *From the Soil*, Fei Xiaotong therefore develops both a focused characterisation of Chinese society and a set of concepts and themes that allow for its sociological analysis.

What is the social in the 21st century?

In this chapter, we have so far proposed five simple statements to characterise the social:

- The social consists of social structures. (Émile Durkheim)
- The social lies in individuals' actions and the meanings they attach to them. (Max Weber)
- The self is social, and its features are a result of our interaction with others. (Charles Horton Cooley)
- The social is thus a site of inequalities and conflicts at multiple levels. (Karl Marx, Friedrich Engels, W.E.B. Du Bois, Charlotte Perkins Gilman)
- The concepts and theories that constitute sociological knowledge are very rarely universally valid and generalisable to human societies across historical, geographical and sociocultural distance. Sociological analysis must account for differences in modes of social organisation and social location. (Fei Xiaotong)

Together, these statements might be usefully understood as a kind of baseline of all sociological knowledge or as the background assumptions framing how sociologists came to imagine human life.

Yet the mid-19th century and the beginning decades of the 20th century are not the 21st century. This then leaves us with a serious puzzle – in what ways do the present realities from the description of a runaway world in our introduction modify the well-known and long-standing account of the social in the sociological canon presented in this chapter? How, for example, can we translate what has long been understood as the classical definition of the 'social' in Western sociology for a 21st century imagination and globalised world? Yes, social structures, individual actions, and the meanings individuals put to those actions are always important considerations shaping each of us, and our social worlds. This is also true of interaction with others, the importance of the social as a site of inequalities and conflicts, and the various differences in modes of social organisation found in different nations and societies.

But in the ominous and runaway world of the 21st century we described in Chapter 1 what does the *social* mean? For example, what is the journey map for a young man who joins ISIS or shoots up a school and chooses a path of violent extremism? What are the ways the social and its various characteristics come together in such a context? What is social in a context where much social contact and action take place online, erasing eye contact and making social connection more about touching screens than being in actual physical touch distance with each other? What is the social when nation-states create 'hostile environments' to remove citizenship illegally from some citizens while making it harder for all citizens to access their rights (Jones et al 2017; Wardle and Obermuller 2019)? How do the various characteristics of the social relate and interact in the rise and development of fascism? How might sociological analysis of the social support or not support claims for reparations for many nations excluded from the fruits of the 'developed' world? What is the social when the practice of democracy itself in its current Western form of 'liberal democracy' becomes a system of elite control with minimal public ratification (Latour 2004, 451)? Are mindfulness, populism and psychologisation, as the dominant ways to understand the world, really enough to understand how the various elements of the social relate, connect and interact? How can and should the sociological understanding of the social be modified to help us better understand contemporary 21st-century moments?

In later chapters we will introduce important sociological ideas and considerations to better understand our 21st-century world, many of which have emerged in the last few decades These ideas include the notion of connected-sociologies raised by Gurminder Bhambra and familiar to the notion of assemblage theory in sociology. It also includes the importance of discourse and discourse analysis and the cultural turn in sociology to better understand and reveal the cultural logic some people now rely on to build false pictures and fake news of various groups and people, such as racist and sexist stereotypes and prejudices. Actor-network theory, meanwhile, is neutral with regard to human and non-human actors in a network, and is an example of a relational sociological framework that allows researchers to analyse relationships and underlying mechanisms of networked actors and their social relations. In recent times sociologists have built on this approach through social network analysis, a research strategy that quantifies the pattern of relations among a set of actors that includes non-human actors as well as people. Nor should we forget that with the spread of Western liberal democracy around the world there also arrived new institutions, forms of life, habits, media, courts, values and feelings. All of which formed new structures of exclusion and transnational structural inequalities to shape and affect the social.

But rather than run before we can walk, let us pause for a moment and travel to the Caribbean island nation of Jamaica to investigate via a brief case study of what was the 'social' in a low-income area of urban Kingston in the late 1990s. Think about these questions as you read the next section and try to answer them at the end.

- How was the garrison organised socially?
- How does its organisation relate to the definition of the social in classical sociology?
- 'Citizenship' is a term that is frequently used in everyday language. What might it mean from a sociological perspective? In which ways might it be useful to think about the following case from the perspective of citizenship?
- More specifically, what happens to the social when the rights of citizenship are removed?

You should be able to answer most of these questions just by reading the following discussion and considering it. However, it would greatly enhance your understanding of the matter at hand it you did some background research of your own, about Jamaican society and history, and about sociological terms such as citizenship, colonialism, neocolonialism and postcolonialism (Gardner 1971). At the end of this chapter, we suggest some starting points for background research on Jamaica; the companion website is also a useful resource.

Demeaned but empowered: a case study of Kingston, Jamaica

In Kingston, Jamaica, as in other urban centres of many Caribbean cities, some areas referred to historically as 'garrisons' have, after a long periods of underdevelopment and in socioeconomic climates of low-paying jobs and unemployment, little social mobility, poor infrastructure, life skills deficits, and a retreat of the state and its various rituals such as protection, social services and citizenship, been 'reconfigured through criminal actors and mechanisms' (Jaffe 2009). What happens to the social in the context of a state unwilling or unable to fulfil its obligations to its citizens? How do people respond? What meanings will people then put to the events around them?

Obika Gray, Deborah Thomas and Rivke Jaffe have all researched and written on these questions in the context of Jamaica – and the title of this section is borrowed from Gray's own study (2006). All three suggest that when we talk about the state we are also talking about 'society' and 'the social' (Thomas 2006). This is because the state is a 'social fact'. It has sovereignty over each of us. It dominates and is a social structure in Durkheim's sense. A state structures what is socially possible through its laws, rules, distribution of resources and the use of legitimate violence (Weber 1965).

Following independence from the UK in 1962, for Jamaica the social facts of Émile Durkheim became the macro-structures of postcolonial, inter-state relations and participation in an unequal and globalised political economy; and, most recently since the 1980s, high levels of violence connected to transnational organised crime. These 'social facts' also reflected the structural and unjust legacies of colonialism, and the failure of postcolonialism and independence to repair the social, political and economic damage done to Jamaica and its people pre-1962, such as the actual violence, the symbolic violence, and the production of racial hierarchy and domination/subjugation more generally of the colonial encounter.

In a Weberian sense these social facts and realities produced a response by some who suffered and were subjected to the punishment of capital accumulation via colonialism and neocolonialism, such as processes of pauperisation, dispossession and the production of social hierarchies. Many responded, as humans often have, to this perceived oppression with resistance and rebelliousness (Prashad 2007). Where some saw criminality in such actions, some local residents interpreted it as resistance and a chance for 'badness-honour' instead (Gray 2006).

> The dominated have the capacity to resist and often find the means to elude power, constrain its effects on them, bargain with it and adapt it to conform to some of their needs. Disadvantaged groups therefore exhibit a social power that can be identified and examined

for its compulsion on power and for its impact on social change. (Gray 2006, 3)

In the face of social relations disconnecting many low-income residents of inner-city Kingston from other residents of Kingston, and Jamaica more generally, many individuals came to define themselves in relation to those they could and did interact with. Society fragmented, and poverty became a stigma. After Jamaica became independent in 1962, the new democratic state struggled to fulfil some of its functions, including its ability to include all citizens in policy concerns and political decision making. Political parties and politicians might court voters in the run-up to elections, a tactic known in Caribbean sociology as 'clientelism' (Stone 1980; Austin-Broos 2017). The term refers to the exchange of votes in elections for material benefits, such as jobs or infrastructure projects in specific communities. Beyond this clientelism, the political class and the state failed to engage comprehensively with all sectors of Jamaican society. In particular, poor people came to be excluded, were viewed with fear and disdain, and therefore stigmatised as a result of their social position.

In response, some of those who had been excluded came to view their social position as lying outside the boundaries of mainstream society and the reach of the state. In particular, this created informal social spaces through which criminal actors and their methods came to dominate in some areas of Kingston and came to stand in for more traditional 'rituals of statehood' (Jaffe 2009), and also redefined what was social power.

Into this context, the larger enduring social realities of class, race and gender inequalities handed down from colonialism and its attendant social class hierarchies, produced an ongoing context of social conflict that also developed as a form of social consciousness among many of those dispossessed. For Gray, in this situation of social conflict the urban poor amassed a form of social identity, social capital and social power – complete with creative arts like music, dance, slogans and posters – which were anti-state and pro-informal social relations (Gray 2006, 13). This social power was and still is often deployed as a challenge to the state via blocking roads, criminality, counter culture and a more general anti-state stance.

> Contrary to the widely held view that the social actions and moral sensibility of the rebellious poor are outside the pale of Jamaican culture, these shared traditions, in which the poor participate, show that what the rebellious poor do politically ought not to be regarded as moral aberrations inflicted upon a civilized society by a criminal and barbaric class. Rather, much of what the rebellious poor do, and the moral sentiments they exhibit, should be regarded, in part, as expressions of the banal, everyday attributes of a widely shared social sensibility in late twentieth-century Jamaica. (Gray 2006, 16)

In response to this informal social power, the state itself, and the various politicians that fought to control state resources via becoming a government were transformed in turn. The concepts and theories that constitute sociological knowledge of the garrisons of Jamaica are not generalisable to all locations but they do reveal the particular ways in which history, sociology and political economy in one Caribbean context can relate to each other to organise a society and the social hierarchies and relations people have with each other.

Jaffe, Thomas and Gray's research illustrates how informal systems and 'positive deviance' (Pascale et al 2010) emerge in a context where many inner-city residents of Kingston experienced 'the formal justice system as deeply unequal and prejudiced' (Jaffe 2013, 741). Among the urban poor in Jamaica it has been widely accepted 'that state agencies such as the police and the judiciary discriminate against people who live Downtown, against those with a darker skin colour, and who speak Jamaican Creole rather than English' (Jaffe 2013, 741). Jaffe concludes that because inner-city residents perceive the non-formal system of justice in their local garrison as more impartial than the formal system, they perceive it as more legitimate than state justice, which they suggest to be only available to specific segments of the population.

Relational sociology

In their descriptions of the social the ethnographic researchers in the previous section did not stop at the five levels that classical sociologists covered and instead saw a much more relational picture of the social. This includes such things as affect, popular culture, spectacle, defiance, resistance, language, global economics, history, international relations and more, in a complex process of what sociologists call *relationality*. This is because the individual problems that some people living in a garrison of Jamaica experience, endure and feel are never simply about their own individual choices and biography, even though of course these are important. Their social location and experiences are also about larger public issues like the economic inequality between nations in the Caribbean and the rest of the world; the lack of an era of industrialisation for the Jamaican economy to grow, develop and diversify; the impact of IMF (International Monetary Fund) economic policies and the damage they did to the Jamaican economy and society; the impact of transnational organised crime and much more.

Relational sociology tries to step away from the classical binaries that have defined sociology for so long, such as the relationships of social facts and social action (Doucet 2018). From the early days of sociological enquiry onwards, scholars such as Émile Durkheim (2013a) and Max Weber (1978) have been concerned with the questions to what extent human life is organised by large-scale social structures and processes whose reach may often be inescapable, and to what extent individuals and social groups are able to creatively change and remake the world in which they live. Relational sociology attempts to move beyond this duality of structure and agency.

Relationality in sociology is connected to the idea that humans are defined by their social relations and are never able to completely step outside the social relations within which they are embedded (Gergen 2009). And social relations themselves are connected to far more elements than we typically imagine, including emotions, feelings, non-human entities, technology, rules, traditions and more. As such, 21st century sociology has constructed new ways to consider and envision social congregation, and hence democracy. In a world of climate change and disasters these new assemblies and assemblages entail a rejection of the anthropocentric prejudices and philosophies on which the human position in and conception of the world is founded (Latour 2002, 2004). They include developing genuine models of relationality, cosmopolitanism and cosmopolitics today, not least for our present global and interconnected context of climate change and ecological disasters that embrace, literally, everything – including all the vast numbers of non-human entities such as animals, ecology, environments, nations, organisations, as well as the ideas, conventions, rules, emotions, feelings, intimacies, and intangible matter acting as new technologies of rule shaping the contexts in which humans act (Latour 2002, 454; O'Donnell et al 2004, 8).

Hence the social today is no longer simply a conundrum of five general principles, it is also more than that. Relationality suggests our perspective on humans and social phenomenon is but one perspective of many strands. Yes, elements such as structure, agency, power, and conflict may provide the roots from which to understand the social, but we need to also acknowledge the many categories and possibilities based on where one is located physically, socially, and historically.

So what does this detour via Kingston, Jamaica tell us about what is the social in our 21st century worlds? It tells us that in order to understand why certain individuals and members of social groups act in certain ways, we must understand their relations and relationality to the social around them – and that the social itself, is a vast combination of relations, including politics, which individuals are never able to step out of. Thus sociological inquiry and research needs more than mindfulness to understand and imagine the relationality of social life in the early 21st century. We need more than psychologisation, and explanations dependent on individuals' thoughts, feelings and actions, yet disconnected from larger social processes and relations such as history, inequalities, and conflict. Yes, understanding psychological processes and qualities like depression, anxiety, happiness, wellness and so on are of course important, but not if you disconnect such individual problems from their relationship to larger social issues.

From the themes we have considered in this chapter, various strands of sociological analysis branch out, and various fields of sociological enquiry have developed since the time of the early sociologists we have cited here. In the following chapters, we will explore some of these branches and fields. The next chapter considers the questions of structure, agency and change, and five other dimensions of sociological enquiry.

THINKING SOCIOLOGICALLY

We may, for our present purpose, consider the theological and the metaphysical polities together, – the second being only a modification of the first in its relation to social science. Their attributes are the same, consisting, in regard to method, in the preponderance of imagination over observation; and, in regard to doctrine in the exclusive investigation of absolute ideas, the result of both of which is an inevitable tendency to exercise an arbitrary and indefinite action over phenomena which are not regarded as subject to invariable natural laws. In short, the general spirit of all speculation at that stage is at once ideal in its course, absolute in its conception, and arbitrary in its application; and these are unquestionably the prevailing characteristics of social speculation at present, regarded from any point of view whatever. If we reverse all the three aspects, we shall have precisely the spirit which must actuate the formation of positive sociology and which must afterwards direct its continuous development. The scientific spirit is radically distinguished from the theological and metaphysical by the steady subordination of the imagination to observation; and though the positive philosophy offers the vastest and richest field it, human imagination, it restricts it to discovering and perfecting the co-ordination of observed facts, and the means of effecting new researches: and it is this habit of subjecting scientific conceptions to the facts whose connection has to be disclosed, which it is above all things necessary to introduce into social researches; for the observations hitherto made have been vague and ill-circumscribed, so as to afford no adequate foundation for scientific reasoning; and they are usually modified themselves at the pleasure of an imagination stimulated by the most fluctuating passions. (Comte 2000, 177)

Try to explain Comte's statements in your own words. What does he mean, in particular, by the 'theological and metaphysical' polities? How are these different from 'social science' and the 'scientific spirit'? Answering these questions, consider the historical period in which Comte lived and worked. How might it have informed his arguments on the importance of social science? (In this context, also see Chapter 6.)

MINI PROJECT

1. The social consists of social structures. (Émile Durkheim)

2. The social lies in individuals' actions and the meanings they attach to them. (Max Weber)

3. The self is social, and its features are a result of our interaction with others. (Charles Horton Cooley)

4. The social is thus a site of inequalities and conflicts at multiple levels. (Karl Marx, Friedrich Engels, W.E.B. Du Bois, Charlotte Perkins Gilman)

5. The concepts and theories that constitute sociological knowledge are very rarely universally valid and generalisable to human societies across historical, geographical and socio-cultural distance. Sociological analysis must account for differences in modes of social organisation and social location. (Fei Xiaotong)

Explain each of these statements in your own words and provide examples. Do you agree with these statements? Why (not)? In which ways, if at all, are they important to understanding human life today?

TALKING POINTS

1. What do sociologists mean by social facts? And by social action? How might the two terms be related?

2. What are social facts? How are social facts created? How do they become widely established in society? How do they acquire compelling power? Answer these questions in reference to the Korean Hangeul alphabet. Do further background research on Hangeul and its history, as required to answer all three questions in detail.

3. 'The social self is simply any idea, or system of ideas, drawn from the communicative life, that the mind cherishes as its own' (Cooley 1983, 179). Explain this statement in your own words and provide examples to clarify your argument.

4. To what extent and in which ways can large-scale social conflict be characterised as a central feature of contemporary human life? Why (not)?

5. In which ways does Fei Xiaotong's work reflect the social realities of China in the early 20th century?

6. What happens to the social when socialising goes online? When you connect with people without having to make eye contact with people? The following is a good three-minute spoken word video that asks such questions: www.youtube.com/watch?v=GAx845QaOck

7. 'Relationality in sociology is connected to the idea that humans are defined by their social relations and are never able to completely step outside the social relations within which they are embedded.' [p 55] Try to explain in your own words what might be meant by relationality. Give examples to illustrate your argument.

8. The social does not exist. There are only individuals. Discuss.

READ ON ...

In this chapter, we have explored a very wide array of key concerns in sociological enquiry. Many of these are explored in greater depth in two fairly recent books, Anthony Elliott and Bryan Turner's *On Society* (2012) and John Scott's *Conceptualising the Social World* (2011). For an important recent account of the sociality of the self, see Vanessa May's *Connecting Self to Society* (2013). To further explore the issue of relationality, Kenneth Gergen's *Relational Being* (2009) makes for a dense albeit very readable starting point as is Francois Dépelteau's *Handbook of Relational Sociology* (2018). Finally, on the development of sociology from a global perspective, see Gurminder Bhambra's *Connected Sociologies* (2014b).

Check the companion website at https://bristoluniversitypress.co.uk/imagining-society-online-resources **for a suggested project and writing task.**

4

Seven key moments in Western sociology

Sociology can be usefully understood as an *intellectual formation*, a distinctive body of knowledge that is characterised by its common themes, such as the notion of the social and engagement with questions of structure, agency and change, social solidarity, community and more, as we have seen in the previous chapter. Moreover, the intellectual features and processes that characterise sociology cannot be adequately understood if we do not take into account key moments in the development of the discipline. In order to understand sociological knowledge and its variations over time and between places, we need to look not only at the world of sociological themes, but also, importantly, some key moments in the history of Western sociology's emergence and development.

In this chapter we discuss seven key moments in the history of Western sociology, which in various ways make for a partial account of sociology's history in the West. We do not offer an in any sense comprehensive history of the development of sociology, and we often gloss over, rather than exploring in detail, the work of key figures within this history. At the same time, we believe that the seven moments we discuss here make for a useful point of departure in an effort to understand the intellectual and institutional forces that define sociology today.

Positivism

Our first moment in this history begins with classical social theory and in particular the early *positivism* of Auguste Comte. Then we move on to look at other scholars, such as Herbert Spencer and Émile Durkheim, who worked to improve on Comte's original ideas. Positivism in early sociology had two main characteristics. First, it parted from the assumption that the social sciences were, in methodological terms, not so different from the natural sciences. Positivism therefore stressed the need for sociologists to discover patterns and regularities that drive the development of society – similar to laws of nature in the natural sciences. Second, positivism stressed the importance of mirroring the empirical methods of the natural sciences, such as the importance of statistical inference in the framing of hypotheses and modes of validation, and also the importance of experimental studies. These early characteristics gave shape to the some of the methodologies sociology would come to embody: empiricism, observation, validity, hypothesis testing, deduction, social theory, inspection, comparison and more. The latter positivism of Spencer, Durkheim and others also gave sociology the concepts of structure, system and function.

At the same time, the notion that sociological enquiry is scientific and in some sense objective has resulted problematic. Early sociologists like Auguste Comte (2000) and Herbert Spencer (Offer 2010; Spencer 2017) compared society to an organism, and they argued that each part of society exists because it has an important function for the whole organism. Therefore, where there are social problems like crime, deviance and racism, these can be fixed by sociological engineering. In the positivistic sociology of Durkheim (2005, 2013b), for example, social behaviour was not fully explainable in terms of individual behaviour and ideas; rather social behaviour was supposedly driven by structural realities like the division of labour, population pressures and social facts. As we mentioned previously, social facts for Durkheim (2013b) were coercive social and behavioural rules transferred via the law, education and morality that people were obligated to follow. The analogy of the living organism with its many organs and functions that must work together for the organism to live, be sustained and reproduce is often offered as a definition for how positivist sociologists understood *functionalism* in the context of society.

Today positivism is critiqued for not including historical context, the micro-individual level of life, political economy, or sociocultural relativism in its worldview. It is also noted how this created various problems of bias and prejudice against certain social groups, not fully understood in relation to the wider socioeconomic realities, historical events, and other sociological concepts. For example, in Comte's era white European society was considered the pinnacle of humanity and this supposedly justified its right to rule over all other human societies. Some also suggested that positivistic social Darwinism gave justification for the racism that led to the Holocaust as the Nazis borrowed such ideas when speaking of cleansing inferior genetics from society. Meanwhile, from a Global South perspective Aimé Césaire suggested that it was the brutal and genocidal treatment of the indigenous and the enslaved in the colonies during colonialism, which laid the terrain for murderous Nazism and the Holocaust in Europe, something he described as 'the boomerang effect of colonialism' (Césaire 1955, 176–7).

Positivism was important in the beginning of Western sociology because it advanced ways of understanding the world distinct from religion and metaphysics. It gave early sociology a form. For example, Durkheim's classic *The Rules of Sociological Method* showed others how to do sociology, how to connect empiricism to theory, how to work with empirical data and test its validity, how to do more than simply describe social events but also understand their significance for individuals and the society (Bulmer 1984). However, positivism was based on problematic ideas and incomplete knowledge about the world. Sweeping general biological laws of nature, and their role in the development of society, were a poor way to understand society and individuals. Without acknowledging the role of historical events in social development, early sociologists had no sociological imagination to work with and many of the rules and laws conceived by positivists are of little value to sociologists today.

Postmodernism

Another key moment in sociology, but a much later one than positivism, is the *postmodern turn* experienced in sociology and across the social sciences in the 1980s. Postmodernism challenged the idea of singular objective truth about the social world and in some ways can be seen as an interpretivist counterweight to the assumptions of positivistic social science. The term 'postmodernism' was first coined in 1964 by Fredric Jameson, a literary critic, philosopher and Marxist political theorist, and has been used to describe a general change in society and social outlook from the 'modern era' and its ethos, which is often dated from the Enlightenment period to the 1960s. Jameson (1991) saw postmodernism not just as a change in worldview but also as the 'cultural logic of late capitalism'.

The sociological study of modernity and modernism combined with the principles and values handed down from the Enlightenment became within sociological research the values of order, rationality and science as the central means by which human beings could improve society by solving social problems. This was sociology declared as 'the science of society'. However, modernity also suggested that history was a grand narrative of constant 'progress' and social betterment. It assumed human civilisation only ever advances upward over time. Postmodernism pushed back against such ideas and called for the end to such grand narratives of human becoming. It pointed out how history is not simply a linear process toward some final ultimate human freedom and utopia – not to mention that history for many groups and nations of the world has been a series of brutal defeats, such as slavery, the Holocaust, the atom bomb and economic underdevelopment. For postmodernists, positivistic claims to universal, objective knowledge and singular truth were not possible because truth always has a subjective and social constructionist component.

Yet such postmodern claims also came with cautions, such as that of feminist philosopher of sexual difference Adriana Cavarero (1995) who warned against being seduced by a mirage of a 'feminised' postmodern male philosophy whose arrival and timing could itself be the hidden figuration of Western hegemonic power (Berger 1993, 178; Braidotti cited in Cavarero 1995, xi). By this, Cavarero was suggesting, as Mascia-Lees translates it: was it not strange that just at the time 'when women and non-western peoples have begun to speak for themselves and, indeed, to speak about global systems of power differentials' (Mascia-Lees et al 1989, 14–15) that the Western white male, who traditionally has commanded the authority to produce knowledge, claims that there is no truth to be found (Clough 2000, 113)? While the merits and existence of postmodernism are still fiercely debated and many sociologists reject the term postmodern, suggesting we have not really moved beyond modernity, there were general themes and lessons learnt from postmodernism that Western sociology has adopted including: a break with the modern and modernity as the central ways to understand the world; the need for a cultural turn within the social sciences that addresses the centrality of consumption to most postmodern societies as opposed to the more traditional model of production; the need to develop models of cultural logic and aesthetics for the times; a recognition of the need for varied forms of epistemology reflective of the local historical, social and cultural contexts; and the importance of combining sociological research with advocacy. Furthermore, postmodernism brought the concepts of globalisation, the culture industries, consumer society, technological change, multiculturalism and the collapse of previous forms of social organisation into the centre of sociological investigation.

The cultural turn

The next step on our journey of key moments in sociology brings us to *cultural studies* and *the cultural turn* in sociology. Let us begin by discussing the latter. The cultural turn in sociology is often attributed to the interpretive work of Max Weber in the late 19th and early 20th centuries. Interpretivism acknowledges that objectivity is always to a certain degree contaminated by subjectivity, hence when we understand our sociological work there will be always be a level of interpretation and reflexivity in how we come to view the work and results. Weber's sociology brought the individual, the study of cultural phenomena, and qualitative methods to sociological analysis, and was an intellectual counterweight to positivism. Weber showed that sociologists had the ability to understand the quality of the social phenomena they studied by observing the actions of individuals and both asking those same individuals about the meanings attached to those behaviours and examining the meanings suggested.

> In the great majority of cases *actual* action goes on in a state of inarticulate half consciousness or actual unconsciousness of its subjective meaning. The actor is more likely to 'be aware' of it in a vague sense than he is to 'know' what he is doing or be explicitly self-conscious about it. In most cases his action is governed by impulse or habit. Only occasionally, and, in the uniform action of large numbers, often only in the case of a few individuals, is the subjective meaning of the action, whether rational or irrational, brought clearly into consciousness. ... [I]t is the task of the sociologist to be aware of this

motivational situation and to describe and analyse it, even though it has not actually been concretely part of the conscious 'intention' of the actor: possibly not at all, at least not fully. (Weber 1978, 21, emphasis added)

For many sociologists Weber is recognised as the father of qualitative methodologies in sociology, and it is via the cultural turn that the sociological tools of interviewing, focus groups and ethnographic observation emerge. As mentioned in the previous chapter, Weber himself noted, 'Sociology … is a science concerning itself with interpretive understanding of social action and thereby with a causal explanation of its course and consequences' (Weber 1978, 4). And for Weber, understanding the quality of people's life experiences, how they felt about their lives, and the relation this had to a person's agency and actions were important sociological criteria to understand and explore, something sociologists still believe today.

For UK sociologist Kate Nash, in recent times 'there has been a well-documented "cultural turn" in social theory' too (2001, 77). She suggests this turn has taken 'two forms: the "epistemological" case in which culture is seen as universally constitutive of social relations and identities; and the "historical" case in which culture is seen as playing an unprecedented role in constituting social relations and identities in contemporary society' (2001, 77). For Nash this is important because it offers understanding of the relationship between culture and politics as being 'the central focus of political sociology' away 'from structural determinism and relations between the state and society' (2001, 77).

Years before the actual emergence of cultural studies in the UK in the late 1950s and 1960s, the immense political relevance of taking popular culture seriously from a Marxist perspective – what the Trinidadian sociologist C.L.R. James called the 'popular arts' (Agozino 2011), and the Frankfurt school of neo-Marxists such as Theodor Adorno (1991) called the 'culture industries' (cultural productions like Hollywood movies, books, comics and music) – was already emerging as a concern in the field for sociologists around the world who recognised the relationship between culture and larger social forces and trends. This sociology of culture was an important development in Western sociology because it presented sociologists with an entry point into the connections between the social, politics, identity and culture. It also allowed for the study of culture as a commodified and economic object.

The cultural turn in sociological research also opened up Western sociology to different sociological traditions from other parts of the world. Mass culture, its commodification, and also the ways social domination and social power played out culturally and through mediated forms were also brought into the mainstream of sociological enquiry. Cultural processes and ideologies akin to Gramsci's ideas about domination and cultural hegemony being achieved via the consent of the masses also became central in understanding how power and resistance play out within and via popular cultural forms in a society (Gramsci 1971).

Feminism and queer studies

From *feminism* and *queer studies*, 'reflexivity' and a concern with the diverse spectrum of human sociocultural differences became central to contemporary sociology. Simone de Beauvoir's social constructionist insight from her book *The Second Sex* (1949, 267) that '*On ne naît pas femme: on le devient*' ('one is not born, but rather becomes a woman'), for example, symbolised among many things a feminist cultural critique concerned with the neglect of women's experience in the discipline. This move disrobed unrepresentative sociological narratives, highlighting the experiences described by the majority of sociological texts and theories as based on and against experiences that from the outset 'were an unrepresentative subset of human experiences, not only in terms of gender, but also in terms of class, race and culture' (Garry and Pearsall 2010, 292).

From feminism and feminist theory sociology learnt there is no one universal subject of knowledge, and marked such a worldview as a falsely generalised, patriarchal standpoint (Doucet 2018). Feminist sociologists also demonstrated 'how discourses of science, religion, law, and the general assumptions' governing the production of knowledge tacitly implied a subject that is male, white, middle-class and heterosexual (Braidotti 1993, 322; see also Martin 1991). Such reflexivity acknowledged the material conditions involved in experience, providing a model of culture where there is 'recognition of the respect due to the infinite singularity of each and every one; a combination of multiplicity and interconnection, which defies easy dichotomies and allows voices, echoes, and traces to emerge' (Braidotti cited in Cavarero 1995, xviii).

The historical movement of feminism in the West has been traditionally understood as various waves. First-wave feminism appears in the mid-19th century and included the first women's rights convention, held in Seneca Falls, New York, in 1848. It also brought about political rights and legislation that by the 1920s allowed women in many Western nations the right to vote. The second wave of Western feminism is often tied to the 1960s and 1970s, but would include the ideas of Simone de Beauvoir and others like her to recover women's experience and viewpoints within the mainstream of social science. Feminist cultural critique implicated the self as an important consideration within not only the practice of ethnomethodology and qualitative data production but also the wider Western intellectual canon (Doucet and Mauthner 2006).

These two earliest waves have been described as particularly white waves of feminism. Third-wave feminism introduced intersectionality and was led by many women of colour such as bell hooks (1981, 1984), Angela Davis (1983), Alice Walker (1983), Audre Lorde (1984), Patricia Hill Collins (1990) and Rhoda Reddock (1990a). Third-wave feminism also introduced queer studies and queer theory into sociology, such as the work of Judith Butler (1990), Eve Kosofsky Sedgwick (1990), J. Jack Halberstam (2005) and others, who have been important in refreshing the sociological imagination to not only be cognisant of the variety of human social and cultural differences, but also to work for a world where such a variety of human difference can live safely with each other.

Queer theory brought sexuality studies into the mainstream of sociology and sexuality as another mechanism of difference-making and stratification for sociological attention and concern. It suggested new ways to imagine and conceive of the human subject such as a plurality of untapped possibilities for identity formation and a 'surge of inner impulses of which it is never immediately clear whether they stem from pre-social drives, the creative imagination, or the moral sensibility of one's own self' (Heidegren 2002, 438). For example, queer theory asked how and why in day-to-day life sexuality, as in who you are – a mode of 'being' and identity – appears constant yet in real life there are also infinite moments each of us as a subject pass through wherein 'years of corporeal training [can] vanish in a movement from a body solidly placed on the sociocultural map to a febrile flesh full of surprises' (Lambevski 2004, 304). This is one explanation from queer theory of the concept of 'becoming'. It is the idea that fixed concepts of identity and subject positionality around bodies and what they are capable of, fail to acknowledge fluid everyday transgressions, the deterritorialisation *of the subject-form*, and the body's inherent potential for variation and change that takes place constantly but is constrained by the norms and conventions around human possibilities (Deleuze and Guattari 1977).

Fourth-wave feminism emerged in the early 2000s and has developed a social justice frame for women, particularly to fight violence against women including sexual harassment, domestic violence and intimate partner violence. From queer and feminist critiques of the sociological project the underrepresentation of women and queer bodies, and their lives and experiences within sociology, both as subjects of research and the producers of theory, became a central concern of sociology. Feminist cultural critique also supported the self as an important consideration within not only the practice of ethnomethodology and qualitative data production but also the wider Western intellectual canon.

The global turn

Another important moment in the development of Western sociology was its incipient *global turn*. This shift from the 1960s as colonialism declined and ex-colonies gained independence is discussed in Chapter 6. However, by turning global Western sociology has been forced to start a process of *decolonising* itself. This includes looking at its canon, its history and its current forms in the university. Western sociology has had to join and connect to a wider sphere of sociological traditions, epistemologies and conditions from around the world that are not identical to Western sociology (de Sousa Santos 2012; Bhambra and Santos 2017).

Today thanks to this more global focus and imagination, Western sociology is now often a project and process of understanding local entanglements of global inequalities. For example, Iain Wilkinson and Arthur Kleinman, two Western sociologists, study social suffering of workers in factories around the world and using the sociological imagination bring together in their analysis 'the human costs exacted by our social arrangements, economic organization, cultural values, and modes of governance' (Wilkinson and Kleinman 2016, 3)

The ethnographic research of Spanish sociologist Encarnación Gutiérrez-Rodríguez into migrant domestic workers and their employers in four European countries is another example of the importance of decoloniality and understanding sociologically how historic global inequalities manifest locally (Gutiérrez-Rodríguez 2010). Using a feminist lens Gutiérrez-Rodríguez explores the lives of undocumented, female migrants from ex-colonies in their Latin American journeys to Spain, the UK, Germany and Austria to work as domestic helpers. The book does not simply describe the lives of the women and their employers but demonstrates how undocumented female domestic labourers suspended in global webs of capitalism are racialised and othered, exempted from rights and citizenship, exploited and abused due to their social position in various long-standing and more recent global hierarchies of social class (economic class, race, gender, nationality, status, education, language and more).

For Gutiérrez-Rodríguez this is the 'coloniality of power', how sociocultural discourses and systems of hierarchy established during colonialism are still alive and well, playing out in the heart of Europe and elsewhere (Escobar 2004; Kamugisha 2007; Bhambra 2014a). Middle- to upper-class heads of households describe their domestic help as part of the family and 'friends', yet their workers are still nonetheless denied basic rights, paid a minimum wage, and for all intents and purposes become 21st-century indentured labour for the European family. In the interviews undertaken by Gutiérrez-Rodríguez she illustrates how most employers saw themselves as fair, socially conscious and never racist. Yet the undocumented domestic workers described what they experienced as exploitation and did not reciprocate the idea of being friends with their employers. Two different worlds collide and reveal the processes, mechanisms and hierarchies of social power in the world.

This is the sociological imagination at work, digger deeper and elaborating on what might at first seem on the surface to be an everyday working relationship between employer and household labourer – when in actual fact the structural relations and social forces of the colonial and global capitalism have forced some women to leave their homes in Latin America and travel to Europe to earn a basic wage under 21st-century indentured labour conditions. These are local entanglements of historical global inequalities. This is one illustration of the kind of work that has emerged in sociology since its global turn.

Academic capitalism

Another key moment in sociological enquiry has been the corporatisation of universities and the emergence of *academic capitalism*. Sociology, of course, is most often found within a university space and field, and traditionally this space and field has been one supposedly focused on the production of value-free knowledge in the social sciences for the general betterment of society, although of course as we have seen knowledge is never truly value-free (Becker 1967; Gouldner 1968). However, in recent times the space and field of the university such as in the UK and the Caribbean has been remade into one of business. This has had a transformative effect across the university sector; for example, the governing structures of the university are now market oriented and focused on capital accumulation rather than solving social problems. Vice chancellors are more like chief executives. Students take on huge economic debt to study, which of course changes the purpose of learning and instantly makes them into consumers, constantly answering surveys about service and satisfaction. Course content is no longer driven by intellectual rigour but by management metrics and these student satisfaction scores. The marketisation of the university also means students are only interested in learning what they must for assessment.

As the university has changed around the sociologist, so have the ways and labour practices of the sociologist within the university been changed. Sociologists working in the neoliberal university must meet productivity targets as factory workers once did. Meanwhile the language, institutional structures and labour practices of the neoliberal university are shaped by audit cultures, performance targets and entrepreneurial modes of thought, which are quite a shift from the ethos of the sociological imagination to be creative, critical and driven to solve the complex and often far from obvious social questions of the time. What is worse, these shackles on the sociological imagination have become commonsensical and accepted as part of the status quo. Alas, if he were writing today, we would have to tell C. Wright Mills that his notion of the sociological imagination as our major way to understand our cultural lives and social features (1959, 14) is in crisis.

Today academic capitalism has had significant impacts on who sociologists are, what sociologists do and what sociology may mean. Hence the need for this book remaking the case for sociology and the sociological imagination. Today sociologists in the academy are constrained by performance criteria and by business-minded administrators. Many are overworked and many need to take time off from work due to stress-related illnesses. A lucky few sociologists are able to play the capital accumulation game and bring in highly sought-after research grants. But again, this transforms academic labour into a search for funding and not the pursuit of knowledge as was once the central criteria for a university's existence and excellence. Academic capitalism forces sociology into a contradiction that damages the potential and potency of the sociological imagination.

New forms of data, new areas of study

The final stop on our journey of seven key moments in Western sociology centres on the importance of new forms of data and the fields of study such as *sensory sociologies*, *digital sociologies* and *big data*. According to UK sociologist Jon Dean, sensory sociologies, or the sensory turn in Western sociology, refreshes and brings new ideas and ways to conceive qualitative methodologies to the discipline. Sensory sociologies

> aim to move sociology beyond the verbal, the reliance on interviews and surveys, and move into a way of communicating research about people's lives through sounds, smell, and the visual. As Law and Urry (2004) have argued, surveys and interviews are perhaps unsuited to grappling with global complexity, particularly those movements in social life which are fleeting, sensory, emotional, or kinaesthetic: Sometimes sounds bring into mind places the viewer does not know, and collages and photo-animations stimulate new understandings of work. (Dean 2016, 163)

This is a similar observation some Caribbean sociologists have made about the importance of using spoken word poetry for data collection, presentation of findings and as a sensory sociology device in Caribbean sociology (Crichlow 2015). Such new ways of telling sociological stories offer a way to make the discipline more open to others with less experience of the technical language of sociology.

> For instance, [on a recent academic panel] Alex Rhys-Taylor played a sound recording he had created from the vibrancy of the Radley Road market in East London. Those of us listening in the audience could hear the chatter, buzz, and hubbub of customers and stall-owners as both went about their daily business, with the fractious cosmopolitan energy of such a street scene made evident. The piece served to explore the sensorial elements of spice and society in order to communicate the lived experience of multiculturalism. (Dean 2016, 163; for an exploration of the smells of that market see Rhys-Taylor 2013)

According to the UK sociologists Susan Halford and Mike Savage, big data is both 'an empirical phenomenon and an emergent field of practice in which claims to knowledge [about the social] are made' (Halford and Savage 2017, 1132–3). Big data was the name given originally given to large datasets too massive for 'conventional computing analysis and storage'. Today big data

> encompasses a range of other qualities immanent in the digital traces of routine activities – for example, as we consume utilities, browse the Web or post on social media – not least their variety and velocity. These data offer insights into the daily lives of millions of people, in real time and over time, and have generated a surge of interest in social research across the academy and, especially, in commerce. (Halford and Savage 2017, 1133)

Big data such as the data sets produced by 'DNA sequencers, Twitter, MRIs, Facebook, particle accelerators, Google Books, radio telescopes,' Tumblr, #thetenyearchallenge and much more (Shaw 2015) are seen to be both liberating and disempowering: the magic bullet to our social problems and the very reproduction of society's worst traits, a gift to capitalists and a curse of constant big brother surveillance (Zuboff 2019). The more accurate observation is that big data cannot replace all forms of knowledge or answer all our social problems, and does come with certain larger societal structures internalised in its assumptions and algorithms, such as inequalities of race, class and gender, built into it. That said, big data is another important and partial data point for sociological inquiry, testing and researching. It is partial because big data only captures

> some activities, of particular people, using certain devices and applications intended to record specific information: the data are biased and partial, although often lacking in demographic detail and other information about their provenance that allow us to be clear about this. Furthermore, sociologists are critical of the dependence of big data analytics on computational methods, particularly speculative data mining using variants of pattern recognition and correlation. Discovering patterns in data, with little sense of meaningful questions, or means of conceptual interpretation, and reliance on 'black-boxed' analytical tools is linked to limited, sometimes mistaken and ethically concerning, claims to knowledge. Not least, the emphasis on patterns and correlations bypasses theoretically informed research questions and displaces the hermeneutic and critical analysis so central to sociology. (Halford and Savage 2017, 1133)

Some sociologists are now working with big data to build and enhance methodological rigour and credibility by developing an ethical framework for big data (Varley-Winter and Shah 2016). Others are producing insights into such work, including the inaccuracy of personal self-tracking data, the controversies and oppressions of digital surveillance, the history of big data, big data as commodities, the false sense of security created by big data, and lots more (Aradau and Blanke 2015; Bolin and Andersson Schwarz 2015; McFarland and McFarland 2015; Mützel 2015; Lupton 2016; Pink et al 2018; Smith 2018).

In their recent edited collection, *Digital Sociologies*, sociologists Jessie Daniels, Karen Gregory and Tressie McMillan Cottom (2017) illustrate how digital technologies transform and remake the relationship between the individual and society and that the study of this reconfiguration is at the heart of 21st-century sociological enquiry. As they note in their introductory chapter:

> Digital technologies simultaneously offer liberatory possibilities for destabilizing old hierarchies while at the same time the create mechanisms for retrenching well-established patterns of inequality, stratification, and domination. It is through the recognition of this tension that we have come to see the need for the critical practice of what we now call 'digital sociology'. Digital sociology provides a lens through which to understand the individual and society after digitization. (Daniels et al 2017, xviii)

They go on to note that there is not one digital sociology methodology or concern, nor a digital sociology that is not interdisciplinary; hence the title of their collection, digital sociologies, as an accurate umbrella term for the field. As such, digital sociologies has refreshed the sociological imagination, the methodologies of the discipline and the internal peer-review processes of sociology (Daniels et al 2017, xxiv).

Sociology: a changing discipline

As a body of knowledge and as a way of making sense of the social world, sociology has changed considerably throughout its history. Some of sociology's core assumptions have changed little over time. Many contemporary sociologists would not find it difficult to agree with, say, Émile Durkheim as to his conceptualisation of the social, and positivist and scientific approaches to sociology, which are still widespread in our discipline today. At the same time, our narrative in this chapter documents how sociology has been responsive to dominant social and political discourses, and how these discourses have contributed to its intellectual organisation. Herbert Spencer's account of social Darwinism and rendering of society as an organism are examples of this; they reflect as much Spencer's personal scholarly proclivities as the intellectual preoccupations of Victorian Britain. In this sense, the ways in which sociologists conceptualise society and social processes always must be understood as a reflection of much broader discourses. Sociology is concerned with the critical analysis of common sense. At the same time, however, it is also always immersed in and infused with the common sense of its times.

It is for this reason that we think it is useful to think of sociology not only as the systematic, theoretically and methodologically informed study of society, but also as a body of knowledge that has significant political implications. Its theoretical and methodological rigour allow sociology to move beyond common sense, to look at the world sideways, and to make sense of otherwise intractable or taken-for-granted social processes and problems. However, sociology is never fully independent from the common sense of its times, and it is for this reason that academic trends, fads and fashions require sociological analysis and critique as much as non-academic social processes. In other words, we argue that the sociology of sociology has an important part to play in how we understand and practise our discipline.

THINKING SOCIOLOGICALLY

1. We claim that positivism gave a false sense of objectivity about sociological work. What is meant by objectivity? What might be meant by the claim that sociological enquiry is objective? Do you agree with our negative assessment of this claim? Why (not)?

2. 'Postmodernism challenged the idea of singular objective truth about the social world.' [p 63] What is meant by this statement? Explain it in your own words, drawing on relevant background research of your own.

3. What is meant by the term 'culture industry'? Through background research of your own, try to clarify its meaning. Then consider how it might be useful to make sense of one of the following:
    a. Instagram
    b. Superhero films
    c. Romance novels

4. Consider: What are the *social conditions* that may have facilitated (or inhibited) the emergence of queer studies as an area of sociological enquiry?

5. On the preceding pages, we have argued that a global turn is taking place in sociology. Yet all the sources we have cited regarding this global turn have been published by large mainstream publishers in the Global Northwest. What, if anything, does this suggest about the scope and reach of this global turn?

6. What is academic capitalism? How does it organise the labour of university students and their lecturers? In which ways, if at all, does academic capitalism affect sociological enquiry today?

7. What is big data? How is big data reshaping contemporary social life? Answer this question in reference to one of the following:
    a. Online social networks, such as Facebook
    b. The Chinese social credit system
    c. Supermarket loyalty cards
    d. Public health
    e. The sharing economy (for example, Uber, Airbnb and other sharing platforms)

MINI PROJECT

Textbooks on classical sociology often focus on the male founders of the discipline in certain Western countries: Émile Durkheim, Max Weber, Karl Marx and others. Much less attention is given to the female sociologists who were involved in building sociology from its beginnings. Look into the life and work of the following early female sociologists. Consider how their work is important to sociology today. Why do these early female sociologists hardly feature in contemporary textbook narratives of sociology's origins? What does this say about sociology today? Summarise your findings on a poster or handout.

1. Harriet Martineau

2. Marianne Weber

3. Charlotte Perkins Gilman

4. Jane Addams

5. Ida B. Wells

6. Beatrice Potter Webb

7. Olive Schreiner

8. Suzanne Césaire

9. Elma Francois

10. Claudia Jones

TALKING POINTS

1. What is meant by the characterisation of sociology as an 'intellectual formation'? In which other ways could we describe the discipline? How does sociology as an intellectual formation differ from other fields of academic knowledge that describe human life, such as biology, economics and psychology?

2. Give examples of how sociological knowledge has changed over time. In which ways has sociology remained the same?

3. What are the seven key moments in the development of sociology? How is each of them important for an understanding of contemporary sociology? Do you agree with our choice of key moments? Why (not)?

4. Is it useful to think of sociology as 'a body of knowledge that has significant political implications'? Why (not)?

READ ON ...

There is a very wide variety of publications that survey each of the seven key moments we have discussed in this chapter. We have cited some of these, and you can find the full references for this text in the bibliography of this book. For an overview of sociology's development over time, many textbooks are useful. In particular, Ken Plummer's *Sociology: A Global Introduction* (2016) and James Fulcher and John Scott's *Sociology* (2011) are useful in this regard. There are likewise surveys of more specific aspects of sociology's history. For example, on the gendered nature of sociological enquiry and the work of early female sociologists, see *The Women Founders* by Patricia Madoo Lengermann and Gillian Niebrugge (1998). On the Eurocentrism and incipient global turn of sociological enquiry, see Raewyn Connell's *Southern Theory* (2007).

Check the companion website at https://bristoluniversitypress. co.uk/imagining-society-online-resources **for a suggested project and writing task.**

5

Sociologies in a global world

One everyday feeling that suggests to many of us a sense of living in a runaway world is the high level of insecurity many people feel about their personal safety. Around the world, security and insecurity are major concerns of the 21st century. Whether it's terrorism, gun violence, military policing, school shootings, radicalisation, violent extremism, domestic violence, stabbings, street crime, racism or much else, security and *securitisation* has become an important field of study across the social sciences. Yet no two societies and cultures are identical, and as such sociologists from different parts of the world cannot offer one all-encompassing analysis with little regard for variance and nuance across different countries and contexts. Every society around the world has its own points of origin, development and localised context; and every society gives voice to its own entanglements of cultural and historical significance within humanity's global story (Young 2008). This suggests that sociology is neither identical nor monolithic across the world's various nations and societies, and this is the central focus of this chapter.

Social problems and the sociological imagination

In sociology, insecurity/security or rather 'securitisation', as academics call studies of security and insecurity, can be understood as a *social problem*. Sociologists understand social problems as negative social realities, cultural values and social conditions affecting individuals, society and the wider environment, which require sociologists to explore, examine and understand (Best and Harris 2013). All individuals in a society might not experience these negative consequences equally; but many will experience negative consequences as a result of a wider social problem, and the society as a whole or in certain social segments, is harmed.

For example, in contemporary societies around the world people sometimes look at individuals who are experiencing economic hard times, such as unemployment or homelessness, as the fault of the individuals themselves rather than a larger social problem structuring the wider society and affecting individuals in the society. You might see this when some politicians or elites or media persons blame those living in poverty for their own difficult situation and suggest that perhaps some people are inherently lazy and simply do not want to work. However, in such a scenario the social context and socioeconomic conditions giving rise to situations of poverty that many individuals find themselves in are ignored. The impact of public issues on individuals by those producing situations of poverty and curtailing opportunities for individuals beyond their personal control becomes forgotten; for example, institutional and structural forces, such as unemployment brought on by the arrival of automation and automated drivers, the rise of online shopping and the closing down of shopping centres, or unsustainable and punitive government policies such as austerity measures, among many other wider social factors. For sociologists, however, doing research to investigate and recognise the wider social context, structural forces and socioeconomic system within which individuals make choices and exert their agency or have their agency constrained, is the central way in which we imagine the world (*ontology*) and understand the people who live in it (*epistemology*). The sociological imagination is well positioned to understand and explain how the macro-level structures of the modern world affect, shape and are related to micro-level experiences and 'social action'.

That is to say, much like you cannot understand a fish without the water around it and within which it swims and lives, so it is important to understand an individual's personal troubles via the social context and public issues the individual moves through from birth to death. This invisible social water is analogous to the sociological imagination. It reminds us that social problems are far more than individual failures but are very much connected to wider societal, structural and transhistorical forces, and how they play out and develop around the world in relation to each of us as individuals and our individual biographies.

The global problem of securitisation

A global and pluralistic sociologies lens must recognise the multiple and varied application of the sociological imagination across time and geographical space to social problems in many different societies in the world. By way of example, let us imagine via a global sociologies lens the social problem of securitisation. Whether it's crime, drugs, terrorism, guns, refugees, violent extremism or some other concern, securitisation as a process can be understood as how top-down authorities such as governments, security forces and politicians name and identify a security concern, and educate the public about what should be considered as genuine threats to personal safety (Balzacq 2011). Authorities often then call out their emergency solution and response to such threats – often some sort of armed state violence – and attack the threat, usually a single human or group of humans who might be described by those in power as 'bad people', 'dangerous', 'mentally ill' or a 'gang'. Yet in the weaponised solutions chosen by state actors to fix issues of violent insecurity the context of the social problem, the background to the social problem or the historical evolution of the issues are removed. Historical racism, structural poverty, hegemonic masculinity and cumulative local economic disadvantages, for example, are ignored and often replaced by ungenerous rhetoric about individual failures of morality, parenting or education. Lawbreakers simply become 'bad people' that a society needs to be protected and secured from. In this scenario governments stop looking for long-term sociological 'solutions' to social problems and the context behind them, and instead increasingly talk about security responses and 'wars' on crime, poverty and drugs. In this sense social problems become security problems of bad individuals. The sociological imagination as a solution to the social problem is erased and replaced by repressive state apparatuses such as the police, the court system and prisons.

Trinidad and Tobago

Trinidad and Tobago (T&T) is a dual-island Caribbean nation. Based on 2015 figures, T&T, population 1.4 million, was named the eleventh most murderous country in the world (UNODC 2014). Is such a high murder rate to be imagined simply as a problem of individuals waking up one day and choosing to become killers? Is this really a simple matter of individual madness and extreme social deviance? Or are the social context and forces at play, based on the sociological evidence collected, better understood via the relationship between sociological structures and institutions – for example, the economy, history, cultural values, social and familial supports, law, geography, individual agency and more. Is this a more realistic and accurate social science explanation than simply one of bad individuals? This is the approach the sociological imagination would take.

Consider this. T&T also has a relatively high rate of inequality and socioeconomic imbalance, which not only makes local job opportunities hard to find and social mobility impossible to achieve, but can eventually, based on other contextual factors, lead some people into crime (UNDP 2016). Such inequality can also have a significant impact on the development of an individual's life skills and psychosocial competencies, such as communication and interpersonal skills, decision making and problem solving, creative thinking and critical thinking, self-awareness and empathy, assertiveness and self-control, and resilience and the ability to cope with stress.

T&T is also geographically only seven miles from the South America mainland, and as a minor energy economy with global clients has sea and air routes to the Americas, Europe and Africa. This makes it an important geographic node in the transnational drugs and weapons trade (Townsend 2009). T&T does not manufacture drugs or weapons. Furthermore, it does not have a relatively high drug consumption rate, so the demand for drugs is from consumers elsewhere, generally North America and Europe; the guns are made elsewhere before being illegally transhipped to T&T (Seepersad 2016). When drugs arrive in T&T to be moved to some other part of the world according to consumer demand, the guns, which have accompanied the transhipment of drugs, sometimes as protection and sometimes as payment, do not leave the country. Once guns are in a society they become hard to eradicate; some describe this as the weaponisation or 'pistolisation' of civil society (Agozino et al 2009). Guns also mean that where once fights, crime and disagreements took place via words, knives, bottles and other weapons, guns are now the weapons of choice. This new technology then, the gun brought to T&T via the transnational drug trade and global flows of money, has over the last thirty years changed the ways in which violent behaviour takes place in T&T and transformed the murder rate: from 6.9 murders per 100,000 people in 1980 to 40.1 murders per 100,000 people in 2008 (Seepersad 2016). For comparison purposes the United Nations Office on Drugs and Crime reported for 2013 a global average of 6.2 murders per 100,000 people. The US had a rate in 2015 of 4.8 murders per 100,000 people. The UK murder rate in 2015 was 0.9 people per 100,000 and the South Korean rate was 0.74 per 100,000 people (UNODC 2014).

Using the sociological imagination the sociologist from and of the Caribbean would also be aware that the war on drugs itself, which gives rise to the consumer demand for a criminal transnational drug trade, is a human creation brought to life through social structures and institutions such as the law, the criminal justice system, the military, illegal capitalist enterprise and historically racist US government policies supported by many nations in the Global North (Lowe 2016). Moreover, other social structures and contextual factors have been identified:

- In the Caribbean, transnational organised crime has its greatest impacts, in terms of crime and violence, in communities which are already underdeveloped, traumatised and poor (Morgan 2014; Seepersad 2016; Seepersad and Wortley 2017).
- The transnational drug trade raises levels of general, police and institutional corruption in a society (Bagley 2004).
- The illicit trafficking of firearms from the US to the Caribbean (Young and Woodiwiss 2019).
- The structural racism and positional difference between global nations wherein the Global South has been underdeveloped relative to the Global North (Rodney 1972; Young 2008).

The sociologist can now start to imagine that the reasons for such high murder rates in T&T are not simply about the individual making a criminal and violent personal decision – although of course this is still an important contextual factor here – but rather, the public issue and social problem of high murder rates is a complex social whole within which the agency of individuals is entangled and their cultural values around what is right or wrong develop with tangible social consequences. For the sociologist, can such a social problem of a never-ending cycle of violence be solved by more security, repression and state violence, or would the social problem of high murder rates in T&T be more successfully tackled by sociologists applying the sociological imagination, and developing long-term sustainable solutions across many different levels not centred simply on repression and violence?

The UK

As is the case with sociology when it is understood as global and pluralistic, the social problem of securitisation in the UK takes on a slightly different form, concerns and nuance from the social problem of securitisation in T&T. Yes, securitisation is a serious social problem in the UK. For example, knife and gun crime rose between 2014 and 2018 (ONS 2019, 26). Yet national laws make gun crime in the UK, relative to T&T, far less common, while the social problem of securing the society has a distinct sociological context too. In the UK, one major security threat identified by the elites, politicians and the media is not a sky-high murder rate, but rather the threat of terrorism, violent extremism and radicalisation, which has played out for generations in different ways, first with the Irish Republican Army during the 1960s to 1990s, and latterly in the 21st century with attacks in the UK by both foreign and local people claimed by ISIS and Al Qaeda.

For example, those in government and the UK media have adopted 'radicalisation' as the isolated, hold-all explanation behind why people become ripe and socially deviant to being involved in terrorist activities. In the main, the media has represented radicalisation as extremist indoctrination, which supposedly only develops primarily in an individual or 'lone wolf' because of religious or political fundamentalism (Heath-Kelly 2013). This 'single issue causality' can be found in public health, criminological or legal approaches to the problem. Yet the sociological imagination can suggest this is a simplistic reading. Radicalisation to the sociologist is not a simple and neat causal relationship wherein a particular religion or political ideology radicalises and creates violent extremism in an individual – because it ignores the social context. Rather those most ripe to adopt non-normative and socially deviant pathways are shaped by a complex combination of sociological factors before they become vulnerable to the dangers of extremist rhetoric. Why does the mainstream definition by Western governments and some researchers of terrorism dismiss the sociological back-story of individuals and groups who turn to terrorism (Pantucci 2011)? Why does it also seem blind to white, far-right forms of terrorism too?

For example, marginalised young men in a society who do not have social supports like job opportunities, strong familial ties and friends, money, social mobility, and who live under the pressures of a broken social system defined by austerity and social inequality, of bullshit jobs, damaged masculine archetypes, a lack of life skills, and criminal activity can join gangs as a supposedly quick fix to questions of material need and sense of alienation (Baird 2018). What happens to young men who are socialised by popular culture and social media with the promise that masculinity and accumulating 'masculine capital' brings power, a job, wealth and respect (Carlson 2015; Bridges and Tober 2017)? That picture of masculinity is often about being a provider. Yet many of the men in gangs spoken to by sociologists suggest being shut out of such realities due to socioeconomic factors, the legacies of regional development and other problematic realities (Barker 2005; Baird 2012, 2018; Carlson 2015). This means many economically challenged young men do not have access to jobs and money and no way to access the promises they were socialised into believing that men would and should have from a young age. This is a public issue of the global socioeconomic system called capitalism (the word we typically use to describe the dominant economic system of our times) and its socioeconomic arrangements playing out in individual lives. Under such structural pressures derived from the failure of the socioeconomic system to distribute social goods like jobs, money and opportunities fairly in a society, a loss of social connection and a low sense of personal worth can develop in individuals (Baron-Cohen 2012). Individuals can feel like they have failed to achieve socially, and do not recognise how the socioeconomic system is structurally required to create a low-paid, precarious, zero-hours-contract surplus labour force that keeps wages low and always keeps some people excluded and vulnerable (Sassen 2014). Under such forces, like the racism and economic deprivation found in UK inner-city areas, some people become ripe for non-normative pathways and influences such as violent extremism. For the sociologist this is not simply religious fundamentalism and radicalisation as cause. Rather this is the socioeconomic exclusion and social prejudice inherent to the current socioeconomic system, with religious radicalisation and fundamentalism as a symptom and not cause. These pressures and more can turn some inward and create the social conditions within which an individual can become vulnerable to reasoning that violent extremism such as terrorism is a viable option.

In such scenarios vulnerable young men may not explicitly realise that what they are missing is the desire to belong, social connection, homo-sociality and love. The gang experience of being a family is one sociological context for why an individual might initially join a gang or become involved in terrorism (Decker and Van Winkle 1996). It is the same contextual factors that can lead vulnerable young men into both. So, for the sociologist the social problem of securitisation that UK society faces is not simply one of religious radicalisation, but rather one of socioeconomic radicalisation more generally among some, brought on by the failed politics of austerity and its broken socioeconomic system, and this sometimes plays out in gang membership and terrorism; but it can also lead in other directions too – including knife crime – and often does. For example, the sociological fact that the majority of domestic terrorists overlap with perpetrators of gender-based violence and sexual assault, which are also two types of radicalisation and violent extremism (Mayors Against Illegal Guns 2013), means for the sociologist it is not simple religious fanaticism, anti-Western, Jihad or far-right ideology shaping young men who become terrorists, but rather larger public issues of socioeconomic conditions, cultural values and problematic ideas relating to masculinity and social exclusion/inclusion, which some young men are exposed and subjected to (Carlson 2015). Social psychologists (sociologists who are interested in the psychology of group behaviour) and criminologists (sociologists who study crime) both point out that social alienation, where young men become socially disconnected from the wider society around them, leads to a lost ability to empathise with others and the norms of the society (Cacioppo and Patrick 2008). Thus the structural reality of local socioeconomic inequality, social and communal isolation, and ideas of masculinity as a provider that cannot be actualised are also important social conditions and considerations produced by the larger society, shaping the agency and social action of some individuals that sociologists include in their analyses.

The US

On 14 February 2018, a 19-year-old male, and ex-student of Marjory Stoneman Douglas High School in Parkland, Florida, returned to his former school, heavily armed, and proceeded to shoot his former classmates and teachers. The mass shooting took seventeen lives, fourteen of which were 18 years old or under. Unlike in the vast majority of other nations around the world, mass shootings and school shootings are a regular occurrence in the US. For example, between January 2013 and February 2018 there were nearly 300 school shootings, which is an average of almost one per week (Everytown for Gun Safety Support Fund 2018).

For the National Rifle Association (NRA), the problem of school shootings is not one that has a social component; rather, school shootings are the work of isolated, mentally-ill individuals. For example, this is what NRA spokeswoman Jennifer Baker had to say in relation to the Parkland shooting: 'While today's meeting made for great TV, the gun-control proposals discussed would make for bad policy that would not keep our children safe. Instead of punishing law-abiding gun owners for the acts of a deranged lunatic our leaders should pass meaningful reforms that would actually prevent future tragedies' (Phelps 2018)

While the sociologist would certainly understand mental illness and gun control as two components of the social problem of school shootings in the US, the sociological imagination also provides for a more nuanced, complex and accurate understanding of the issues beyond 'deranged' individuals and gun control. For example, US sociologist Jennifer Carlson has noted that 'without understanding not just *why* Americans own and carry guns but also *how* guns matter in their day-to-day lives, scholars, pundits, and politicians risk imputing a whole host of assumptions about the social life of guns in the United States' (Carlson 2018). This observation is an example of how sociology is both plural and global at the same time. The US has its own history of gun culture, unfamiliar in many other nations, and this must be considered and included in relative terms whenever deploying the sociological imagination anywhere in the world.

US sociologists Tristan Bridges and Tara Tober also note that,

> a great deal of commentary attempts to tie mass shootings to a single issue. Often, that seems like the easiest way to make sense of atrocities. That's why we get sound bites that lean on mental health (when shooters are white), terrorist ties and affiliations (when shooters are brown), gang violence and 'urban decay' (when shooters are black), bullying (when it happens in a school), and overwork (when it happens in a workplace). (Bridges and Tober 2017)

As they go on to discuss, however, the 'deranged' individual and other single-issue explanations dominating the gun lobby and those politicians it funds, suggest a randomness to acts of violence. Yet the high frequencies of school and mass shootings in the US is not found elsewhere in the world. As such, mass shooting events like school shootings are not isolated personal issues; rather the issue of individuals who become mass shooters is one that is more accurately understood through the lens of a sociological public issue and social problem of the wider society.

Sociological research demonstrates that many distinct contextual factors come together to produce the social problem of school shootings in the US. For example, Bridges and Tober highlight research data demonstrating a positive correlation between the number of guns in a society and the number of mass shootings in a society. Furthermore, they suggest mass shootings and school shootings in the US appears to be a social problem deeply tied in some way to men and masculinities, as nearly all mass shootings in the US are committed by men, some of whom, but not all, were socially alienated and isolated for a variety of reasons, including bullying at school (Celis 2015; Bridges and Tober 2017). Social psychologists suggest one reason this might be true is connected to 'social identity threat' and 'masculinity threat', wherein some men who are unable to actualise their masculinity based on the scenario and narratives fed to them by society, which they are socialised into, react to such loss of agency and 'masculine capital' (Baird 2018) with an 'exaggerated display of qualities associated with that identity' (Bridges and Tober 2017). One way the sociological imagination fills in the gaps about gender and gun violence would be the suggestion from the sociological research undertaken by Colombian sociologist Jorge Celis (2015, 520) that 'shooters see school as a social entity that has diminished their masculinity, and the way to reaffirm their masculinity is to attack randomly students and teachers in full view of the rest of school members during school hours'. Celis has also noted from the data collected on high school shootings that 'the majority of perpetrators have had parents who were gun collectors and that 'shooters mostly use family guns to commit the massacres' (Celis 2015, 536). Carlson too points out from her sociological research that 'gun carrying' in the US transforms 'the gendered and racialized meanings of citizenship' (Carlson 2015, 29). She developed the term 'citizen-protector' in her research 'to capture how men use guns to assert their authority, dignity, and relevance to their families, and even their broader communities, by embracing a duty to protect – up to and including the willingness to kill' (Carlson 2018).

US culture provides a reason why an erosion of masculine capital can play out in such violent ways in that society as compared to other societies where the consequences of a threat to masculine capital have not become a social problem of weekly school shootings. For Bridges and Tober, and Carlson, violent masculinities are produced and often glorified in US culture and in most other nations too. Think about all the types of violent media from music lyrics and films to video games and TV, which pivot on the identity of aggressive masculine archetypes and are consumed endlessly. At the same time, as these mediated narratives of what it is to be a man filter through the mediascape, the privileges traditionally accompanying masculinity in the US are being eroded by transformations in gender equality. Alongside such transformations Carlson also points out that as a consequence of the current economic climate men are losing another 'core pillar of masculinity – breadwinning – due to a neoliberal shift away from manufacturing' (Carlson 2018). For another US sociologist, Michael Kimmel, such changes have produced an 'aggrieved entitlement' among some men who believe they are entitled to the male privilege of their fathers and grandfathers (Kimmel 2013).

None of these reasons by themselves, such as being angry about losing male entitlements, watching violent media, having parents with guns, being bullied and more will lead to mass and school shootings; however, the work of sociologists like Tober, Bridges, Celis, Carlson and Kimmel add sociological context to the social problem of securitisation in US society to illustrate that the social problem of school shootings is far more than one of mentally-ill individuals. Additional sociological research, for example, demonstrates that most family, friends and other people who interact with the perpetrators of mass and school shootings describe assailants as 'normal' and not isolated people (Celis 2015). School shootings in the US are shaped by social forces and public issues. However, the predominant way school shootings have been analysed is by using psychological and individualist approaches. These approaches cannot and do not capture the social values, environmental forces and cultural situations within which the individual is shaped and their agency and choices become understood. For example,

> [e]mpirical research clearly reveals that school shooters tend not to present life-long histories of mental illness, [psychological] approaches usually put a strong emphasis on the perpetrator's individual pathologies, ignoring the influence that social values such as masculinity exert on perpetrators' actions. Consequently, perpetrators are viewed as lone wolf shooters and school shootings as isolated cases. (Celis 2015, 520)

The sociological imagination presents a different picture of the social problem of mass and school shootings in the US from that of the psychological imagination, with its pure focus on individual pathologies that blames the individual perpetrator solely and ignores the larger social context within which the individual exists. The focus on individual pathologies plays into the hands of those who do not want gun control, for a variety of reasons, including guns sales and economic profits. For the sociologist, understanding the social problem of school shootings in the US is a combination of different social factors, including: transformations in gender relations; larger issues of inequality; racial politics; a society within which guns are readily available and upheld as a right more than anywhere else in the world; assertions of damaged masculinity; the high number of suicides associated with the perpetrators of mass homicides; the capital accumulation motives of the gun lobby; and the many US politicians who received donations from the NRA, and more (Lankford 2015). Clearly, then, for the sociologist the issues are multiple, and action on all levels, including gun control, is needed but this is also a social problem that needs a larger shift in the culture for many in the US, regarding such ideas as gun control, gun culture and, equally, male dominance, violence and supremacy.

Social democracy and sociology

As our detour of the different ways how the social problem of securitisation can play out in different societies and sociologies, no matter what the social problem, sociology requires sociologists from many different geographic places and backgrounds to have nuanced local and global knowledge in order to employ the sociological imagination effectively. So, where did the social go in terms of inclusion in top-down analyses of social problems across the world's various societies? What has happened to the social imagination in trying to understand poverty, the war on drugs, terrorism or school gun violence?

Social democracies are founded on the idea that the state, and the government in control of the state, should use its powers to temper the extremes of capitalism and rebalance capitalism's natural tendency toward monopolies and socioeconomic inequalities. As Wolff (2016) makes clear, social democracy was understood as a political choice to keep the productive aspects of capitalism such as innovation and wealth creation, while also ensuring such factors as free education, universal healthcare and opportunity more generally were still available to all, irrespective of a person's negative financial standing. Today, social democracies can still be found in northern Europe and in particular Scandinavian nations. They were also once dominant in mainland Europe too, as well as in the US during the era of the New Deal in the 1930s and 1940s, and in emerging ex-colonies around the world from the 1950s to 1980s. This was the era before Global North institutions such as the International Monetary Fund, the World Trade Organization and the World Bank, in a quest for increased capital accumulation for companies, corporations and shareholders mainly based in the Global North (Meeks and Girvan 2010), forced many small economies in the Global South to convert to neoliberal policies centred on competitive individualism and austerity cuts to public and social services. This led to growing inequalities, both within and between different nations around the world, as central features shaping everyday life, in contrast to the more socially democratic ideas from the thirty-year period prior to the late 1960s and early 1970s such as national health services, welfare nets and reducing social inequalities. As Marxist sociologists note, capitalism is not capable of realising 'economic equality and democracy, rather it is the great obstacle to their realization' (Wolff 2018). Social democracy was once seen as one solution to this obstacle

In this prior political context, sociology, sociological research and sociological evidence was essential to the temperance needed for social democracies to function successfully. This was because individuals and their opportunities in social democracies were always imagined and understood by sociologists in relation to the wider public issues in a society. Today a central way to imagine individuals in society is often to disconnect them from the wider social context of their lives. Such imagination, centred on the myth of individuals as free-floating atoms, each with identical potential for social mobility and economic opportunities, supports and develops a different type of economic and political system from social democracy. This is the form of capitalism often referred to in its many different geographical contexts as 'neoliberalism' (Davies 2014). Today in Anglo-US politics and media, it is common to hear that crime is caused by immigration, or that poor people are pathological and willingly dependent. These simplistic populist explanations promote the dominance of individual pathologies and culpability over the possibility that history and wider social factors have a part to play in social phenomena. Such lessons often dominate classrooms too. Clearly the choice is not an either-or option between a psychological lens or a sociological one. However, the sociological imagination may pose something of a threat to the dominant economic model of our time by providing evidence that individual pathologies cannot by themselves ever explain social events and problems (Cottom 2019).

However, based on the size and power of US culture industries, not least in education, media and popular culture, individual pathologies today have come to be the preferred way to imagine the world (Davies 2015) – not because they provide the most accurate explanation of social events but because ideas such as the Protestant ethic (Weber 2001) and a spirit of capital accumulation have become the normative cultural values into which people are socialised and educated (Giddens 1970). As such, for much of the second half of the 20th century capitalism was beyond reproach as the dominant socioeconomic system available. Under a type of capitalism called neoliberalism, the push for 'profit over people' around the world – in less-developed societies such as the Caribbean, Africa and other parts of the Global South, as well as those less affluent groups in developed nations of the Global North – accelerated from the 1970s and has meant people have ceased to be the most important considerations in development projects.

Instead, politically, profit and capital accumulation became more important considerations than people.

This is quite clearly seen in the transformations universities around the world have gone through, as they have shifted from developing people and nations to concentrating on making money and customer service (see Chapter 10). As the university environment has changed so has the production of sociology and sociologists. For example, over the last forty years among many sociologists in the Global South, consultancy work and the US or European money it paid and the social mobility this granted became more important than developing the discipline locally. As a combination of these factors and many others that we discuss in Chapter 6, during the 1970s to today the sociological imagination was fractured, diluted and splintered. The British sociologist Frank Furedi has noted other changes that sociology has gone through in the last twenty years in the UK, including an infantilisation of pedagogy, the growth of paternalism and a demand for conformity regarding any responsibility towards social change. Not to mention limitations to free speech, an increase in intolerance, an increased focus on self-esteem and maximum risk avoidance, and continuous emotional validation and affirmation over intellectual freedom and the pursuit of truth (Furedi 2014).

Under various pressures over the last forty years, sociological studies of social problems using the social imagination became partial and incomplete, divided into silos, but no less important in studying the world (Tett 2015). For example, the sociology of social problems became 'social work', the sociology of crime became 'criminology', and the sociology of social conflict became 'mediation'; and in terms of the availability of scarce resources in universities, disciplines began to compete with each other rather than provide a holistic sociological lens on social problems. For Furedi, over time such realities have transformed UK sociology at the university from a discipline nurturing radicalism and intellectual experimentation to one that is conformist and censorial (Furedi 2014).

The time is long past due to reintroduce the social, and the holism of the social imagination, back into how we understand and develop our societies. The market and competition, as central cultural values and social norms based around the individual, have been the dominant value system for over fifty years now, and while many social problems have disappeared during this time many new ones, and many unintended social consequences such as climate change, environmental destruction, increases in social alienation and the death of the university as a place of social change, to name a few, have left the planet and its people in precarious times. It is time for a return to the sociological imagination.

The dynamics of globalisation

So how did the world and sociology become unequal? Once, globalisation and the way it plays out in similar but different ways or 'multiple modernities' as sociologists called such differentiation, were all the rage (Bhambra 2007; Lee 2008;

Welz 2008; Pieterse 2016) and highly praised as a process of global humanity coming closer together. Yet with time what once glittered in academic discourse began to be described by some, especially those in the Global South, as a form of neocolonialism and a new imperialism led by transnational global elites who continued to hoard a disproportionately large share of the total global wealth while destabilising the environmental, sociocultural and economic fabrics of life (Harvey 2007; Piketty 2014; Wolff 2016). As such, globalisation is an ambiguous concept, with negative consequences as well as positive ones.

If you plot the word 'globalisation' into Google's Ngram Viewer, the word begins to appear initially in the late 1960s and early 1970s. Sociological theorising on globalisation begins in the Global North's culture industries at around the same time and the term has been used heavily in academic literature and popular culture since the mid-1980s. One sociological definition of globalisation is the processes involved in making the world a global society (de Sousa Santos 2002). This includes flows of people, trade, markets, ideas, capital, labour, technology and more, moving back and forth around the world. Another understanding of globalisation from the Global North is 'globalisation … is unifying the world into a single mode of production and a single global system and bringing about the organic integration of different countries and regions into a global economy' (Robinson cited in Connell 2007, 53). From a varied, nuanced and pluralistic global sociologies' perspective, however, this latter definition seems too void of socioeconomic and cultural difference to capture the world and all the people in it. Is this humanity's sole aim, to become one big capitalist regime? Who made that decision for everyone? As the Australian sociologist, Raewyn Connell (2007, 53) has noted, 'the concept of the global society was built on the idea that boundaries were rapidly breaking down and there was a new intensity of links across distance among people, social entities or regions'. That is to say, globalisation understood as simply an economic project is to underutilise our sociological imaginations.

For many nations outside of the Global North, and the sociologists produced from and in such societies, globalisation is not something that started simply from the 1960s; because from the 'darker side of Western modernity' – slavery, colonialism and imperialism – were earlier forms of globalisation (Mignolo 2011a). Some sociologists of the Global South also describe colonialism and imperialism as state-led white-collar crime (Fanon 1965; Friedrichs 1997). For example, at the end of slavery in the British Caribbean in 1833 it was not the formerly enslaved who were compensated for their enslavement; rather, it was the slave owners who were compensated for their loss of human property. The British government, using taxpayers money, paid £20 million to 3,000 slave-owning British families as compensation for this supposed loss of property. Today that figure would be equivalent to £16.5 billion, and while the formerly enslaved were forced into destitution and poverty at the end of slavery many British families who were compensated at the time, such as the Camerons, the Gladstones and the Hoggs, would go on to have family members at the heart of the British establishment over the next one hundred and eighty years, some of who went on to become prime minister, lord chancellor and politicians in the UK. All this information and much more can be seen on the University College London website, which you'll find a link to on the companion webpage for this chapter. The compensation given to many slave owners was central to building the industrial society of 19th-century Britain, including national rail networks, cultural societies, universities, factories, insurance companies and banks (Williams 1994). Yet nothing was given to those societies traumatised by European colonialism and slavery, which today form part of the many nations globally described as less developed and underdeveloped, and which constitute, according to the United Nations Office on Drugs and Crime, the twenty highest national intentional homicide rates per 100,000 people in the world (Morgan 2014). This bigger picture of transnational phenomena, historical change and social connections is a good example of the sociological imagination at work.

For de Sousa Santos (2006) and many other sociologists in the Global South, globalisation was and is seen as a 'set of unequal exchanges in which a certain artefact, condition, entity or local identity extends its influence beyond its local or national borders and, in so doing, develops an ability to designate as local another rival artefact, condition, entity or identity' (de Sousa Santos 2006, 396). The history and genealogy of this cumulative unequal exchange has produced many unintended consequences and social problems, such as a dramatic rise in inequality between and within developed and underdeveloped countries, environmental degradation, ethno-racial racism and conflict, international migration, refugee crises, civil wars, ethnic cleansing and genocide, and global organised crime. This is what some sociologists mean when they describe globalisation as a form of 'neocolonialism'. Yet in the other part of de Sousa Santos's definition of globalisation is the always-successful globalisation of a particular localism that brings cultural ideas, practices and artefacts with it, such as the globalisation of US movies, of Caribbean Carnival, of Chinese food, of tea and coffee cultures, of electronic dance music, of yoga and so much more.

'Glocalisation' is a term suggested by the sociologist Roland Robertson, from the Japanese word *dochakuka* (Smith 2007). Robertson (1997) believed glocalisation better captures the relationship between the global and local under globalisation. For Robertson, globalisation is not the opposite of localisation. Rather they are two parts of one whole. The US sociologist George Ritzer (2004, 73) describes glocalisation as 'the integration of the global and the local resulting in unique outcomes in different geographic areas'. One example he uses is the way in which Global North fast-food restaurants like McDonald's and KFC offer local variations of their menus abroad rather than simply trying to Anglo-Americanise foreign taste buds. In this sense glocalisation is a marketing process embedded in globalisation to market foreign products in local forms and variations so they better fit and sell in local marketplaces, which, understood in sociological imagination terms, is connected to a larger project of capital accumulation rather than global harmony. Ritzer also adds to this picture by describing how glocalisation is about more than simply markets, business and making money. Glocalisation is also about cultural hybridities and heterogeneity, as the global and local combine.

Social problems in an interconnected world

From the social problem of securitisation in different societies and a critical reading of globalisation in this chapter we have begun to see how the sociological imagination can be applied to a variety of social problems in various geographic and historical contexts. We have seen how the world is interconnected, and that explanations of social events involving gun crime and radicalisation are not adequately explained by narratives solely focused on personal problems and individual failures, because such social problems are broader and far more social and transhistorical than simply being a case of 'bad' people. People and their individuality are shaped and developed within larger social and public contexts. In recognising such complexity about human social action and outcomes, we also began to see the idea of sociology, as a singular project from the West and by the West, as no longer tenable – if it ever was. Today sociologists and the sociological imagination are found all over the world. And as sociologists use the sociological imagination in various national and social contexts to better understand their social problems, the idea of a singular Western sociology as the only sociology available to them has been slowly dissolved. That said, our discussion of globalisation and glocalisation raises questions of an uneven playing field in the production of sociological knowledge between the Global North and South. In the next chapter we look further at this issue in inequality as we continue the story of global sociologies by looking at the development of sociologies around the world in the 20th century.

THINKING SOCIOLOGICALLY

1. In this chapter, globalisation is described as 'an ambiguous concept, with negative consequences as well as positive ones'. Describe what the chapter suggests globalisation can look like for people living in the Global South and in particular the ex-colonies of Europe. What have been the benefits and negatives of the globalisation process for these ex-colonies?

2. What is the relationship between colonialism, slavery and the development of Western societies? And how might the past influence the fact that, according to the UNODC, nearly all of the fifty most murderous nations in the world per capita are former and current European colonies or dependencies?

3. How and why might the terms 'glocalisation' and 'neocolonialism' be more or less accurate terms for the sociologist than 'globalisation'?

MINI PROJECT

This exercise illustrates the collective socialisation of men and women into gender roles and cultural ideas concerning masculinity – what it supposedly means to be a man – and femininity – what it supposedly means to be a woman. Watch these videos made by Promundo, a Brazilian non-governmental organisation promoting gender justice and preventing violence by engaging men and boys in partnership with women and girls. They offer a sociological perspective on gender in a cross-cultural comparison to illustrate how our ideas about being a man or a woman are intimately social and connected to who we know, how we know and what we know.

1. Understanding Masculinities in Morocco: Ahmed's Story (4:10) www.youtube.com/watch?v=CvLvkyA_B6Y&feature=youtu.be

2. Understanding Women's Economic Empowerment in Morocco: A Drama (4:45) www.youtube.com/watch?v=irQkDil7IFM&feature=youtu.be

3. Understanding Masculinities in Lebanon: Adnan's Story (5:43)
    www.youtube.com/watch?v=2IcZelV6gZ0&feature=youtu.be

4. Understanding Gender Norms in Palestine: A Drama (6:27)
    www.youtube.com/watch?v=qnTMMgDjrS4

5. When Men Change: A Promundo Film (3:55) www.youtube.
    com/watch?v=DXaFRrl-I70

You may also find these online resources useful:

https://promundoglobal.org/resources/man-box-study-young-man-us-uk-mexico/

https://goodmenproject.com/featured-content/what-is-inclusive-masculinity-wcz/

TALKING POINTS

1. How did Max Weber suggest the Protestant ethic helped in the development and emergence of capitalism? [p 87] What are the characteristics of the Protestant ethic as a moral grammar?

2. What is neocolonialism? In which ways, if at all, is the term useful to understand contemporary social life?

3. What is meant by the notion of 'global sociologies'? Why are they varied, plural and connected at the same time?

4. Why is the sociological imagination essential in understanding, imagining and developing our societies?

5. What events have transformed the world so that many governments and elites around the world now imagine social problems as never-ending wars, and not as long-term sociological problems to be resolved for the betterment of all in society?

6. 'A global and pluralistic sociologies lens must recognise the multiple and varied application of the sociological imagination across time, cultures and geographical space to social problems in many different societies in the world.' [p 78] What is this statement trying to say? In which ways is sociology global but also plural, singular but also multiple at the same time? Why might this be?

READ ON ...

Through personal experiences of black womanhood in US society Tressie McMillan Cottom's *Thick* (2019) explores relationships between self and social structure to illustrate the intersectional complexity of modern social problems. On globalisation, Boaventura de Sousa Santos in the *The Processes of Globalisation* (2002) and *Globalizations* (2006) offers insights about the pros and negatives from both top-down and bottom-up perspectives. Walter Rodney's 1972 historical sociology classic *How Europe Underdeveloped Africa* provides a Global South vision of globalisation (1972). Walter Mignolo too in *The Darker Side of Western Modernity: Global Futures, Decolonial Option* (2011b) offers a vision of modernity acknowledging distinctions in development processes between Global North and South. Iris Marion Young in 'Structural Injustice and the Politics of Difference' (2008) explains how difference in historical global processes produces distinct social, economic and cultural outcomes. Frank Furedi looks at the infantilisation of the university under neoliberalism (2014). Raewyn Connell explains the influence of divergent sociological processes on ideas in *Southern Theory* (2007). Saskia Sassen's *Expulsions: Brutality and Complexity in the Global Economy* (2014) provides examples of this in socioeconomic terms. Thierry Balzacq in *Securitization Theory: How Security Problems Emerge and Dissolve* (2011) explores how social problems become security problems. Men, masculinities and gangs is the topic of Adam Baird in 'The Violent Gang and the Construction of Masculinity amongst Socially Excluded Young Men' (2012) and 'Becoming the "Baddest": Masculine Trajectories of Gang Violence in Medellín' (2018). Gun culture is tackled in Jennifer Carlson's *Citizen-Protectors : The Everyday Politics of Guns in an Age of Decline* (2015).

Check the companion website at https://bristoluniversitypress. co.uk/imagining-society-online-resources **for a suggested project and writing task.**

6

Decolonising sociology

In Chapter 5 we saw how sociology is far more than a singular entity; rather, it is a plural, varied and multiple discipline. We turn our attention now to the processes of change that early Western sociology underwent during the 20th century. In this context, we look at the globalisation of sociology and the development of varied global sociologies. Finally, we explore a 'connected sociologies' paradigm that emphasises the diversity and interrelations of different forms of sociological knowledge.

Sociology and imperialism

Sociology as an academic discipline has its own origin myths and the actual truth of the matter is shrouded in contradictions. Yet, understood through its genealogy and family tree as outlined in Chapter 4, most agree the sociology taught at universities first emerges as a Western and Global North bundle of ideas, methods, language and social science discipline, and it was given birth to by empire. As vast economic and social changes were happening in 19th-century European societies such as France, Britain, Germany and Russia, sociology emerged in such societies as an attempt to understand the change from traditional societies to modern ones. As Connell reminds us, sociology was 'a science of the new industrial society' (2007, 6).

A basic definition of empire, according to US sociologist George Steinmetz who has written critically about the imperial entanglements and contradictions of the discipline, is to describe it as a relationship 'of political control imposed by some political societies over the effective sovereignty of other political societies' (Steinmetz 2013a, 9). He describes European nations such as Germany, Britain and France as the metropole and centre of empire. This relationship included much more than politics simply defined. Rather, it included ideologies involving tastes, cultural values and social norms. In many ways empire can be imagined through the Marxist sociological lens as a relationship not simply between centre and periphery but between ruling-class ideas about the world and colonial subjectivities.

The ideas of the ruling class are in every epoch the ruling ideas, i.e. the class which is the ruling material force of society, is at the same time its ruling intellectual force. The class which has the means of material production at its disposal, has control at the same time over the means of mental production, so that thereby, generally speaking, the ideas of those who lack the means of mental production are subject to it. The ruling ideas are nothing more than the ideal expression of the dominant material relationships, the dominant material relationships grasped as ideas. (Marx and Engels 1998, 67)

Sociology's point of creation, then, were the 19th-century urban and cultural heartlands of the major imperial powers at the high point of modern imperialism, wherein capitalism had emerged from the social relations and global structures of colonialism (Williams 1994). In this sense, some postcolonial historians like Manu Goswami and critical sociologists like Steinmetz have described the early sociology of Europe as 'imperial sociology' (Steinmetz 2005, 302; see also Goswami 2013). For Steinmetz, 'imperialism is a form of political control of foreign lands that does not necessarily entail conquest, occupation, and permanent foreign rule' (Steinmetz 2013a, 59). One reason for defining imperialism in this way is that the territories had already been conquered in earlier times and were now administered from the metropole. For Steinmetz (2005, 342), imperialism is 'a more comprehensive concept' than colonialism, since it 'presupposes the will and the ability of an imperial centre to define as imperial its own national interests and enforce them worldwide in the anarchy of the international system'. Or phrased by those on the periphery, colonialism was about the dispossession and robbery of resources such as land and labour (a process Marx called 'primitive accumulation'), which laid the groundwork for imperialism, which in turn used such resources to accumulate capital, and then put such capital in motion through investing it to make larger profits (Lenin 1917; Rodney 1972; Evans and Buhle 2015).

Sociology was one element in the global expansion of North Atlantic and European popular culture and intellectual life from the metropole to the colonies (Said 1993). Connell explains that imperial sociology, as a discipline, was 'formed within the culture of imperialism, and embodied an intellectual response to the colonised world. This fact is crucial in understanding the content and the method of sociology, as well as the discipline's wider cultural significance' (Connell 2007, 9). As she notes, in the imperial era the main justification for empire was no longer missionary religion but the belief in the evolutionary superiority of the settlers. It is from within these problematic scenarios of ethno-supremacy and ethnocentrism that Western sociology and anthropology first emerges, with all the 19th-century baggage this entailed.

The European intellectuals who first imagined and created imperial sociology as a 'science of society' were aware of the global expansion of North Atlantic power and believed in the supposed superiority of their own societies; it was a foundational aspect of their epistemology. Therefore early ideals of 'modernisation', including the belief that European society was the pinnacle of social evolution, influenced the genre of their writing and justified imperialism as a civilising developmental project. As Connell (2007, 7) notes of the times, 'the formula of development from a primitive origin to an advanced form was widespread in Victorian thought'. For instance, early European sociologists like Émile Durkheim were interested in the beliefs of non-Western peoples, but there was no interest in learning the social truths or insights contained in non-European understandings of the world with a view to considering whether they might contribute to improving life in Europe. Instead, as Connell (2007, 221) points out, such colonial societies and their individuals were in the main treated as curiosities, 'as exhibits in a museum of primitiveness' with little to offer the metropole. Even though such evolutionary ideas are seen within global sociologies today as empirically feeble and politically conservative, at the time of empire and imperialism such ideas were important and supported the political agenda and ruling class ideologies of the times.

Fall of the sociology of empire

According to historical research by Steinmetz (2005, 302), the years immediately after the end of the Second World War were when sociology as a 'fully fledged discipline' was firmly established in British universities. Sociology's purpose at such time was linked not just to social democracy and the welfare safety-net needed at home, but also to huge energies put into fortifying the declining empire through 'colonial developmentalism' in which sociological 'research and higher education' played key roles. One of the most significant groups of colonial sociologists, Steinmetz (2014, 440) reminds us, were the 'Government Sociologists' who conducted research for British governments in the colonies alongside anthropologsts conducting ethnographies as a means of colonial control and documentation (Thompson 1960).

Between the 1940s and the 1970s, colonialism and empire were central research areas for many British academic sociologists, whether they were located in the major universities and sociology departments of the UK or in the newly emerging universities in the British colonies, such as the University of the West Indies, which was first founded in 1948 as a branch of the University of London (Steinmetz 2013a, 371). For Steinmetz, this sociology of empire as a sociological practice took one or more of the following forms:

- ethnographies, surveys, and other applied research conducted in colonies at the behest of governments;
- autonomous social research in and on the colonies;

- theoretical and historical analyses (by sociologists) of ancient or contemporary empires;
- comparative sociological research based on information generated in colonial settings;
- sociological activities other than research that are nonetheless directly related to imperial rule, such as the instruction of colonial officials or membership on government colonial science commissions. (Steinmetz 2013a, 356)

Some North American sociologists such as Ivor Oxaal (1968, 1971), a sociologist of development working in the 1960s and 1970s, suggested that a coherent programme of public diplomacy to transfer power to suitably prepared colonial elites was developed by the colonial powers starting in the late 1930s. 'Island scholarships', for example, a scheme for Caribbean academics to attend universities and institutions in the UK and the US, were an original form of 'public diplomacy', diplomatic propaganda and 'soft power'. According to Oxaal (1971, 17), such scholarships were designed by imperial powers to shape the future leaders, educators and professionals in the colonies and to produce people who followed the ways, views and ruling ideas of the metropole and their capital interests. The winners of island scholarships on their return to the Caribbean, for example, got involved in local electoral and parliamentary politics or became educators at elite schools, and in Trinidad and Tobago were described by local sociologists such as Lloyd Best (1997) as the 'Afro-Saxon' architects of postcolonialism in the islands.

This early form of public diplomacy gelled well with a short revival in British imperialism, which 'gained a new lease on life and reasserted itself under the shelter of the new empire – the American one', as Steinmetz (2013a, 355) suggested. By the 1970s, most British ex-colonies had achieved independence and imperial sociology was in decline. A new, more anti-imperialist and fractured sociology diffused around the world. This included changes in British sociology too, which reacted to colonialism's abrupt loss of legitimacy by turning away from its former empire and concentrating on domestic matters in the former metropole itself.

In the context of the diffusion and emergence of global sociologies under this new American empire, Connell suggests that the new post-war era of US global hegemony contributed significantly to the creation of a classical canon in US sociology, and by extension the growth of pluralistic global sociologies, as US power began to sweep across former colonies and as the former colonial powers of Europe declined (Connell 2007). In 'countries that could afford to have sociology, the discipline was created or remade in the 1950s and the 1960s on the basis of research techniques, research problems and theoretical languages, not to mention textbooks and instructors, mostly imported from the United States' as it extended its geo political power, control and public diplomacy around the world (Connell 2007, 24). US sociology's involvement in the initial development of a global sociology can be understood via a framework of global history, its own history of imperialism, and its use of 'modernisation theory' – a Global North sociological theory used to explain the process of modernisation within societies. Modernisation theory in effect provided a rod with which US officials tried to enforce their worldview on less powerful nations.

Modernisation theory was dominated initially in the post-Second World War period by a body of knowledge emerging around 'development' as a supposed step-by-step process in any given society. Modernisation theory assumed incorrectly that, with assistance, 'traditional' countries could be brought simply to development in the same manner as more developed countries had been. See for example US economist Walt Rostow's 'five stages of development' (1960) and Caribbean economist Sir Arthur Lewis's 'industrialisation by invitation' (1950). Both Global-North-inspired development theories would later be challenged from the 1970s onwards by a new wave of global sociologists, as being processes which actually increased dependency, overexploitation, and underdevelopment in the peripheries, rather than provided social and economic development (Rodney 1972). Modernisation theory was closely associated with US foreign policy, which soon after the Second World War came to reject European colonialism in favour of the view that all cultures and societies in the world are equally suited for democracy, capitalism and the US way of life (Turner 2003), a form of US imperialism and intra-nation 'structural violence' most ex-colonies have never recovered from (Farmer 2004; Young 2008). As such, modernisation theory itself has come under scrutiny from global sociologies as a new imperialism and neocolonialist.

Neo-Marxist sociologists such as the German-American Andre Gunder Frank, the New World Group in the Caribbean and Latin America, and Pan Africanists among others began analysing the exploitation of the global peripheries through mechanisms that bypassed colonial rule, such as unequal conditions of exchange and the 'development of underdevelopment' (Frank 1971). However, given the history of sociology and its relationship to first empire and then imperialism, along with its problems of 19th-century-derived scientific autonomy, the discipline as it had been initially conceived soon faced crises of legitimacy. Steinmetz identifies these crises by using the example of the US and connections between the crisis of empire, and the crisis of universities in North America (Steinmetz 2013b). From the Second World War until well into the 1970s the US military was the largest contributor of social science funding. In *The Sociological Imagination*, C. Wright Mills (1959, 106) discussed the consequences of such entanglements of social scientists with empire, '[I]f social science is not autonomous, it cannot be a publicly responsible enterprise'. The French sociologist Pierre Bourdieu too has called on intellectuals to 'take their "irresponsibilities" seriously' (1999, 27).

Who funds sociological research and for what purpose is an important consideration for global sociologies today and the sociological imagination? During the first two decades of the 21st century, for example, US military funding for social science involving counterinsurgency has again expanded, this time as university jobs are disappearing. Today, as during the times of empire and imperialism, there is increasing pressure to make academic research serve political ends. The most extreme example is the involvement of ethnographers and other social scientists as 'embedded' advisers on the local 'human terrain' with US military troops in Afghanistan and Iraq (Whitehead 2009). The US Defense Department's Minerva Project called on sociologists and other social scientists to use their methods for 'more effective, more culturally sensitive interactions between the US military and Islamic populations' (Steinmetz 2013b, 868). In military circles, this was known as 'enhancing the kill chain' (Lucas Jr 2009).

On the other side of the spectrum, a pluralistic global sociologies lens recognises that imperial sociology's focus on empire, social evolution and development has also made it impossible for sociologists to overlook in their work the systemic class, gender and racial disparities, and the social hierarchies in global power. For example, Steinmetz uses the example of South African, anti-colonial anthropologist Max Gluckman's 'extended case method' and 'situational analysis', which were inspired by the social complexities of race, ethnicity and class in South Africa. Such bottom-up methodologies, Steinmetz points out, contributed 'to the downfall of earlier static and context-free forms' of ethnography and forced many to reassess their earlier ethnocentric approaches. Such realities are the subject of the next section.

Epistemologies of global sociologies

The term 'epistemologies' refers to ways of knowing and investigating the world. Epistemologies are built on the assumptions we each implicitly make about the best way to understand and ask questions about the world. Individual sociologists as well as various global sociologies around the world all possess an epistemology derived from local experiences of the world and this will influence and shape the questions they ask about the world and the subsequent production of knowledge. Sociologically, epistemologies are not context-free theories of truth, and to truly understand the premise of 'global sociologies', it is important to recognise and understand the notion of various vistas and viewpoints on the world being possible. This is distinctly different from the origins of sociology in empire and imperialism with its initial positivistic way of seeing and imagining the world, something we cover in detail in this chapter (see also Chapters 4 and 5 . A global sociologies epistemology accommodates social constructionist, relativist and decolonial viewpoints.

Epistemologies express the common beliefs of various groups of scientific and social science researchers at different locations and times. Social science in this sense can be imagined as embodied practice. Sociological research is done by groups of sociologists in particular settings. Metropolitan social science, which can be seen in the early works of positivist sociologists such as Auguste Comte, Herbert Spencer and Émile Durkheim established early on a need to approximate in sociology the language and objective conceptual style of the natural sciences. Metropolitan social science also tried to reproduce theory as monolithic and top-down, rather than dialogic and exploratory where all voices might be heard. Generally, positivists and realists have preferred the former approach, which means more quantitative and deductive methods of investigating the world, while social constructionists and relativists have preferred the latter, which means more qualitative and inductive ways of investigating and knowing the world. But this is of course not a fixed rule and there is much overlap. In basic terms, deductive reasoning or the deductive approach starts with a hypothesis or social theory that the sociologist finds important. Research is then done to test and decide whether such a hypothesis is correct or not. This means moving from the general to the specific. Alternatively, sociologists using inductive reasoning or the inductive approach reverse the steps taken by deductive research and move from the specific and collect lots of data relevant to their area of research in order to analyse and develop a general theory to explain the patterns such analysis might reveal. This is more traditionally understood as a bottom-up approach and is in general more exploratory.

In global sociologies, mainstream sociology is, as Connell suggested, more accurately 'an ethno-sociology of metropolitan society' and Anglo-American capitalism. What this means is that mainstream sociology is parochial, limited and particular. According to Connell (2007, 226) this is concealed by the language of mainstream sociology, 'especially the framing of its theories as universal propositions and tools'. Other social constraints including publication opportunities, funders and one's historical standpoint and social location, which also determine the ways social science work gets done. Another factor is the unequal power relations and resources of the phenomenally productive Northern culture industries; not to mention academic voices in the Global North tend to be louder and travel further than academic voices from the Global South.

Connell further suggests that imperial sociology did not have as its core concern 'truthfulness'. This created an 'incompleteness of knowledge in, and problematic truthfulness of, metropolitan theory – given its hegemonic position,' something Connell identifies as a 'structural difficulty in world social science' (2007, 227). One of the core mechanisms historically constituting Northern theory in sociology was the erasure of experiences from the periphery – what other sociologists have come to call a 'sociology of absences' (de Sousa Santos 2012). For Connell, to undo this erasure involves reworking relations and borders between periphery and metropole to make a shared learning process possible (Connell 2007, 213–14). Southern theory by contrast embodies a bottom-up view on a global, historical scale, and as Connell points out has a complex relationship with dominant systems of knowledge including a need to engage the relationships between knowledge systems, cultural systems and systems of hierarchies in 'a mutual learning process on a planetary scale' (Connell 2007, 222; see also Mignolo 2011a).

Notwithstanding the contrast between the epistemologies and theories of the North and South, their epistemologies and theories are neither monolithic nor singular. So, if you wanted to grasp global sociologies as a singular concept, 'contradictory' is probably a more honest descriptor. In Northern theory for example, there are different blends of knowledge between the US empirical tradition (that is, accepting the conditions of the world) and the German critical tradition (that is, drawn from the Marxist tradition and the later neo-Marxist Frankfurt School, in which both promoted critical knowledge about the conditions of the world). In the UK sociology tradition, while it is fair to say that sociology was used by civil servants destined for the tropics for the administration of empire (Holmwood and Scott 2014), it is also true that there is a distinct strand of British sociology that was from the beginning critical of imperialism (Steinmetz 2013a, 358). And today in global sociologies of the 21st century there are infinite overlaps between various traditions because individual sociologists in all societies now overlap, blend and blur.

According to US sociologist John Turner, critical theorists saw ideas fuelled from the Enlightenment such as the 'use of science for constructing a better society as naive, as pursuit of an illusion, or even as harmful'; because for critical social science the very cause of many of our social problems, rather than part of their solution, is the broader culture of commerce and capitalism (Turner 2003, 198). In contrast to this critical epistemology, another US sociologist, Talcott Parsons, a structural functionalist, provided a different view to illustrate the less critical US sociological tradition of the 1940s to 1980s. 'By visualizing societies as systemic wholes with basic requisites necessary for survival in the environment, functional theory provided a way to examine complex social systems' (Turner 2003, 34). While structural functionalism was once a dominant US sociological perspective of the mid-20th century, by the 1970s it went into retreat as its deficiencies became more evident.

Sociologists in the Global South further developed the critical theorist approach in understanding their social world. For example, Caribbean sociologist Lloyd Best argued for the need for 'independent thought' in order for ex-colonies to define their own paths and ideas of development (Best 1997). Such a sociological imagination was curtailed around the world by the shift to one ubiquitous and global economic system, that of neoliberal capitalism, which was less concerned with social development and more focused on accumulating profits, with all the social problems such a system brings for societies who started their supposed 'independent' social and economic development from broken colonial systems, poor sociocultural infrastructure and traumatised populations. Furthermore, for small island nations of the Caribbean and the Pacific, neoliberal capitalism and its processes are simply not socially, economically or environmentally sustainable (Girvan 1967; Conway 1997; Freeman 2000; Hendrix and Salehyan 2012). For Best, under such circumstances 'The education programme cannot but be regional in scope, it must be anchored in the landscape, impregnated by ethnic tradition, practical in job creation and skill orientation and adequately funded whatever the national income or the budget balance' (Best 1997, 19). Or to phrase it another way, sociology, global sociologies and the sociological imagination must be relative and varied to the society within which the sociologist works to understand.

Among social scientists in the Global South and the Global North overlaps and flows of ideas, methods and research are constant yet uneven with much more of a knowledge transfer from Global North to South than the other way around, although Global South to South knowledge transfer in sociological terms has increased in recent years. In this sense and as many sociologists in both the North and South recognise there is a need to 'provincialise' Northern theories, 'Eurocentred knowledge' and monolithic sociological premises in order to better recognise 'the epistemic and cultural diversity of the world' (Bhambra and de Sousa Santos 2017, 4). For the sociologists Gurminder Bhambra and Boaventura de Sousa Santos, 'epistemologies of the south concern the production and validation of knowledge anchored in the experiences of resistance of all those social groups that have systematically suffered injustice, oppression and destruction caused by capitalism, colonialism and patriarchy' (Bhambra and de Sousa Santos 2017, 5).

De Sousa Santos's 'ecologies of knowledge' challenge Western sociological theories and knowledge production with non-scientific, popular, vernacular knowledge, with a view to building what he calls new 'ecologies of knowledges' (Bhambra and de Sousa Santos 2017, 5). For Bhambra and de Sousa Santos, 'radical alternative theorising implies other epistemologies (ways of knowing), other ontologies (ways of being in the world), and other methodologies (how to advance knowledge within a given way of knowing)' (Bhambra and de Sousa Santos 2017, 6). They also note UK sociologist Martin Savransky's call 'for a deeper questioning of the metaphysical structures of the imagination to profoundly alter the standard relationship between epistemology and ontology' (Savransky cited in Bhambra and de Sousa Santos 2017, 6). Savransky also called for 'a re-engagement of sociology and anthropology, and a more thoroughgoing engagement with the work, and more specifically, the realities of social movements' (Savransky cited in Bhambra and de Sousa Santos 2017, 6–7). This is something that has already happened in the Caribbean sociological tradition where anthropology and sociology have reconciled and anthropology is a subdiscipline of sociology rather than in opposition, contrast or competition; and race, class and ethnicity have taken on Caribbean-derived interpretations (Best 2001).

Global sociology and its methods

What does a global sociology, or more accurately today, 'global sociologies' look like? As Steinmetz's critical and historical sociology has documented, research on various 'academic sociology fields' such as postcolonial India, contemporary Mexico, postcolonial Africa, the Caribbean and contemporary Europe all underscore the point 'that academic sociology does not mature in a linear fashion or converge on a singular approach. National, regional, and local "colorations" will persist. Even the model sometimes held up as a universal one, US sociology in the 1950s, is better analysed as a conflictual space of differences' (Steinmetz 2007, 303).

So it was that in the 1950s and 1960s distinct and varied global colourations of sociology first began to emerge. At first many early non-Anglo-European sociologists straddled two worlds, that of the metropole and their own societies. This early wave of internationalisation was a 'global sociology'; however, by internalising colonial categories and ideas on modernity and development in many ways it was a global sociology that reinforced the power differentials and inequalities previously seen in the era of sociology and empire between the metropole and the colonies. However, over the next forty years, various national and regional traditions slowly began to take shape, especially in newly independent ex-colonial nations. With new engagements with colonialism and imperialism, new more radical sociological vistas emerged and breathed vitality into the discipline and the original sociological project continued splintering, with such additions as critical race theory, racial liberalism, critical whiteness studies, intersectionality, reparations and many more (Reddock 2014).

Attempts to hold global sociology together have been thoughtfully debated as a means by which to nurture, enrich and develop a discrete formation. One such example is that of Michael Burawoy's, who suggested a form similar to US anthropology with four distinct fields: professional sociology, policy sociology, critical sociology and public sociology (Burawoy 2005). However, there continues to be concern from many located outside Europe and North America that the internationalisation of a generic sociology in such a formation is an ongoing process of Western modernisation rooted in the discipline's imperial diffusion around the world. One reaction is that far from sociology remaining singular, as in 'global sociology' with a single dominant methodological perspective, sociology's splintering has given birth to global sociologies.

Over time and well into the 21st century, new waves of sociologists have emerged from their societies and spread out around the world for research, scholarly collaboration and education purposes. However, 'brain drain' remains a serious problem and means many successful sociologists have not returned to their countries and places of origin. Amina Mama, Professor of Gender, Sexuality and Women's Studies, noted the brain drain reality in the African academic context:

> At present, an estimated 100,000 African academics are located in the North; ironically, the same number of expatriate experts is imported to advise African governments each year at annual costs of 4 billion dollars to foreign exchange reserves (see Mkandawire and Soludo, 1999). What could this vast expense, spent differently, have contributed to retaining or returning desperately-needed African faculty, some of

whom might have provided sounder advice than all those expatriate experts? (Mama 2002, 3)

Of course, some sociologists do return; others with sociological training also return to infuse local traditions while trying to build networks between scholars in the Global North and Global South. Such networks, however, are often hampered by inequalities in funding and resources between North and South.

In contrast to what was once a singular sociology, many of the colourations of sociology today have left behind imperial sociology and have developed anti-imperialist epistemologies and forms of sociological enquiry that are comfortable with acknowledging the larger social contexts and economic structures that shaped our worlds, such as slavery, colonialism, imperialism and various forms of capitalism. But global sociologies have also become much more than simply accusatory of the sins committed by empire and new forms of imperialism or stuck in national formations and traditions. Global sociologies offer new ways to use the sociological imagination and to understand the world, such as intersectionality, transnational social phenomena, the essential need for decoloniality, and a redefinition of what constitutes 'academic' knowledge to include various non-academic publications and platforms. Global sociologies are diverse in epistemology, diverse in methodologies, and have splintered well beyond the original whole (Tilley 2017).

Around the world today the International Sociological Association (ISA) lists 68 national sociology associations as members (Table 6.1).

Yet Immanuel Wallerstein, ISA President from 1994 to 1998, lamented at the turn of the century that while the

> ISA is the principal organizational mechanism by means of which sociology is an international activity. As you will see when you read the history, the ISA is only very imperfectly international. Of course, this is part because the numbers of institutions and practitioners are quite disproportionately distributed across the globe, although the disparities are less great than when we started out 50 years ago. No doubt this is also in part because the efforts to make our activities truly international have been less intensive and less persistent than they ought to have been. (Wallerstein cited in Platt 1998, 9)

Not to mention that at many of ISA meetings and conferences those who are representatives of the various national sociological associations are based in metropolitan locations and do not hold academic positions in a university of the Global South (Platt 1998, 51). This of course suggests that sociologists in the Global South find it much harder to link with and travel to international conferences, which are most often hosted by metropolitan universities in the Global North.

Table 6.1 List of international sociological associations

Country	Sociological associations	Founding date
1 Albania	Shoqata Sociologjike Shqiptare	2006
2 Argentina	Asociación Argentina de Sociología	2009
3 Armenia	Армянская социологическая Ассоциация	1992
4 Australia	Originally: Australian Sociological Association (TASA) Currently: Sociological Association of Australia and New Zealand (SAANZ)	1963
5 Austria	Österreichische Gesellschaft für Soziologie	1950
6 Azerbaijan	Azərbaycan Sosioloji Birliyi	1996
7 Bangladesh	Bangladesh Sociological Association	2003
8 Belgium	Vereniging voor Sociologie	1975
9 Benin	Association des Sociologues et Anthropologues du Bénin	Unknown
10 Brazil	Originally: Sociedade Paulista de Sociologia (1937) Currently: Sociedade Brasileira de Sociologia (1951)	1937/1951
11 Bulgaria	Българска социологическа асоциация	1931: established 1939: ceased 1959: reinstated
12 Canada	Canadian Sociological Association	1965
13 Croatia	Originally: Sociological Association Currently: Hrvatsko sociološko društvo	1918 1992
14 Cyprus	O Syndesmos Koinoniologon Kyprou	1996
15 Czech Republic	Originally: Masaryk's Sociological Association Currently: Česká sociologická společnost	1925 1993
16 Denmark	Dansk Sociologforening	1965
17 Ecuador	Federación Ecuadoriana de Sociólogos	Unknown
18 Estonia	Originally: Estonian Sociologists Academy Association Currently: Eesti Sotsioloogide Liit	1990 1999
19 Ethiopia	Ethiopian Society of Sociologists, Social Workers and Anthropologists	1996
20 Finland	Westermarck Society	1940
21 France	Association Française de Sociologie	2002
22 Germany	Deutsche Gesellschaft für Sociologie	1909
23 Greece	Ελληνική Κοινωνιολογική Εταιρεία	2007
24 Hungary	Magyar Szociológiai Társaság	Unknown
25 India	Indian Sociological Society	1951
26 Iran	انجمن جامعه شناسی ایران	Unknown
27 Italy	Associazione Italiana di Sociologia	1983
28 Japan	日本社会学会	1924
29 Kazakhstan	Қазақстан социологтарының Ассоциациясы	2002
30 Korea	한국사회학회	1956
31 Lebanon	Lebanese Association of Sociology	Unknown
32 Lithuania	Lietuvos Sociologų Draugija	Unknown
33 Macedonia Rep	Здружение на социолози на Република Македонија	Unknown

34 Mexico	Asociación Mexicana de Sociología	1939
35 Moldova	Asociația Sociologilor și Demografilor din Republica Moldova	Unknown
36 Netherlands	Nederlandse Sociologische Vereniging	Unknown
37 New Zealand	Sociological Association of Aotearoa New Zealand	1988
38 Norway	Norsk sosiologforening	1949
39 Pakistan	Sociological Association of Pakistan	Unknown
40 Palestine	Palestinian Sociological Association	Unknown
50 Philippines	Philippine Sociological Society	1952
51 Poland	Polskie Towarzystwo Socjologiczne	1931: established; 1939: ceased; 1957: reinstated
52 Portugal	Associação Portuguesa de Sociologia	1985
53 Romania	Asociația Română de Sociologie	Unknown
54 Russia	Российского Общества Социологов	1989
55 Slovakia	Slovenská sociologická spoločnosť	1964
56 Slovenia	Slovensko Sociološko Društvo	2006
57 South Africa	South African Sociological Association	1993
58 Spain	Federación Española de Sociología	Late-1970s
59 Sweden	Sveriges Sociologförbund	Unknown
60 Switzerland	Société Suisse de Sociologie	1955
61 Taiwan	Taiwanese Sociological Association	1968
62 Tanzania	Taasisi ya Sayansi Jamii	2013
63 Turkey	Turkish Social Science Association	1967
64 Uganda	Uganda Sociological and Anthropological Association	2006
65 Ukraine	Sociological Association of Ukraine	1968
66 United Kingdom	British Sociological Association	1951
67 USA	American Sociological Association	1905
68 Venezuela	Asociación Venezolana de Sociología	Unknown

Sociology splinters: feminist sociologies

For Caribbean sociologist Rhoda Reddock (see Chapter 4's discussion of feminism and queer studies), feminism can be defined as 'the awareness of the subordination and exploitation of women in society and the conscious action to change that situation. Feminists differ in their understanding of the nature of the problem and therefore on the strategies for its solution' (Reddock 1990b, 62). For Canadian sociologist Gillian Creese, feminist sociologies shed light on 'sociology's history of exclusions in the production of knowledge' (Creese et al 2009, 604). For Creese, feminist sociologies are part of a broad enterprise of feminist theorising and research across the social sciences that are inherently interdisciplinary, intersectional and diverse. Creese and her colleagues (2009, 606) also remind us that, 'feminist sociology, while diverse, has been shaped by critical theory that aims to be reflexive and contextual stemming from the fundamental premise that knowledge, being socially embedded, is always political'.

Beginning with the 'second wave' of the women's movement in the 1940s the challenge by feminist theorists to 'mainstream' sociology really started to make headway in the 1960s. Early feminist critiques focused on the underrepresentation of women and women's experiences within sociology, the canon and professional outputs, both as the subjects of research and the producers of theory. As US sociologist John Turner describes it,

> Feminist theorists examined the construction of gender and sex roles in modern society to demonstrate the existence of a 'female world' that sociology had ignored. Feminists used the concepts of gender and patriarchy to reveal masculine (or androcentric) stances in social research methodologies and in sociological theory. These more radical critiques questioned the capacity of sociological research and theory, as a body of knowledge constructed from the experiences of men, to address the experiences of women. (Turner 2003, 249)

Consequently, most critical feminist theorists worked to extend the emancipatory dimension of feminist theory – that is, its ability to offer a call to action as well as a mode of understanding. This combination of theory, method, politics and praxis, with its focus on gender and patriarchy as the main sources of oppression and inequality, are the common factors distinguishing the feminist critique of sociological theory, according to Turner (2003, 250).

Early feminist critiques of sociological research and theory, such as popular feminist sociologist Ann Oakley's (1974) work on housewives and their opinions of housework, made the case for broader issues of representation and sexual bias within sociological research and theory. Oakley connected the inbuilt sexism within sociological theory and research 'to the male-oriented attitudes of its founding fathers' (Oakley 1974, 21). She argued that the discipline held stereotypical assumptions about women's social status and behaviour and 'these stereotypes will only be overcome if women's experiences are made the focus of analysis and viewed from their perspective' (Turner 2003, 576).

Today this legacy of feminist critiques of the Western sociological project is symbolised in the variety of feminist sociological knowledge produced by Global South intellectuals from within the Global South. These include the 'coloniality of gender' (Lugones 2016), 'the sociology of gender in Southern perspective' (Connell 2014), and 'Third World women' as 'a viable oppositional alliance' who are held together cohesively by 'common context of struggle rather than colour or racial identifications'(Mohanty et al 1991, 7), and many more. By way of a global sociological splintering, critical feminist theorists have also developed several methodological approaches designed to address the topic of gender asymmetry and to avoid the possible gender biases in standard sociological practices (Doucet 2018). For instance, the 'feminist standpoint theories' of the 1980s as promoted by Dorothy Smith (1987), Hilary Rose (1983), Patricia Hill Collins (1990) and others built on epistemological and methodological principles by explicitly focusing on women and their direct experience as the centre of the analysis (Doucet and Mauthner 2006). Turner explains that, 'standpoint theorists argue that they can use women's experiences to analyse social relations in ways that overcome the androcentric dichotomies of "positivism" – such as culture vs. nature, rational mind vs. irrational emotions, objectivity vs. subjectivity – that structure knowledge production in the social and natural sciences' (Turner 2003, 259). Standpoint theory emerged thirty or forty years ago as a critique of the relationship between power relations and the production of knowledge, and it empowered oppressed social classes by illustrating how politics does not necessarily impede or obstruct sociological research. This was especially relevant to the rise of feminist scholarship at the time (Harding 2003, 2).

As Doucet (2018) notes, from a global sociologies perspective it is important to recognise that feminist empiricism – in the form of feminist methodologies, epistemologies and standpoints – challenged the key tenets of traditional empiricism embodied in 'positivistic' science and imperial sociology and were the foremothers of what is today called 'relational sociology' (see Chapter 3) (Lorde 1984; Albiston et al 2002; Powell and Dépelteau 2013; Redshaw 2013). As Creese et al (2009) note, critical theoretical concerns about power, privilege, inequality and marginality provided feminists with analytic frameworks, methodologies and epistemologies for exploring social justice.

For example, Caribbean feminist, Rawwida Baksh-Soodeen has noted the critical potential of feminist epistemological and methodological principles:

> Standpoint epistemology is the concept that less powerful members (individuals and groups) are potentially capable of a more complete view of social reality than the privileged, precisely because of their disadvantaged position(s). Feminist standpoint epistemologies focus on the specificity of women's oppression, linking this to women being able to see the viewpoints of both women, and men, and hence having an understanding that is potentially more complete, deeper, and sensitive than men's. (Baksh-Soodeen 1998, 77)

She went on to write that critical theory and standpoint epistemologies are elements of a relativist and social constructionist mode of sociological enquiry because 'there is no single truth; the location of individuals and groups in the social structure determines their construction/interpretation of truth and reality, and the oppressed have a more powerful claim to complete understanding' and the necessity of inclusive knowledge production than dominant groups and elites (Baksh-Soodeen 1998, 77).

Baksh-Soodeen's research highlights the distinctions and variety across global sociologies, including within sociology's various splinters like feminist sociologies. For example, the Euro-American feminist movement in the 1970s developed varied explanations of women's subordination. Consequently, this led to splits and fractions within Euro-American feminism such as 'liberal feminism, Marxist feminism, radical feminism, and socialist feminism' (Baksh-Soodeen 1998, 75). Race and ethnicity via such theories as critical race theory also became a central 'platform for exposing differences in women's lived experiences of subordination' (Baksh-Soodeen 1998, 75). They were revealed as not being monolithic; rather, they varied across sociocultural differences such as 'black, native American, Asian, women of colour', Caribbean and many more (Baksh-Soodeen 1998, 75). A good example of this tradition today is US sociologist Tressie McMillan Cottom's (2019) thick description collection on the experiences of black womanhood across a variety of spaces in North American society; for example, childbirth, where stark inequalities in treatment and care are clearly identifiable and the impact of sociological concepts like intersectionality and white fragility are brought to life.

As Reddock goes on to point out 'Feminism has not been a 1960s import into the Caribbean' (Reddock 1990b, 67). Rather, from a global sociologies framework, the 'second wave' of the feminist movement in the Caribbean, a multicultural region, in the 1970s intersected with post-independence discourse and had to build issues such as race and class and the experiences of the 'creole' or black/ brown/mixed/white populations of Caribbean societies into Caribbean sociology. One reason contained in Baksh-Soodeen's research is that the dominant discourse 'within Caribbean feminist politics (theory and practice) [w]as Afro-centric, as opposed to either a Euro-centric or multicultural paradigm' and 'there was no multicultural framework (despite a sociological theory of "cultural pluralism" developed by M.G. Smith in the 1960s) within which the specific experiences and interests of non-African women could be viewed or contextualized' (Baksh-Soodeen 1998, 78). Since such times, there has been far more engagement with inclusion and making Caribbean feminism a more multicultural feminist platform, as the most recent splinter of Caribbean sociology, 'Indo-Caribbean feminism' indicates (Hosein and Outar 2016). As Reddock suggests of Caribbean feminism in the 1990s, so it is a similar scenario for the wider colourations of global feminist sociologies too: '[t]he modern women's movement in the English-speaking Caribbean is the continuation of a rich struggle for women's emancipation, a struggle fraught with contradictions but one nevertheless firmly based within the socio-political and historical context of the region' (Reddock 1990b, 63).

Feminist sociological research has multiple 'roots and routes' in academia and in broader social movements. For example, the social media #MeToo movement in 2017 shed light on the prevalence of sexual assault and harassment widely experienced by girls and women in media professions and later led to the downfall of sexual predators such as Harvey Weinstein, Bill Cosby, Jeffrey Epstein and others. While this does not indicate, as Creese et al remind us, 'that all feminist sociologists subscribe to epistemological positions of critical theory or align themselves with progressive social change framed by social justice issues', it does illustrate how feminist theoretical and methodological debates shaping feminist sociology lead to progressive social movements. However, as Creese et al (2009, 611) go on to note, for feminists around the world there is also a grave concern today that the 'strings attached to state funding can serve to domesticate sociology to serve dominant structures of power under the guise, for example, of the nebulous tax payer, rather than citizens of civil society'.

Sociology splinters: indigenous sociology and decoloniality

In their examination of Nigerian sociologist Akinsola Akiwowo's indigenous sociological theory of 'sociation' from the 1980s, also known locally as the 'Asuwada theory' and derived from a sociological problematic of trying to understand the local context for association in Nigeria, Nigerian sociologists Ayokunle Omobowale and Olayinka Akanle note how this local sociological theory first gained local attention in Nigerian sociology before gaining global attention (Omobowale and Akanle 2017). However, they go on to describe how in the long run the theory now receives little attention in Nigeria and has been replaced by 'the dominant Western-orientated theories' and their 'universal positions' over more relative epistemologies. One reason for this erasure, they suggest, is 'academic dependency' on imperial and universalist sociology that dominated sociology in the Global South. 'Academic dependency' according to Malaysian sociologist, Syed Farid Alatas, is

> a condition in which the knowledge of certain scholarly communities are conditioned by the development and growth of knowledge of other scholarly communities to which the former is subjected. The relations of independence between two or more scientific communities, and between these and global transactions in knowledge, assumes the form of dependency when some scientific communities (those located in knowledge powers) can expand according to certain criteria of development and progress, while other scientific communities (such as those in the developing societies) can only do this as a reflection of that expansion, which generally has negative effects on their development according to the same criteria. (Alatas 2008, 9–10)

Alatas also goes on to note the need for global sociologies to develop a sociological theory of 'irrelevance' in contrast to the Western universalist sociological theory of 'relevance' dominating global sociology and determining what get to be sociological problems, methods, valid theories and more for sociological consideration. Another Nigerian sociologist, Muyiwa Sanda, in discussion of the merits and development of Akiwowo's 'Asuwada theory,' also pointed out that universalist sociological theories fail to properly explain indigenous cultures (Sanda 1988). For example, the indigenous concepts contained within Asuwada attempted to

> emphasise contextual values of social beings who would contribute to social survival and community integration and development. Th[e] theory postulates that among Africans in general and the Yoruba in particular, the need to associate or co-exist by internalising and rightly exhibiting socially approved values of community survival and development, is integral to local social structure, as failure to co-exist potentially endangers the community. A deviant who defaults in sociating values is deemed a bad person (*omoburuku*), while the one who sociates is the good person (*omoluabi*). This theoretical postulation contrasts Western social science theories (especially sociological Structuralist (macro) and Social Action (micro) theories), which rather emphasise rationality and individualism (at varied levels depending on the theory). Western social science ethnocentrically depicts African communal and kin ways of life as primitive and antithetical to development. Western social science theories have remained dominant and hegemonic over the years while Akiwowo's theory is largely unpopular even in Nigerian social science curricula in spite of its potential for providing contextual interpretations for indigenous ways of life that are still very much extant despite dominant Western modernity. (Omobowale and Akanle 2017, 43)

As Omobowale and Akanle go on to discuss, since the early 20th century there have been many attempts to indigenise the social sciences. This has given us, according to Mignolo such sociological ideas as dependency theory, 'internal colonialism, structural heterogeneity, pedagogy of the oppressed, research action, intellectual colonialism, philosophy of liberation, coloniality' of power, decoloniality and more (Mignolo 2014, 587). Today, the indigenising of the social sciences is most often found in the body of sociological research and knowledge production around 'decoloniality'. Decoloniality is a sociological concept whose point of origin was the 'Third World'. (We more commonly refer to the terms Global South and North today.) For Argentinian sociolinguist Walter Mignolo (2011a, 273) 'Decoloniality has its historical grounding in the Bandung Conference of 1955 in which 29 countries from Asia and Africa gathered. The main goal of the conference was to find a common ground and vision for the future that was neither capitalism nor communism.' That common ground and vision he goes on to discuss was 'decolonisation'. Decoloniality is important to indigenous sociology and global sociologies because it provides a way to delink from major Western macro narratives such as rationality and the individual as being the only ontology and epistemology available to a sociologist. It also, as we saw earlier in the chapter, provided new ways to look at dominant paradigms like modernisation theory and capitalist development

Mignolo and other sociologists of decoloniality are concerned with 'reformulating the principles and structures of knowledge, revamping categories and belief systems that Eurocentric social sciences have disavowed' (Mignolo 2014, 587). This they suggest requires epistemic disobedience and 'border thinking'. Border thinking is the idea of thinking beyond the limitation of an imperial and global sociology defined by a 'self-narrative of modernity invented as its outside to legitimise its own logic of coloniality' (Mignolo 2011a, 282). As Mignolo goes on to discuss, modernity is not an unfolding of some universal notion of progress with Western ideas of development at its heart, but rather the hegemonic narrative of Western civilisation. By hegemonic, we mean the socioculturally dominant and normative narrative – or accepted common sense and taken-for-grantedness – about the world and how it might or should be (see Chapter 8 for discussion of cultural hegemony).

Dependency theory was a reaction around the world to the sociology of development and the modernisation theory accompanying it. For Mignolo it was a response to a myth meant to conceal the fact that 'Third World' countries could not develop and modernise under the imperial conditions of their establishment. The New World group who wrote in the 1960s and 1970s from a Caribbean sociology and political economy vista made similar arguments (Meeks and Girvan 2010). Much of their research was around independent thought and Caribbean freedom. According to Mignolo (2011a, 276) 'independent thought requires border thinking for the simple reason that it cannot be achieved within the categories of Western thought and experience'. Once border sensing and thinking emerged, then 'the decolonial option came into being, and by coming into being as an option it revealed that modernities are just options and not the "natural" unfolding of history. Modernity and postmodernity are options, not ontological moments of universal history, and so are subaltern, alternative or peripheral modernities' (Mignolo 2011a, 279).

Edgardo Lander (2000), a sociologist from Venezuela, and many other Global South sociologists we have mentioned before such as Best, Reddock, Mama, Akiwowo and Alatas indicate the need for independent thought and the decolonisation of knowledge to confront 'imperial assumption that knowledge is universal and is not connected with historical configurations (Western knowledge, Chinese knowledge, Islamic knowledge, etc.)' (Mignolo 2014, 586). Global sociologies and its splinters such as indigenous sociology are not 'against' Western social sciences; rather, they seek to restore knowledge and the 'ways of knowing that the Western social sciences silenced, suppressed, repressed or disavowed' (Mignolo 2014, 589).

> Once we enter in the realm of the geopolitics of knowing, sensing and believing and we do not believe any more in the universality of the

social sciences to solve, from the experience of Europe that grounded their foundations, the problems of non-European histories, local histories that were destabilized by the interference of local European designs, the meaning of de-Westernization and decoloniality has to be seen first in their loci of enunciation. (Mignolo 2014, 589)

As Mignolo reminds us, indigenous sociology and decoloniality in the social sciences are important because they problematise the implicit 'universal pretensions of the narratives that Europeans told to themselves':

> The social sciences emerged to solve problems in Europe and contributed to make of Europe what it is in terms of institutions of knowledge, actors, and categories of thoughts. It contributed to European and US imperialism. It is doubtful the social sciences would be of help to non-Europeans who want to solve their problems, one of them being Western imperialism economic, political, cultural, and epistemic. (Mignolo 2014, 595)

This argument can be read in several ways. On the one hand, Walter Mignolo here points to the Eurocentric origins of the social sciences. He presents the social sciences as narrowly focused on understanding social life in the Global Northwest. Moreover, he suggests that in their Eurocentric form the social sciences are ill-suited to understanding problems in the Global South, which in significant ways stem from Western imperialism. On the other hand, Mignolo's argument also signals a shift away from this Eurocentric narrative, in that it highlights for a global audience that there are alternative possibilities for knowing about the social world.

All sociology is connected

For critical sociologist Gurminder Bhambra, the singular 'global sociology' proposed by those in the Global North such as Michael Burawoy 'as a way to redress the previous neglect of those represented as "other" in dominant "Eurocentric" constructions of modernity within sociology – and as a path towards a rejuvenated sociology for a newly-global age … do so under terms which are inadequate' (Bhambra 2015, 8). Bhambra, building on the work of historical sociologists such as Steinmetz whom we discussed at the beginning of this chapter, also makes the important observation 'that the way in which we understand the past has implications for the social theories we develop to deal with situations we live in today' (2007, 11). Under such realities Bhambra argues for a 'connected sociologies approach', one 'that can be built on postcolonial and decolonial critiques of Eurocentrism, as a better way of understanding a shared global present' (2015, 8). She adds that the main focus of 'connected sociologies' must put 'histories of dispossession, colonialism, enslavement and appropriation at the heart of historical sociology and the discipline more generally' (Bhambra 2015, 8). These are similar arguments we have made in this chapter in connection with our global sociologies framework, such as the criticism of modernisation theory from Marxists and Global South scholars of dependency, coloniality and underdevelopment. Bhambra takes this further with her critique of the 'multiple modernities' paradigm, which replaced modernisation theory in the 1990s as a paradigm that reproduced European modernity

> as the reference point in their examination of alternative modernities. In this way, they effectively defend the dominant approach by suggesting that the 'fact' of the European origins of modernity cannot be denied. In contrast, I suggest that it is precisely this 'fact' that must be denied, once global interconnections are properly recognised and understood. (Bhambra 2015, 9)

For Bhambra the central failure of 'global sociology' is its inability to recognise the

> plurality of possible interpretations and selections, not as a 'description' of events and processes, but as an opportunity for reconsidering what we previously thought we knew. The different sociologies in need of connection are themselves located in time and space, including in the time and space of colonialism, empire, and postcolonialism. These new sociologies will frequently appear discordant and challenging, and they may be resisted on that basis (a resistance made easier by the geo-spatial stratification of the academy). The consequence of different perspectives, however, must be to open up examination of events and processes such that they are understood differently in light of that engagement. Put another way, engaging with different voices must move us beyond simple pluralism to make a difference to what was initially thought; not so that we all come to think the same, but that we think differently from how we had thought before our engagement. (Bhambra 2015, 9–10)

A fundamental aspect of Bhambra's 'connected sociologies' approach is the recognition that using the sociological imagination requires all sociologists to recognise how and why the contemporary world came into being and the processes involved in that emergence.

> A 'connected sociologies' approach requires that we locate Europe within wider processes, address the ways in which Europe created and then benefitted from the legacies of colonialism and enslavement, and examine what Europe needs to learn from those it dispossessed in order to address the problems we currently face. The 'connected

sociologies' approach points to the work needed to make good on the promise of a reinvigorated sociological imagination in service of social justice in a global world. (Bhambra 2015, 10)

This chapter has covered a wide range of sometimes difficult and challenging materials. From the 20th-century genealogy of Western sociology's development and uneven diffusion to the emergence of the current global sociologies formation, we have seen sociology as an academic discipline and epistemology on the world that is varied in methods, concerns and theory, which leads us to the conclusion that in today's 21st-century world 'global sociologies' is a more accurate version of the discipline than 'global sociology'.

For sociologists in the Global South, whose sociological theories are not taught or read in the Global North, a global sociologies lens and imagination asks how do people from the North learn about sociologists who are not from the North, in similar ways as those in the South have learnt and been educated about the North? Not least because the world we all live is a connected one, much like all sociology is 'connected sociologies'. Without such discussions about how theory from the South can become a central aspect of the global sociologies project, the reality remains that globalisation and glocalisation as unequal processes are for many in the world new forms of imperialism and colonialism, of cultural appropriation and homogenisation. Historically, 'less-developed' nations of the world, the 'underdeveloped' and over-exploited nations and the sociological research produced in them, record power differentials and inequalities wherein ideas, commerce and culture from the Global North have significant negative impacts on policies, life and economies in the Global South in disproportionate ways. Not to mention that rather than recognise the vast cultural and social heterogeneity of, say, African countries, the powerful entities of the Global North often lay down one-size-fits-all, force-to-fit solutions such as policing situations and austerity measures on all societies regardless of their inherent sociological, economic and cultural distinctions.

While we have been able to touch on the global phenomenon of sociology's decline from the 1970s, we have also acknowledged that the sociological imagination under its various global-sociologies colourations is needed if we as a global society are going to attend to the many social issues and problems we face. That said, we must also acknowledge the inequality in resources between different sociological colourations, associations and departments across the planet; this of course includes the vast economic cutbacks that sociology as a discipline has recently experienced in universities across the world. Notwithstanding such contextual realities in the production of sociological knowledge in the 21st century it has never been more important to make the case for global sociologies.

THINKING SOCIOLOGICALLY

In this chapter we used some sociological terms that need defining. Using sociology resources please define these terms and their associated questions.

1. **Imperial sociology** Referencing the chapter, what does this term mean? What is the relationship between Western sociology and empire? What types of social structure and social development are implied under empire and imperialism? How is colonialism different from imperialism?

2. **Modernisation theory** What does this Global North sociological concept mean? Why does a fundamental premise of modernisation theory – that all societies can move in a step-by-step process to development – not hold water? Why is the modernisation theory of development criticised by the 'connected sociologies' project?

3. **Epistemologies** What is meant by the term 'epistemology'? Why in a global sociologies framework does Raewyn Connell suggest that epistemology is better understood as plural, as epistemologies? What are the characteristics of Southern theory epistemology? What are the characteristics of the epistemology of your sociological imagination?

MINI PROJECT

I argue for a 'connected sociologies' approach built on postcolonial and decolonial critiques of Eurocentrism, as a better way of understanding a shared global present. The central concern of 'connected sociologies' is to rethink sociology, putting histories of dispossession, colonialism, enslavement and appropriation at the heart of historical sociology and the discipline more generally. Only by acknowledging the significance of the 'colonial global' in the constitution of sociology, I argue, can we understand and address the postcolonial and decolonial present that would be the terrain of a properly critical 'global sociology'. (Bhambra 2015, 8)

As part of her definition of a 'connected sociologies' framework, sociologist Gurminder Bhambra (2015), in her essay 'Global Sociology in Question', written for the International Sociology Association, has suggested the definition quoted here.

For this mini project, you will need to do some background research. Please consult the rest of the essay 'Global Sociology in Question', which can be found here: http://globaldialogue.isa-sociology.org/global-sociology-in-question/.

Once you have read the short essay please answer these following questions to complete this mini project on connected sociologies:

1. Why was the shift from a singular modernity paradigm in Western sociology to a multiple modernities paradigm not successful?

2. Why is building a multicultural sociology for the future not enough to 'address the problematic disciplinary construction of sociology in the past, or the continued ramifications of this construction in the present'?

3. How were and are histories of colonialism and enslavement central in the creation of the 'global'? And why does a connected sociologies paradigm need more than simply the addition of excluded sociological voices and vistas to make it truly decolonial?

4. What is 'connected sociologies'? Why is it important? How and why is the sociological imagination a key component of connected sociologies?

5. Working in groups, in so far as it is feasible, summarise your findings and display them in a poster presentation.

 TALKING POINTS

'The ideas of the ruling class are in every epoch the ruling ideas, i.e. the class which is the ruling material force of society, is at the same time its ruling intellectual force. The class which has the means of material production at its disposal, has control at the same time over the means of mental production, so that thereby, generally speaking, the ideas of those who lack the means of mental production are subject to it. The ruling ideas are nothing more than the ideal expression of the dominant material relationships, the dominant material relationships grasped as ideas' (Marx and Engels 1998, 67).

1. What is this statement trying to say? How are 'ruling ideas' learned, produced and consumed? Why might this be the case?

2. What is meant by the notion of 'Southern theory'?

3. What do the terms 'academic dependency' and 'brain drain' mean? How have they affected the development of global sociologies?

4. How can people from the North learn about sociologists who are not from the North, in similar ways as those in the South have learnt and been educated about the North?

5. What are the most pressing problems in your society that you want to use your sociological imagination to solve and why? How is this local or regional problem connected to the larger historical unfolding of the world and world events?

READ ON ...

On imperial sociology and the Anglo-American development of sociology during the 20th century please see George Steinmetz's various outputs including 'American Sociology before and after World War II: The (Temporary) Settling of a Disciplinary Field' (2007) and *Sociology and Empire: The Imperial Entanglements of a Discipline* (2013b). For a Global South view of the development of sociology Raewyn Connell's *Southern Theory* (2007) offers insights from both a gendered and ideological perspective. Maria Lugones also offers an insightful text on the gender system in her work the 'The Coloniality of Gender' (2016). Alatas offers insights in Asian sociology in *Alternative Discourses in Asian Social Science* (2006). The impact of underdevelopment in the Global South and particular social locations in the Global North is well captured by Andre Gunder Frank in 'The Development of Underdevelopment' (1971) and by Paul Farmer in his 'Anthropology of Structural Violence' (2004). Relational sociology can be read up on in Powell and Dépelteau's *Conceptualising Relational Sociology* (2013) and also more generally in Dépelteau's edited collection *The Palgrave Handbook of Relational Sociology* (2018).

Check the companion website at https://bristoluniversitypress.co.uk/imagining-society-online-resources **for a suggested project and writing task.**

7

Structure, agency, power and conflict

As we have seen, in the 21st century the importance of C. Wright Mills's sociological imagination and its ability to reveal what is hidden in plain sight about the relationships between personal issues and public problems has eroded. In its place other ways of imagining society, such as populism and psychological theories of self-determination and individual pathologies, have emerged and have pushed the sociological imagination and the importance of understanding the role that context (history and individual biographies) and social structure (social forces) play in socialisation and the relationship between the individual and social structures into the background.

Yet as British sociologist Tracy Shildrick notes in her work for the Joseph Rowntree Foundation, 'sociological thinking focuses on the structure and organisation of society and how this relates to social problems and individual lives' (Shildrick and Rucell 2015, 1). As such, sociologists have understood concepts such as power, poverty and social inequalities via 'social structures (how society is organised) and the role of individual agency – people's independent choices and actions' (Shildrick and Rucell 2015, 1). Specifically, a majority of sociologists have come to understand power, poverty and social inequalities in society as based on 'how resources in society are distributed' (Shildrick and Rucell 2015, 1). For example, the Spanish sociologist Manuel Castells, explicitly a sociologist of power most well known for his theory of communication power, notes that 'power is the key to understanding the primary source of social structuration and dynamics' in society (Castells 2016, 2). Earlier, US sociologist Joel Charon had noted that inequalities shape and define the order of our societies:

> Is it (inequality) inherent in the nature of organisation? How does it arise? How is it perpetuated? What are the problems it brings, and how does it affect the individual? Marx saw inequality as inherent in all class societies; Weber saw it inherent in the nature of lasting organisation. Some sociologists see it as contributing to order. All see it as one source of social change. (Charon cited in Shildrick and Rucell 2015, 10–11)

As we will see in this chapter, in sociology power is understood as complex, multi-layered and diffuse. Power does not just repress and use force against you, power is also seductive and productive; it offers us what we want too – even when this puts others at socioeconomic disadvantage; for example, the UK housing market and the incentives governments have given to asset holders over non-asset holders (Piketty 2014). The study of power and inequalities in sociology requires a variety of ways to imagine power and the role inequalities play in organising and ordering our various societies. For example, why structurally in modern Western societies does whiteness have power over blackness, does the city have power over the countryside, the West have power over the rest, the rich over the poor, men over women, and capitalism over other forms of socioeconomic design? It is also important to understand the new ways in which power is unfolding in the 21st century, such as digital power and the attention-surveillance economy (Zuboff 2019), audit cultures and the quantification of performance (Espeland and Sauder 2016), and the ways in which ranking, new metrics and surveillance cultures stretch and extend inequalities.

In this chapter we provide readers with some basic sociological frameworks and concepts of power to help readers think about these questions and how power unfolds in various economic, social and cultural ways. We ask how sociologists and the social imagination have explained the ways in which power and social class operate ideologically and materially in hidden and invisible ways, distinct from the visible forms of power that make and enforce rules and laws in society, which produce and perpetuate social inequalities and social stigma about others more generally. We also explore poverty and inequalities through history, and from various social divisions such as gender, race, sexuality, class and more.

What is power?

Have you ever thought about what experiences, relationships and knowledge make you feel powerful? Perhaps these include being able to do what you want, without constraint by any social norms, economic realities or cultural values. Perhaps you feel powerful by helping out or working with others, or overcoming sociocultural differences and economic divisions, or having access to the knowledge and information you need to make informed decisions about your life. And what of the reverse? What types of influences, interactions and rules might make you feel powerless and unequal? Take social media entities like Facebook, Instagram, WhatsApp and Twitter; for example, is the negative reaction and sometimes personal rage one can experience online and based on what one sees on social media a form of power over you? Are you reacting to the person who posted something or are you reacting to *implicit* larger, sociocultural discourses and economic realities that come to be embedded in the worldviews and ideologies of those we interact with?

And what might sociologists say about digital technologies and algorithms (O'Neil 2017), which now decide what we are fed online and how our digital lives unfold, or what Zuboff (2015, 2019) calls the next frontier of power – surveillance capitalism? Not least in the sense of digital inequalities, wherein those already suffering from conditions of inequity experience more surveillance, a greater lack of digital resources, and more severe punishments than others, and this can mean that 'digital tracking and targeting, by both state and corporate actors, might contribute to conditions of unfairness and inequality in society' (Gangadharan 2017, 603). In the UK, for example, under the anti-terrorism Prevent strategy universities regularly track all the websites visited by every single student and employee, including tracking students' devices via tracking the various access points they use.

What too might we say about all those entities who have *explicit* power over us to make and enforce rules and laws we must all follow? These would include nation-states, their people and institutions like presidents, prime ministers, governments, judiciary, the bureaucracy, the courts, the police, the prison system and the military. These are what the French Marxist sociologist Louis Althusser (1971) described as 'repressive state apparatuses' or hard power. 'Repressive suggests that the State Apparatus in question "functions by violence" – at least ultimately (since repression, e.g. administrative repression, may take non-physical forms)' (Althusser 1971, 137).

In today's world, global institutions like the United Nations, the World Trade Organization (WTO), the International Monetary Fund (IMF), the World Health Organization and the World Bank, not to mention multinationals like Facebook, Google, Coca-Cola, Nike, BP, HSBC and many, many more also affect us through their decisions and influences, including using their large wealth to lobby politicians behind the scenes. All these entities use various instruments to make and enforce rules and laws, such as budgets, policies, constitutions, regulations, agreements, conventions, surveillance, force, violence, lobbying and more. What does power as control over you feel like? And are so many rules, laws and regulations really necessary for society to function well? Do all these rules and laws empower you, or do some take power away from you? And what might a society without so many rules look like? How would it function?

Ubiquity of power

For the well-known French sociologist of power, Michel Foucault, 'power is everywhere'. We are never outside or excluded from power because power 'comes from everywhere' (Foucault 1990, 93). It is the air we breathe. In this sense Foucault reminded us that all our social relations are defined in many ways by power. This happens between parents and children, between friends, between teachers and students, between bosses and employees, between university admission boards and prospective students, and in all the social relations we have.

Foucault also pointed out that power isn't simply about explicit coercion and authority to makes us obey. Power is 'strategical' too; it offers us things that we want and desire, thereby implicitly shaping our behaviours and ideas without us recognising how under such processes we can come to consent to our own domination.

As Foucault once wrote,

> [w]e must cease once and for all to describe the effects of power in negative terms: it 'excludes', it 'represses', it 'censors', it 'abstracts', it 'masks', it 'conceals'. In fact power produces; it produces reality; it produces domains of objects and rituals of truth. The individual and the knowledge that may be gained of him belong to this production. (Foucault 1977, 194)

For Castells, power is foundationally about communication power, and he offers a compelling model to understand power not too dissimilar from Foucault's.

> I contend that coercion and persuasion are the two main forms of exercising power. Coercion is enacted by the apparatuses of the state, defining and enforcing law and order. Persuasion is articulated in discourses of power that are produced by a variety of cultural mechanisms (starting with the school and biomedical institutions) and distributed and formalized by socialized communication systems – that is, by communication that relates to society as a whole. (Castells 2016, 8)

Facebook and the digital attention economy is a good example here (Daniels et al 2017). It offers us experiences we might want – social connectivity, memories, attention – while at the same time being driven by a business model sociologists call 'surveillance capitalism'. Surveillance capitalism is the term invented by US social psychologist Shoshanna Zuboff in 2015 to explain how big data via the digital attention economy and large-scale surveillance modifies human behaviour for profit.

> The major means of wealth generation on the Internet and through proprietary platforms such as apps is the surveillance of the population, allowing for a handful of firms to reap the lion's share of the gains from the enormous sales effort in the U.S. economy … Advertisers no longer need to subsidize journalism or media content production to reach their target audiences. Instead, they can pinpoint their desired audience to a person and locate them wherever they are online (and often where they are in physical space) due to ubiquitous surveillance. (Foster and McChesney 2014, 22–3)

Social power

British sociologist Michael Mann, author of the four-volume historical-sociology opus *The Sources of Social Power*, suggests another way to imagine power is to use his IEMP model of social power, which refers to different dimensions of ideological, economic, military and political power. It allows the sociologist to imagine power in society not as something constrained and limited by nations, cultures and societies, but rather that power overlaps and intersects across geographies, time periods and cultures, and as such is far greater than any society.

> I reject sociology's foundational notion of 'society' because the boundaries of the four power sources rarely coincide. Despite the increasing 'caging' of people within modern nation-states (noted in Sources, Vol. II), these have never been powerful enough to constitute whole 'societies'. Human activity comprises multiple, overlapping, intersecting networks of social interaction. This model has become widely accepted since I initially advanced it. It enables us to identify the root of social change, since plural power organizations can never be entirely institutionalized or insulated from influences coming 'interstitially' from cracks within and between them. Social change results from a dialectic between the institutionalization and the interstitial emergence of power networks. (Mann 2006, 343)

For Mann power *is* everywhere, and power most centrally plays out in all our lives via its 'capacity to organise and control people, materials, and territories, and the development of this capacity throughout history' (Mann 1986, 3). Mann defines the four dimensions of his IEMP model as follows:

• Ideological Power derives from the human need to find ultimate meaning in life, to share norms and values, and to participate in aesthetic and ritual practices with others. Ideologies change as the problems we face change.
• Economic Power derives from the human need to extract, transform, distribute, and consume the products of Nature. Economic relations are powerful because they combine the intensive mobilization of labor with very extensive circuits of capital, trade, and production chains, providing a combination of intensive and extensive power and normally also of authoritative and diffused power.
• Military Power. Since writing my previous volumes, I have tightened up the definition of military power to 'the social organization of concentrated and lethal violence'.
• Political Power is the centralized and territorial regulation of social life. The basic function of government is the provision of order over this realm. (Mann 2012, 6, 8, 10, 12)

And what of the individual, what is his or her relationship to social power? One simple way to understand your individual social power is through the wage you are paid for your job. Under capitalism your social power, then, is the wage you earn. In this sense, capital, and access to it, is social power.

For the sociologist Mark Haugaard, Foucault's definition that power is everywhere is problematic because it is agents and individuals who use power – either to dominate or to empower. 'Power is not some kind of metaphysical force which *is* everywhere. Power does nothing, wills nothing and, as a thing in itself, it is nowhere' (Haugaard 2012, 74). For Haugaard (2012, 74), it is agents and individuals 'who are and who will, it is agents who struggle, it is agents who create truth claims and use them to empower themselves to positions of authority'. Yet at the same time Haugaard notes such social agents are not free to do as they please; rather they, and their use of power, are constrained by getting others to see their truth claims as valid. In this sense individuals are able to use power but require the buy-in of the larger social, and this can be either desirable or dominating, but either way power always requires agents and individuals. So, for Haugaard (2018, 93) 'As a sociological fact, power constitutes a normatively neutral term that can either describe emancipation or domination … from a sociological perspective power is a form of social action that is cognitively based and normatively neutral'. That is to say, social power is, across its various dimensions, always in tension with individuals, the social and social structure, wherein the social structure is not external to us and simply a constraint on individual agency and action, but rather the social structure is an active element and process *structuring* our individual lives (Giddens 1984; Haugaard 2018). Finally, let's return to Castells who puts this level of structure and agency and its relationship to power into a poststructural context for us:

> Power over minds is more important than power over bodies. Power over minds, moreover, should not be understood as a pure manipulation mechanism, but as the ability of certain discourses to be internalized and accepted by individuals in an effective communication process between senders and receivers of discourses. (Castells 2016, 9)

Political sociology and the study of power

Traditionally, the study of power in sociology has been studied under the umbrella term 'political sociology'. Whether it was macro-level development of state power via politics and political institutions globally, or meso-level analysis of class relations and their effects on the distribution of resources in society or investigations into the processes that drive social segregation and division, or even more micro-level standpoint epistemologies – all have been described as political sociology. However, to say political sociology is the only sociological splinter to study power within global sociologies would be to misunderstand the sociological imagination in decolonial times. Not least in a global sociologies framework, because once the shackles of imperial sociology were broken all sociologies gained elements of a political sociology frame, because all sociologies involved some element of critical and reflexive epistemology. That is to say, power is a complex sociological phenomenon and requires multiple sociological frames to grasp its varied forms, dynamics and real world extensions.

> Political sociology can trace its origins to the writings of Alexis de Tocqueville, Karl Marx, Emile [sic] Durkheim, and Max Weber, among others, but it only emerged as a separate subfield within sociology after World War II. Many of the landmark works of the 1950s and 1960s centered on micro questions about the impact of class, religion, race/ethnicity, or education on individual and group-based political behavior. Beginning in the 1970s, political sociologists increasingly turned toward macro topics, such as understanding the sources and consequences of revolutions, the role of political institutions in shaping political outcomes, and large-scale comparative-historical studies of state development. Today both micro- and macro scholarship can be found in political sociology. (Manza 2011)

A power matrix

One useful way that activists, political sociologists and political anthropologists working for social change have come to understand power, and in particular political power, is via a 'power matrix' (Miller et al 2006), which breaks power down, much like Mann and Castells, into various dimensions and recruits a large variety of different sociology definitions of power into its discourses. Two dimensions of the power matrix include breaking power down into visible, hidden and invisible forms of power; and breaking power into dimensions of public, private and intimate spheres of power (VeneKlasen and Miller 2002).

The first dimension of the power break down is not dissimilar to how Mills himself understood power manifesting in three main forms: 1) as coercion or physical force – what we might call visible power; 2) as authority (power is tied to various positions and social locations within centralised administrative structures and is justified by those who are obedient to these social hierarchies) – what we might call hidden power; and 3) as manipulation carried out without the awareness of those being manipulated – what we might call invisible power (Mills 1956).

Visible, hidden and invisible power

The metaphor of visible, hidden and invisible forms of power builds on the work of many different sociologists of power including British sociologist Steven Lukes and his three dimensions, or faces, of power, which he suggested sociology should study (Lukes 1990). The three faces included decision-making power, non-decision-making power, and ideological power:

- The first face, decision-making power, is the most overt form of power and can be likened to the idea of whoever is in charge of making decisions has the power.
- The second face, non-decision-making power, can be likened to setting the agenda of what is sayable and discussable; in other words, what can come up for and in discussions. Lukes (1990, 20) suggested the study of this face of power can bring the important idea of the 'mobilisation of bias' and coercion into the discussion of power.
- The third face of power – ideological power – concerns how power can manipulate what people think, and eliminates the discussion or awareness of potential alternatives. This, Lukes suggests, is achieved implicitly and ideologically via 'culturally patterned behaviour of groups' and builds on Marx's famous observation, 'Men [sic] make their own history but they do not make it just as they please; they do not make it under circumstances chosen by themselves, but under circumstances directly encountered, given and transmitted from the past'. (Lukes 1990, 26)

According to VeneKlasen and Miller, in the power matrix visible power is how rules are made and enforced. Visible power makes us comply and do things. Visible power includes the institutions of the state, which are controlled by those elected to form a government. Hence visible power is dispensed from the top downwards via respected positions and institutions like heads of state, legislatures and courts, ministries and the media. Visible power is also something wielded by global organisations and multinational corporations. Visible power gets its way through laws, policies and constitutions, and from budgets, regulations and conventions. And if these don't work visible power falls back on its repressive agents like the police and army to enforce these rules.

Hidden power is how vested interests set the agenda about what is debatable, and dismiss alternatives. Hidden power is about exclusion and delegitimisation. It is the way certain ideas, groups and alternatives to the status quo are kept away from the discussion table. Hidden power suggests how the powerful exclude matters from the media and from public consideration through hiding issues for discussion, spreading misinformation, intimidation, and using mechanisms like steering committees, public relations, advertising and propaganda. Examples of hidden power include the surveillance capitalism and 'psy-ops' of big data (O'Neil 2017; Zuboff 2019), the fossil-fuel industry's control over the global warming debate and environmental policies, state and corporate racism in the war on drugs, and the Catholic Church's influence on global reproductive health policy in Latin America and elsewhere.

The final dimension of the power matrix is invisible power (Miller et al 2006). This is about shaping meaning and values. Teaching people what is normal and socially acceptable. It is also called 'socialised power' or 'internalised power'. It is also one way to imagine how social structures become 'poststructural' by being internalised as ideologies, 'social facts' and 'moral grammars' about the world (Nehring and Kerrigan 2018b). Invisible power comes from the control of information, education, online behaviours, surveillance, and how we are all socialised. It includes things like culture, ideologies, religions, values, norms, rankings, tradition and customs. Examples of invisible power include blaming poverty on laziness, women blaming themselves for domestic violence, and the faith we put in statistics and top-down pedagogy as the best type of knowledge to have about the world – that is, the teacher with all the answers at the front of the classroom presenting the answers for those in the room to remember and recycle them uncritically. Invisible power also explains why many of us consent to, buy into and defend a global economic system that is not in our best interests.

Yes, capitalism has improved life for many in the world, but today many sociologists have come to question the huge social, economic, ecological and cultural costs, and whether these now outweigh capitalism's potential for good (Harvey 2007; Giroux 2010; Sassen 2014; Wolff 2016). Or as French sociologist Pierre Bourdieu once noted, 'Every established order tends to make its own entirely arbitrary system seem entirely natural' (Bourdieu 1977, 163).

Public, private and intimate power

Another frame for the study of power highlighted in the work of VeneKlasen and Miller (2002) comes from the field of gender analysis and gender justice. 'Public, private and intimate power' speak about expressions of power, as in 'power over, power with, power to, and power within.' In the power matrix, various models of power overlap with each other and with other frameworks, helping to illustrate the multiple and overlapping expressions of power. In gender theory, feminist sociologists have developed frameworks to illustrate how power is much more than the visible forms we can see and understand (Hosein and Outar 2016). For example, VeneKlasen and Miller note that in gender analysis:

- The public realm of power refers to the visible face of power as it affects women and men in their jobs, employment, public life, legal rights etc. …
- The private realm of power refers to relationships and roles in families, among friends, sexual partnerships, marriage etc. …
- The intimate realm of power has to do with one's sense of self, personal confidence, psychology and relationship to body and health. (VeneKlasen and Miller 2002, 40)

'Power over', 'power with', 'power to', and 'power within' are all ways that power can be expressed positively and negatively, to dominate or to empower (Hearn 2012). 'Power over' is perhaps the most common understanding of power and can be understood by the sociologist as including elements of social structure in its definition. 'Power over' captures many of the negative aspects of power such as, 'repression, force, coercion, discrimination, corruption and abuse' and class warfare (VeneKlasen and Miller 2002, 39). Understood in this way power is a zero-sum game of 'crabs in a barrel', with winners and losers who gain power by taking power from, and exerting it over, others (Wright 2015). 'In politics, those who control resources and decision-making have power over those without. When people are denied access to important resources like land, healthcare and jobs, power over perpetuates inequality, injustice and poverty' (VeneKlasen et al 2002, 45). Again, this can be related to individual social power and its relationship to capital accumulation and access.

On the flip side, 'power with', 'power to', and 'power within' are understood as positive ways to understand how power operates and can be expressed in the world. 'Power with' refers to solidarity and collectivism with others. It is the idea we are stronger and more powerful when we work with others for social and organisational change rather than when we work alone in silos (Becker 1967; Tett 2015). Multiple people with their multiple talents and skills can achieve power with each other. 'Power to' captures the ideas that each individual has the potential power to make a difference in their own lives and also the wider world. 'Power within' captures the sociological idea of 'agency' and 'has to do with a person's sense of self worth and self-knowledge; it includes the ability to recognise individual differences while respecting others' (VeneKlasen et al 2002, 45).

All this background of differential access to power suggests the playing field of life is not level for all. As such, we now ask in a transhistorical-sociology sense how and why did some people get more power than other people?

Political power: who has it and why?

The sociology of Michel Foucault reminds sociologists that power is more than state power, and that the sovereignty of state power is actually a consequence of the historical unfolding of power rather than its cause. As Foucault wrote, any 'analysis, made in terms of power, must not assume that the sovereignty of the state, the form of the law, or the over-all unity of a domination are given at the outset; rather, these are only the terminal forms power takes' (Foucault 1990, 92).

Notwithstanding this reminder from Foucault, sociologists have had lots to say about state and political power. In fact, another way to think about the label 'political sociology' is that it is the combination of two social science disciplines – sociology and political science – and as such is most interested today in the study of state power and the relationship between nation-states, societies and politics. This includes understanding the macro and micro levels of the political. On the macro level, political sociologists have studied nation-states and the political institutions of the state such as ministries, the police and the courts (Hearn 2012). They have also considered how the many varied institutions of the state emerged, developed, and what they might become into the future. This includes processes like social change, social movements, collective action and resistance to political power. Political sociologists also study the micro level of politics, including such elements as individual political behaviour and voting, democracy and elections, social identities, attitudes and group behaviour, and the general social forces that shape and produce the political sphere. Not least because political sociology, as Max Weber pointed out in his classic essay 'Politics as a Vocation,' explains how the social ingredients a society invests and puts into its political system, will shape and determine 'the political', the types of politics, and the politicians the society ends up with (Weber 1965). This is important to understand because it tells the sociologist how the political is not a separate field from the social, but intensely and inherently an element of, and shaped by, the social.

The question of who has political power and why, is one that Harold Lasswell, a political scientist by PhD, but also a formidable sociologist during his time, as well as a friend of C. Wright Mills, tackled with his 1936 classic, *Politics: Who Gets What, When, How* (Lasswell 1936). For Lasswell, the very definition of politics is a competition about who gets what, when and how. In this sense democracy today can be understood not as an ongoing social and political project of inclusive national development or progress for all but rather as an ongoing competition between various political parties to gain control of the state and its institutions through forming an elected government that then decides how those state resources can and will be distributed to the wider society.

In this sense politics today in many countries has become a battle over money and its distribution, which via taxation and other revenues collected by the state, notwithstanding the ability of many states to issue their own currencies, is a vast amount. So, via the sociological imagination, politics, both in the 1930s and today, can be understood not simply as national development as once suggested, but rather as a competition of state capture to secure resources and the decision making control for how such resources are to be spent and used. But how did we get to this point? What details do the sociological imagination and historical sociology add in terms of context and history to better understand the emergence of the nation-state, government, sovereignty and contemporary politics today? How can the Enlightenment be read in decolonial terms?

The Enlightenment

In the centuries before the 1600s kings and gods ruled Western societies (Graeber and Sahlins 2017). This was an era of divine creation and absolutism, where 'gods' ordained kings and their right to govern over all others. Under such a belief system a feudal order and hierarchy was established based on inherent ascribed status and natural subordination. As political philosopher John Christman (2002, 27) has noted, 'Royalty took their place, not sanctioned from below by the consent of the governed, but by their superior place in the overall structure of humanity (in the "great chain of being").' With time, a countermovement against ascribed hierarchy emerged. This era and countermovement is called the Enlightenment. On the surface the ideas of the Enlightenment suggested anti-hierarchy and fairness, and that through rational thought and empiricism (science) 'man' [sic] could govern and educate 'himself' [sic], through government of the people without need for kings. However, as US anthropologist David Graeber has researched kings 'linger in ghostly form' (Graeber and Sahlins 2017, 12):

> [e]ven when kings are deposed, the legal and political framework of monarchy tends to live on, as evidenced in the fact that all modern states are founded on the curious and contradictory principle of 'popular sovereignty,' that the power once held by kings still exists, just now displaced onto an entity called 'the people'. (Graeber and Sahlins 2017, 1)

The immediate period preceding the emergence of Enlightenment from the mid-1400s to the mid-1600s was accompanied by the growth in wealth and commerce in the market towns of Europe and Britain, and a growing class of merchants known as the *burgs* (and from which the word *bourgeoisie* later emerges), who were excluded from political power by the absolutism of kings and clergy. This merchant class wanted a more democratic system of government and popular sovereignty, whereby many governed rather than a single individual holding sway over all. From the late-1600s this questioning of traditional authority was accompanied by what is called the 'Age of Reason' a socio-cultural period of great Western philosophical, political and scientific transformations extending to the mid-1800s. Famous political philosophers of the Enlightenment era include Thomas Hobbes, John Locke, Jean Jacques Rousseau and Immanuel Kant.

The first three in this list are well known in political philosophy as 'contractarians' for their thinking on the 'social contract'. The social contract was a philosophical thought-experiment used by Western political philosophers to understand how humans might move from living in a 'state of nature' to establish civil society and consent to being governed. Kant is included in the list because for many he is the preeminent philosopher of the Enlightenment, and is also recognised by some sociologists as 'the father of modern concepts of race and scientific racism' (Sussman 2014, 27). The consequences of 'race science' for social divisions and inequalities are a point we return to in Chapter 8.

Social contract theory is the idea that government is founded on the popular consent of individuals taken to be equals, and this is where modern society and politics (or modernity) emerges. However, different contractarians had different conceptions of why such consent was required. For Hobbes, human beings are inherently bad people and live in a brutish and competitive 'state of nature'; as such, they need some form of top-down force and sovereign entity to stop them from reverting to their worst qualities and killing each other. For Rousseau, humans in small-scale societies are inherently good, but as society grows the increases in money, wealth, and possessions change the population who become more self-interested and greedy, and as such humans need top-down government to protect their private property rights and provide justice. And for Locke, humans were neither good nor bad because the state of nature was already one of reasonable equality among 'men' [sic], wherein morality was part of the natural order of things. Locke's version of social contract theory, via the idea that people have natural rights, which through laws and constitutions can be preserved and protected through due process, shared moral values and protecting individual possessions and property rights, has led some sociologists, criminologists and historians to suggest that the contemporary criminal justice system in the US was derived from, or at least influenced by, Locke's social contract thinking (Eze 2008).

One important critique of the story told by social contract theory is that 'the establishment of society thus implies the denial that a society already existed, the creation of society requires the intervention of white men, who are thereby positioned as already sociopolitical beings' (Mills 1999, 13). Another implication of social contract theory is that people require a top-down sovereign to establish and run a society, something that has become common sense today, but which other political models like anarchism or communism might suggest is not true (Scott 2014).

The language of rights and liberal equality from social contract theory is the same language of rights that echoed into and shaped the American and French Revolutions, via the Declaration of Independence and the Declaration of the Rights of Man (Elliott 2007). The Enlightenment and these early revolutions is where the Western liberal norms of freedom, equality, justice and rights that define modern Western politics first emerge and were codified into laws and institutions. Once given to everyone equally, Western liberal norms provide important values to achieve and live by.

However, in decolonial terms, both these historic revolutions and their declarations, not to mention the initial ideas of Rousseau, Hobbes and Locke, were always genderised, racialised and anti-poor (Mills 1999). This is because the rights driving the US and French revolutions did not include women, people of colour or those who did not own land. As such the liberal notion of equality at its feudal and colonial origins is actually one that built social inequality structurally into the social, because some people were seen as sub- or part-human and thus excluded from such rights for all. Today, this history is one element in why many societies are scarred and marked by entrenched social hierarchies such as racial and gender inequalities and class divisions, which in many places became forms of social class and caste distinctions.

Decoloniality suggests that social inequality was an organisational component at the inception of modern societies and politics (Mills 2008). 'Racial liberalism' both fed the justifications for European slavery, colonialism and imperialism, and was fed back into them (Eze 2008; Mills 2008). As we saw from the emergence of imperial sociology (Chapter 6), European slavery, colonialism and imperialism were criminal forms of violence and economic exploitation that extracted much wealth, labour and commodities from colonies (Williams 1994). Karl Marx called these processes 'primitive accumulation', while contemporary British anthropologist David Harvey (2007) calls them, 'accumulation by dispossession'. Both men, alongside others, are clear that the accumulation of resources and capital during European slavery, colonialism and imperialism was a major factor in the expansion and successful emergence of British liberal capitalism from 1820 to 1870 (Bell 2009).

> [D]espite the emphasis on rationality, truth and scientific objectivity, a number of biases of race, culture, class and gender inevitably filtered into the notions of these [Enlightenment] thinkers. For instance, Hamilton (1996) notes that many of the key thinkers (apart from being white males) were from the higher order of society: many were of 'noble birth', or from the gentry classes or from a professional milieu. Thus, ideas about social progress, equality and democracy were inevitably limited by biases and interests that derived from the dominance of property owning white male intellectual elites. In this sense, Buck-Morss (2000) points to the glaring discrepancy between the narratives of freedom and equality in the Enlightenment discourses and the Enlightenment silence on brutalities of coloniality and slavery within European colonial empires. (Salandy 2018, 4)

Yet without the sociological imagination and its drive for historical context, such realities about the foundations of modern societies and polities and their relations to other societies disappear and have often been excluded by hidden and invisible power, suggesting the ahistorical view of 'study the world as you find it', rather than studying the world you find, in ways that include context and backstory, as well as individual agency.

A good illustration of the racism and racial liberalism contained at the foundations of the modern Western political tradition can be seen through the example of the Haitian Slave Revolution, as supported by the Haitian Constitutions of 1801 and 1805, in contrast to the US Declaration of Independence and the French Declaration of the Rights of Man (Buck-Morss 2009). The 1801 Haitian Constitution, often referred to as 'Toussaint's Constitution', after the Toussaint L'Ouverture, leader of the Haitian Revolution, abolished slavery in Article 3: 'There cannot exist slaves on this territory, servitude is therein forever abolished.' In Article 4 it proclaimed equality of all men [sic]: 'All men, regardless of colour, are eligible to all employment.' And in Article 5 it prohibited any classification system based not based on merit: 'There shall exist no distinction other than those based on virtue and talent, and other superiority afforded by law in the exercise of a public function.' The 1805 constitution build on these articles and in contrast to the US and French documents explicitly noted 'all mankind [sic] is equal'.

However, the new state of Haiti soon faced major problems. Haiti was punished with financial violence and the first black republic was denied its freedom. This occurred in 1825, when French monarch Charles X declared Haiti had an 'independence debt' of 150 million gold francs to pay to France in order to compensate former slave owners and enforced it through naval force and political isolation. The French demand for reparations for ex-slave owners was reduced to 90 million gold francs, a debt still equivalent to £14 billion today. There was no freedom for Haiti under the subjugation of such debt, and once again it illustrates how power and inequalities in modern society cannot be understood without understanding how social inequalities and divisions such as race, gender and class are built structurally into contemporary capitalism and the sovereignty of modern political systems. The independence debt subjugated Haiti and has stagnated its development to this day, and has led to racist stigma for Haiti and Haitians. Yet it was the racist social structures and forces of white supremacy in-built into European colonialism that created such problems.

Thus, in decolonial terms, ex-colonies around the world were not founded on similar ideas of a social contract like Western nations and should not be understood in identical ways. Rather, colonialism and slavery seen from the bottom up were state-led white-collar crimes of Western European nations and their elites (Fanon 1965; Agozino 2003). As it was achieved through physical violence, economic terrorism and primitive accumulation there was of course never any consent to colonialism by the colonised (Césaire 1955). It was a 'domination contract' (Mills 2008). A similar point was made by Martinican psychiatrist and sociologist of colonialism Frantz Fanon, and a student of Aimé Césaire: 'Was my freedom not given to me then in order to build the world of the You?' (Fanon 2008, 181). And in the independence constitutions of many ex-colonies there has never been restitution to address the social inequities produced under colonialism within nations, or between nations.

Capitalism and conflict

These social hierarchies and structures established over four hundred years ago at the seedling stage of Western modernity and mercantile capitalism still endure in many ways today, and in fact now extend into the digital world as can be seen in algorithms that are racially biased and not gender-neutral (O'Neil 2017). Furthermore, the social and economic hierarchies produced within ex-colonies and between ex-colonies and their previous European colonialists were compounded on independence by Western-led, global organisations, which were developed to serve and sustain capitalism as the colonial empires of Europe and their power to directly administer life in the ex-colonies began to decline. Such organisations include the IMF, the World Bank and the WTO, and their destructive and socially punishing doctrine of structural adjustment policies punished the global South in neocolonial ways such as 'corporate imperialism' (Girvan 1971, 2017).

Such organisations and various powerful states in the West, alongside international investment law, have since the 1970s worked together to organise the world for a type of predatory capitalism many call 'neoliberal capitalism' (Harvey 2007). Neoliberal capitalists have worked hard to let market forces, rather than democracies, determine the direction of global social and economic development, and while certain individuals, shareholders and elites have become richer the majority of the world's population is facing up to increasing social inequality, the end of social safety nets and social democracy, unsustainable environmental damage, and disastrous increases in social injustice (Slobodian 2018). Not to mention a complete absence of responsibilities from states in the West to pay restitution for the destructive social and economic policies that were enforced both during colonialism and imperialism, and latterly in the post-1960s independence era.

> The relationship between neoliberalism and violence is directly related to the system of rule that neoliberalism constructs, justifies, and defends in advancing its hegemonies of ideology, of policy and programme, of state form, of governmentality, and, ultimately, of discourse. Neoliberalism is a context in which the establishment, maintenance, and extension of hierarchical orderings of social relations are re-created, sustained, and intensified, where processes of 'othering' loom large. Accordingly, neoliberalization should be regarded as integral to violence inasmuch as it generates social divisions within and across space. (Springer et al 2016, 160)

Understood via the social imagination it becomes clear that social inequalities and divisions are foundational organisational elements of modern nations, Western society and global order (Venn 2009). Another way to say this is that racism, patriarchy, sexism, heteronormativity and class inequality are foundational, structural elements of the Western liberal tradition, and are forms of hidden and invisible power embedded in modern polities that define its ideologies (Césaire 1955).

We should never forget that slavery was once legal around the world, that women had to fight and die for men to give them the right to vote, and that people of colour were not allowed to vote in some countries of the world; for example, in the US and South Africa black suffrage was not achieved until 1965 and 1994 respectively. Or that in 2018 in the UK a Conservative government saw fit to stigmatise and deport black British citizens as illegal immigrants. Originally from the Caribbean, they had lived in the UK since before 1974. Records of their British citizenship were destroyed by the same government. Of those members of the 'Windrush generation' wrongly deported, at least eleven are thought to have died (Wardle and Obermuller 2019).

In transhistorical terms this can be described as a return of the racial liberalism of the Enlightenment and the racist politics of colonialism, wherein some people are deemed worthy of full treatment as human beings, while some are 'othered' and marked out by the state itself for violence such as deportation and imprisonment. Under such a hostile and racist climate where right-wing politicians and their media supporters mobilise racism by using the cultural logic of colonialism, and classing outsiders as 'immigrants' even when said 'immigrants' are full citizens, the sociological imagination is required more than ever to counter and combat the use of political power and sensational populism that panders to racist ideas and systems.

None of this critique is meant to suggest that the aspiration of Enlightenment ideals of Western liberalism were wrong or is not something to aspire to. Rather it is to say, from a historical and decolonial sociology vista, that such ideals and values were not applied equally and as such the world today is a place of social inequalities and divisions where some have more wealth, more opportunity and more privileges than others. Today this happens both in online and offline contexts. Sociologists have also shown how these inequalities are often situations of cumulative advantages for some social groups and classes, and cumulative disadvantages for other social groups and classes; for example, intergenerational transfers of wealth and poverty (Rodney 1972; Piketty 2014). Understood via a historically informed social imagination, it now become easier to understand and support the call for reparations and affirmative action by historically underdeveloped populations and nations (Beckles 2013).

Sociology and social change

For Foucault (1990, 93), 'Power is not an institution, and not a structure; neither is it a certain strength we are endowed with; it is the name that one attributes to a complex strategical situation in a particular society.' These 'situations' are arrived at through long processes of historical events, their outcomes and the social processes they produce. Yet if the social world of modernist global capitalism is inherently unequal and unfair for many groups what does this mean for liberal democracy and the laws we live by? Can we even say we have authentic democracy today? And what of the 'public sphere', a collective space where resistance to the dominant model of social organisation can be resisted and social movements – the power of groups and solidarity over the power of individuals – can be harnessed (Gaudio 2003)? Social change for the sociologist is more than individuals; it requires collective action to transform the structural foundations of the modern world. Yet collectivism seems to be in short supply in today's world. In the next chapter we will consider many of the social inequalities and processes that work to stop collectivism and which sociologists suggest drive individuals and social groups apart, making substantial social change harder to achieve.

THINKING SOCIOLOGICALLY

1. Is it (inequality) inherent in the nature of organisation? How does it arise? How is it perpetuated? What are the problems it brings, and how does it affect the individual? Marx saw inequality as inherent in all class societies; Weber saw it inherent in the nature of lasting organisation. Some sociologists see it as contributing to order. All see it as one source of social change. (Charon 1998) [p 121]

What is this statement trying to say? In what ways do sociologists understand inequality as foundational and organisational in the contemporary world? Why might this be?

2. Who has *explicit* power over you to make and enforce the rules and laws you follow? How is the sociological imagination important in understanding and imagining how such power influences your personal agency?

3. What does power as control over you feel like? And are so many rules, laws and regulations really necessary for society to function well? Do all these rules and laws empower you, or do some take power away from you? And what might a society without so many rules look like? How would it function?

MINI PROJECT

'"Big data", I argue, is not a technology or an inevitable technology effect. It is not an autonomous process, as Schmidt and others would have us think. It originates in the social, and it is there that we must find it and know it. In this article I explore the proposition that "big data" is above all the foundational component in a deeply intentional and highly consequential new logic of accumulation that I call surveillance capitalism. This new form of information capitalism aims to predict and modify human behavior as a means to produce revenue and market control. Surveillance capitalism has gradually constituted itself during the last decade, embodying a new social relations and politics that have not yet been well delineated or theorized. While "big data" may be set to other uses, those do not erase its origins in an extractive project founded on formal indifference to the populations that comprise both its data sources and its ultimate targets.' (Zuboff 2015, 75)

For this project, you will need to do some background research. Useful sources to begin with are 'Big Other: Surveillance Capitalism and the Prospects of an Information Civilization' by Shoshana Zuboff which is available for free via SSRN here https://papers.ssrn.com/sol3/papers.cfm?abstract_id=2594754.

Other resources that maybe available in your library university include:
Routledge Handbook of Surveillance Studies (Ball et al 2012)
Discipline and Punish: The Birth of the Prison (Foucault 1977)
Surveillance Studies: An Overview (Lyon 2007)

In this mini project you will apply the sociological imagination to identify what sociologists call the surveillance economy and define its features from a critical standpoint.

1. What is a surveillance society? How and when are we subject to multiple forms of surveillance in such a society?

2. What are the different types of surveillance? What are the overt forms of surveillance that we are all explicitly aware of and what are more mundane forms of monitoring and surveillance that we are less conscious of?

3. What might be the impact of the continuous attention paid to our personal information through these surveillance practices?

4. How do you think the relationship between these overt and mundane forms of surveillance affect and shape our personal lives and behaviours?

5. How might the sociologist understand surveillance as a type of knowledge-generating practice and organising metaphor for society?

6. In your opinion, what do you think the rise of the surveillance economy is a reaction to?

Working in groups, in so far as feasible, summarise your findings and display them in a poster presentation.

TALKING POINTS

Across the world's various societies political sociology encompasses a vast and disparate variety of topics and theoretical perspectives. This means sociologists often find it hard to agree about just what does or does not belong in a political sociology course.

Based on what you have read in this chapter and combined with the important social issues and problems in your own society imagine you are a lecturer for an upcoming ten-week course on political sociology.

What different topics will you include in your political sociology course and why? What will be your core intellectual lens and focus? What concepts, approaches and foundations of the social determinants of political processes, institutions and ideas in politics will you select?

Please draft a ten-week programme for your political sociology course.

READ ON ...

What is politics and who becomes a politician in Max Weber's book *Politics as a Vocation* (1965) is a sociological classic about the issue of politics and power. To better understand the ways in which state power is entangled with ideological manipulation through its institutions Louis Althusser offers some compelling ideas in *Lenin and Philosophy, and Other Essays* (1971). Johnathan Hearn's *Theorizing Power* (2012) is an excellent sociological overview on power. Power in the digital economy and online today is tackled by Jessie Daniels and colleagues in *Digital Sociologies* (2017). How algorithims and digital data create new forms of social inequalities is captured by Cathy O'Neil in *Weapons of Math Destruction: How Big Data Increases Inequality and Threatens Democracy* (2017). Emmanuel Chukwudi Eze in *Race and the Enlightenment: A Reader* (2008) and Charles Wright Mills's *Racial Liberalism* (2008) are excellent texts for understanding the often hidden racial dilemmas embedded in the Enlightenment tradition and the continued influence of racism today. Thomas Piketty explains how wealth and assests shape power and power relations today in *Capital in the Twenty-First Century* (2014). Hilary Beckles in *Britain's Black Debt: Reparations for Slavery and Native Genocide* (2013) asks why reparations for slavery and colonialism are not on the table in the 21st century. Meanwhile, the brutal reality of exclusion in the 21st century due to failure of the social and economic system is the subject matter of Saskia Sassen's *Expulsions: Brutality and Complexity in the Global Economy* (2014).

Check the companion website at https://bristoluniversitypress. co.uk/imagining-society-online-resources **for a suggested project and writing task.**

8

Difference, stratification and inequalities

Whether it's sociological research regarding who profits from the legalisation and decriminalisation of cannabis in the US (Alexander 2012), or which groups are monitored and policed the most under surveillance capitalism or the UK government's Prevent (Heath-Jones 2013; Zuboff 2019), or the inequalities that have given rise to social movements such as Black Lives Matter (Epp et al 2014) and #MeToo (Jaffe 2018; Mendes et al 2018), or the reinvigoration and continuation of the British state's 'hostile environment' for immigration, including the deportation of black British citizens to the Caribbean and the false dichotomy of 'good immigrants' versus 'bad immigrants' (Jones et al 2017; Wardle and Obermuller 2019), one of the most important and vibrant areas of research in global sociologies – both today and in the past – has been that of poverty, inequalities and discrimination. This is because of the ways in which processes of difference making and their historical contexts, and the socioeconomic processes and cultural systems giving rise to them, can be some of the most fundamental social problems people experience in their daily lives.

For example, Tressie McMillan Cottom's work on the US highlights many contemporary forms of inequality and discrimination experienced by black women there, including 'that black women are 243 percent more likely to die from pregnancy or childbirth-related causes than are white women' (Cottom 2019, 7). Sara Ahmed's (2017) work on the science of being a 'feminist killjoy' foregrounds the importance of feminism as a sociological lens and general attitude in focusing on and understanding how racism and sexism function in the academy, as well as in everyday life through the various institutions we each need to engage with to live our lives, from immigration and social services to education and employment. For many people today institutions like the university might be considered spaces where employment is based on merit, yet Ahmed shows how many university practices in the UK are in reality often structured by social inequalities involving socioeconomics, race and gender that have developed over long periods of time.

Saskia Sassen's recent work on the growing conditions for and realities of income inequality and 'bullshit jobs', alongside accelerations in land and water destruction, suggests that traditional sociological concepts like poverty, inequality and discrimination – centred on the economy and its increasing complexity – do not go far enough in understanding and clarifying the current political moment, which she describes as types of 'expulsion' from various spaces of work, living and the environment (Sassen 2014). Sassen also highlights how new levels of complexity in society hide the processes and responsibility for the displacements she identifies, such as expulsion from employment and the land you live on.

Systems and structures of difference making

Patriarchy

Patriarchy is an ideology and social structure referring to the rule of men and male dominance that is consciously and unconsciously built, reinforced and maintained by both individual men and women in society. Patriarchy provides some people with advantage over other people, and as a sociocultural system it persists as the dominant mode of gender organisation in society because of this unequal advantage for some. For Cynthia Enloe, patriarchy persists because it constantly shifts and adapts its sociocultural forms while also giving less weight to women's perspectives (Enloe 2017). It also recruits forms of toxic masculinity and femininity, such as evangelical manliness, internalised sexism and misogynoir, which damage both men and women while discrediting other more progressive forms of masculinity and femininity.

Caribbean sociologist Patricia Mohammed (1994, 144) suggests, 'we must be able to view patriarchy as ideas of superiority which function to control groups and classes in society, and both men and women are victims of the dominant patriarchal contract'. Patriarchy is about social power and control. Feminists challenge the power of patriarchy across all fields and spaces of life by redefining the boundaries of what constitutes femininity and masculinity or 'gender norms' (Ahmed 2017). The dominant notions of femininity and masculinity are sociocultural constructions that shift over time and societies, and provide (in) formal rules on a spectrum of what are the supposedly socially correct ways to act like a man or a woman (Hearn and Morgan 2014).

Gender as a 'social construct' does not mean gender has no real effects in the world. Gender is a long-standing sociocultural system shaping all our lives in terms of how we are subject to power and also how we can use power or not. Gender can be further defined as 'complex systems of personal and social relations of power through which women and men are socially created and maintained and through which they gain access to, or are allocated status, power and material resources within society' (Barriteau 2003, 30).

How do feminists study inequalities and discrimination? Feminists investigate power relations in the institutions and social and economic relations of societies (Ahmed 2017). Over the years, there have been various waves of feminism, and feminists have developed various analytical tools to understand women's lives.

> The methodologies and concepts of gender analysis joined a long and distinguished list of feminist explanatory tools that include biology is destiny, the personal is political, dual systems analysis, sexual division of labour, capitalist patriarchy, the sex/gender system, the public/private dichotomy, multiple consciousness ... the contours of a black feminist epistemology, and identity politics. From their investigations feminists defined the social relations of gender to refer to a complex system of power played out in the different and often unequal experiences of women and men. (Barriteau 2003, 29)

In the patriarchal system, women as a group – in relation to their access to economic resources and political power – have traditionally been placed in a subordinate position in the social hierarchy of society compared with men as a group. For example, unpaid work, which is mostly done by women and includes a diverse range of 'traditional' activities performed without cash payment, such as meal preparation, doing laundry, unpaid care provided for children, and caring for a parent or elderly neighbour tends to be neglected in discussions relating to work, labour and productivity (Gutiérrez-Rodríguez 2010). Gutiérrez-Rodríguez shows how these services are generally excluded from GDP calculations in most countries. Although women are active in paid employment, there is still the expectation for women to perform unpaid care work in the private sphere or at home. As the sociologists Judith Treas and Tsui-o Tai (2016, 495) show in their work on the gendered division of housework across twenty European nations: 'women still do most of the household labour, even in 13 European countries, such as Norway and the UK, where gender egalitarian values receive general support'. The theoretical framework used in their sociological study emphasises 'that gender inequality is maintained by a complex, integrated system of structural and cultural forces that work at multiple levels – from micro to macro – to reinforce women's disadvantage' (Treas and Tai 2016, 505).

Janet Newman's research shows how the conditions of paid work, being uncertain in the 21st-century globalised world in tandem with neoliberal policies of austerity and its cuts in public and welfare services, have intensified 'the time pressures on women, making it more difficult to reconcile care work, paid employment, casual work, study, voluntary or charitable contributions and political activity' (Newman 2013, 217). This makes it difficult for progressive feminist projects to succeed. Women are now 'time poor' and have to bear additional pressures in the unpaid arena due to public and welfare cuts. 'The spaces of power are shrinking, the borders tightening and material constraints coupled with more coercive governance regimes make it more difficult for activists to find the time or resources for creative political work' (Newman 2013, 217). However, the solidarity among feminists working against injustice has resulted in change in the past and continues to be a strong voice, as is evident in many social movements today.

Concepts such as the 'glass ceiling' and the 'glass escalator' are feminist terms for the social inequalities between men and women in the social space of paid employment. The 'glass ceiling' is an invisible boundary that women experience in their ascension into top positions in usually male-dominated professions. The 'glass escalator' refers to the advantages men experience in predominately female professions such as nursing, teaching, librarianship, hair and beauty, social work and the culinary fields because men are 'assumed' to be most competent at higher levels of professionalism than women (Williams 1992).

In 2013, Christine Williams revisited her concept of the 'glass escalator' to include 'intersectionality' as an approach, because previously the concept had referred strictly to white middle-class men (Williams 2013). An example of social inequality not limited to gender inequality is the 'glass escalator' in Wingfield's (2009) study on the experiences of black men in nursing who found no evidence of the glass escalator in their careers. Instead, racial inequality that existed in the traditional profession of nursing reflected the masculine hegemony of white privilege. This rule applied also to homophobia. 'The exclusion of gay men from the glass escalator is not merely an exception to the rule; it is part of the process of reproducing hegemonic masculinity' (Williams 2013, 617).

The intersectionality approach allows for race/ethnicity, class and sexuality to be taken into account in the study of gender. This approach confirms that the 'glass escalator' pivots not only on gender inequality but on the exclusion and marginalisation of those also oppressed on the basis of race, sexuality and class.

The Caribbean-American intellectual Audre Lorde who died in 1992 wrote about this from the experiences in her own life in her famous essay 'There is no hierarchy of oppressions' (Lorde 1983). She pointed out that as a woman she was oppressed in the US social system that she lived in. As a mother she was oppressed. As black she was oppressed. As a poet she was oppressed. As poor she was oppressed. As a feminist she was oppressed. And as a member of an interracial couple she was oppressed. Of this intersecting 'downpression' she said: '… I usually find myself part of some group in which the majority defines me as deviant, difficult, inferior or just plain wrong' (1983, 9). From her membership of these many different social groups and classes Lorde understood sociologically that 'oppression and the intolerance of difference come in all shapes and sizes and colours and sexualities' (1983, 9). And that 'there can be no hierarchy of oppression' (1983, 9). Her answer was simple. All beliefs in the inherent superiority of one value system over other value systems involve a system of human dominance. Whether it is sexism, racism, classism, shadism, heterosexism, ableism or any other prejudice the belief in the inherent superiority of one group of human beings over another for Lorde could only ever be a failure of humanity.

Patriarchy controls people and classifies them into groups with varying degrees of status and privileges. Women are subordinate to men in the patriarchal structure. However, men also suffer in this patriarchal power structure, most notably men who do not fit into the ideals of 'hegemonic masculinity' in their given societies and also men who aspire to toxic versions of masculinity. In gender analysis, it is crucial that race, class/ethnicity and sexuality are all included.

Race science as racism

One consequence of the rise in populism in the US and elsewhere over the past decade has been the steady increase and return of what sociologists call 'race science', which borrows from 19th-century eugenics to claim black Americans are a monolithic group who are less intelligent than white Americans (Eze 2008). 'Race science' recruits biological myths about race – that differences in human bodies (often called 'race') explain social hierarchies, inequalities in the distribution of power or resources, and IQ levels – while ignoring the vast empirical evidence about the historical roots of social inequalities (Chakrabarti and Patnaik 2017) and the research of geneticists that 'human beings are 99.5% genetically identical' (Gravlee 2009). Or as biological anthropologist Agustín Fuentes (2014) notes, 'While different populations vary in some of the .1% of the genome, the way this variation is distributed does not map to biological races, either by continent or otherwise.'

To put it simply, 'race science' seeks to talk about racial inequalities as genetically driven and ignores the sociological imagination around how the social environment and cumulative economic injustices of the past shape individuals and groups in the present. 'Race science' is racism under the guise of pseudo-scientific research and it has been around since colonialism. This is not the same as saying there are not small measurable genetic markers for certain geographic and ethnic population groups, but it is to say those clusters do not overlap with the pseudo-scientific notion of 'race' (Gravlee 2009). It is also to say that 'race science' was used historically to make claims about black inferiority and supposed biological differences in order to justify colonialism, legal slavery and neoimperialism. Ideas of white supremacy are found at the heart of 'race science'.

> Making claims about the existence of biological races won't help answer questions about health, like how the health of racialised groups is harmed by racial discrimination – how it increases the risk of disease, the risk of exposure to environmental toxins, or the risk of inadequate and inappropriate health care.
>
> This doesn't mean that genetic variation is unimportant; it is, but it does not follow racial lines. History has taught us the many ways

that studies of human genetic variation can be misunderstood and misinterpreted: if sampling practices and historical contexts are not considered; if little attention is given to how genes, environments, and social conditions interact; and if we ignore the ways that sociocultural categories and practices shape the genetic patterns themselves. (Kahn et al 2018)

In this sense sociological research has long highlighted how the social construction of race has also been used to turn poor populations against each other, such as through debates on immigration, affirmative action and social justice. This tells the sociologist of the importance of the nexus of race and class, more than simply studies on class or race separately. A connection the Marxist C.L.R. James described eloquently more than fifty years ago when he wrote of the history of Haiti: 'The race question is subsidiary to the class question in politics, and to think of imperialism in terms of race is disastrous. But to neglect the racial factor as merely incidental is an error only less grave than to make it fundamental' (James 1963, 293). Cedric Robinson (2000) has used the term 'racial capitalism' to explain how race gives capitalist inequality its legs.

Peruvian sociologist Anibal Quijano has written of the history of the race concept in the Americas to illustrate that race was always meant to be a tool of division, and while race has become an important pillar of political mobilisation and identity politics this does not erase how the category of race is still used by 'race scientists' to drive groups apart and to create social divisions in terms of opportunities and justice.

> The idea of race, in its modern meaning, does not have a known history before the colonization of America. Perhaps it originated in reference to the phenotypic differences between conquerors and conquered. However, what matters is that soon it was constructed to refer to the supposed differential biological structures between those groups. (Quijano 2000, 533)

'Race science' as racism is what global South scholars mean when they use the term the 'coloniality of power'. The coloniality of power is an anti-colonial theory of power highlighting the extension of practices, discourses and legacies of European colonialism into social orders and forms of knowledge in ex-colonies and ex-colonial powers. The theory explains how the legacies of colonialism live on in contemporary societies in the form of social discrimination via 'systems of hierarchies, systems of knowledge and cultural systems' that outlive formal colonialism and became integrated with independence in successive social orders (Quijano 2000). The coloniality of power illustrates how 'the racial, political and social hierarchical orders imposed by European colonialism' in Latin America and the Caribbean provided value to certain peoples, groups and societies while disenfranchising others.

Caribbean sociologist Rhoda Reddock has written about how intra-race issues have unfolded within the discipline of sociology itself too. Using the example of 'critical race theory', which can be found in Caribbean radical thought from the 1930s onwards and was in use for over fifty years in Caribbean sociology, she shows how it only entered the mainstream of sociological discourse when black US sociologists adopted critical race theories in their own work (Reddock 2014). This suggests another way to think about race and status, is that globally there are intra-race hierarchies and colourism between racialised bodies in different parts of the world.

Finally, it is also important to recognise that race is a Western- and European-derived concept. As such, in using 'race' as understood in the Western Anglo-European tradition, the Western sociologist can also exclude themselves from other ways of knowing the world, as the work of Nigerian sociologist Oyèrónké Oyěwùmí, to name one example, suggests:

> As the Yorùbá are part of a vast and complicated history of Central West Africa, and their linguistic bases facilitate communication across many other African communities, exploring Yorùbá concepts invites a communicative practice of producing African knowledge – including that of self-awareness – than the conceptual frameworks offered by Euromodern impositions in which African peoples function as nodal points of the primitive or cultural practices with no proper place in the present or future. Oyěwùmí's study of motherhood is thus heuristic as well as theoretically original in that as being very much part of the present, since the negotiation of the concept [of motherhood] didn't end during colonialism but instead took on forms to address the Euromodern situation, it offers much for non-Africanists to ponder. (Gordon 2018)

Social inequalities

Traditionally, 'social inequalities' has been an umbrella term to capture that within modern capitalist societies, different groups and individuals are rewarded, protected, supported and have access to resources, unequally. As we came to see in the previous chapter, and in the aforementioned examples of patriarchy and racism, in the context of access to social power, each of us does not start out on the playing field of life from identical social, cultural and economic positions or with the same amounts of social, cultural and economic capital. Different groups and different individuals have distinct amounts of sociocultural capital and economic privilege as groups, and power over other groups and individuals, based on the many different social classes and positions in all societies. In sociology these positions, social locations and amounts of capital in the social hierarchy are often linked to history and the cumulative advantages and disadvantages that different groups, such as rich and poor, experience; and social class differences can often play out with caste-like qualities that often prevent social mobility, which is something that has long been a focus of sociologists (Parsons 1939; Brathwaite 1960; Robinson 2000).

As such, the sociological imagination has long understood realities like poverty, social inequalities and discrimination as being connected to the ways that social goods and resources such as money, education, support, opportunities, political power and status, and also inner cultural resources such as self-esteem, self-worth, self-confidence and more, have been – and still are currently – unequally distributed across society (Hearn 2012; Piketty 2014; Illouz 2019). It is in this sense that the sociologist, using the social imagination, connects personal issues to public problems, and connects social problems to psychosocial injuries, life-skills deficits and the psychological impacts such social problems create.

Consider this crude analogy. Many of us play video games. One fun element of these games is when you struggle to do well you can switch the difficulty level. In most video games usually these levels are easy, medium and hard, but it can also include a many more levels in between such as in Sid Meier's Civilization series, which across volumes I to VI has these different difficulty levels:

- Settler
- Chieftain
- Warlord
- Noble
- Prince Regent
- King/Monarch
- Emperor
- Demigod
- Immortal
- Deity
- Sid Meier

Now clearly, the difficulty setting on a computer game isn't identical to privilege, social inequality or class analysis. But it is one way to imagine and explain how privilege, discrimination and social inequalities work as caste-like categories or 'social races', to give different persons at different levels and in different groups in the social hierarchy and structure, different opportunities, experiences and abilities over others (Wagley 1965).

These positions and social locations are often reproduced and maintained by various socioeconomic institutions like work and education, whose systems of selection and entry suggest 'meritocracy' – a system under which social mobility and advancement is achieved based on merit – but instead inscribe class reproduction rather than permitting open competition (Khan 2012; Rivera 2016). Macro-structural trends shape our micro-individual lives. This is not to say that working hard is not important in life. It is, of course. Or that each of us does not have agency – we of course do, but we do not all have the same agency, or the same choices as each other, and we are not all rewarded the same for the same hard work. As many people experience at first-hand, working hard alone does not automatically lead to economic success.

Privilege does not exempt anyone from facing adversity in life or from suffering hard times and unfair treatment, but it does mean in sociological terms that, based on the colour of our skin, our socioeconomic location, our status, our nationality, our wealth and lots more, that in comparison to some people with different colour skin, class background, status, nationality, education, wealth and more, we may not all have to face the same the exclusions or structural obstacles.

What makes a social class?

The French sociologist Pierre Bourdieu is famous for his conceptual toolkit of ideas and ways to imagine the social. One idea in particular comes from his research on taste, and helps to provide a definition of social class. One question Bourdieu asked was 'Are classes a scientific construct or do they exist in reality?' Or put another way 'Do classes exist or do they not?' (Bourdieu 1987). For Bourdieu the answer was always yes and no.

Yes, because the sociologist can identify classes as social groups composed of individuals with similar relationships to power, opportunities and resources. However, this point of view is often criticised by those who answer 'no' to the same question, because in their view such classes are nothing more than the invention of the sociologist, and that the dimensions of identification used by the sociologist do not exist without the sociologist being there to construct such dimensions. For Bourdieu, however, the answer more accurately was both yes and no – and importantly so: 'In fact, it is possible to deny the existence of classes as homogeneous sets of economically and socially differentiated individuals objectively constituted into groups, and to assert at the same time the existence of a space of differences based on a principle of economic and social differentiation' (Bourdieu 1987, 3).

For Bourdieu the best way to understand social classes was to first view 'the social space' and recognise that the social space is relational. In this manner the sociologist defines reality via relationships. However, it is important to note that these relations and relationships are shaped by and stand-in for the social structures of a society as historically derived phenomena. 'Knowledge of the social world has to take into account a practical knowledge of this world which pre-exists it and which it must not fail to include in its object' (Bourdieu 1984, 466). Bourdieu would develop this insight to become his famous concept of *habitus*. Once the sociologist comes to understand that individuals embody within them the social structures that make the world around them then the task of the sociologist, as Bourdieu saw it, is to construct spaces of explanation, prediction and difference.

> The social world can be conceived as a multi-dimensional space that can be constructed empirically by discovering the main factors of differentiation which account for the differences observed in a given social universe, or, in other words, by discovering the powers or *forms of*

capital which are or can become efficient, like aces in a game of cards, in this particular universe, that is, in the struggle (or competition) for the appropriation of scarce goods of which this universe is the site. It follows that the structure of this space is given by the distribution of the various forms of capital, that is, by the distribution of the properties which are active within the universe under study-those properties capable of conferring strength, power and consequently profit on their holder. (Bourdieu 1987, 3–4, emphasis in original)

What are these powers or forms of capital Bourdieu spoke of? How do they help us to understand the sociological concept of social class? Earlier we noted that many sociologists suggest that power and inequalities in society are related to 'how resources in society are distributed' (Shildrick and Rucell 2015). Bourdieu took a similar perspective and suggested that power in society is related to 'the structure of the distribution of capital' in society. In its most simple definition, capital is often used to refer to money and wealth. 'Capital accumulation' for example means earning revenue and collecting money. For many critical sociologists, social reality cannot be understood without 'following the money': who has it, how did they get it and what do they do with it? Because following the money can often provide insight into the 'why' in terms of motive, social action and agency. Yet Bourdieu, like Weber, was also well aware that capital is more than money too.

[F]undamental social powers are, according to my empirical investigations, firstly *economic* capital, in its various kinds; secondly *cultural* capital or better, informational capital, again in its different kinds; and thirdly two forms of capital that are very strongly correlated, *social* capital, which consists of resources based on connections and group membership, and *symbolic* capital, which is the form the different types of capital take once they are perceived and recognized as legitimate. (Bourdieu 1987, 4, emphasis in original)

'Capital' is also social power, not just in terms of money and wealth, but also on other levels too like cultural, social and symbolic capital. Capital can make people do things. It has power over us. For the sociologist this is why class analysis is so important in the study of inequality, because before inequality becomes a reality on an individual level – say, because your wage is low – it is also a social reality on a larger group level, because statistically as a group systems of race, gender and class discrimination mean some are paid less than others (Pager and Shepherd 2008; Graham 2009). It is also to say that your destiny is never simply about your individual agency, as much as we wish it were, but it is also very much about your relationship to social classes and goods like background, capital, networks, power, wealth, ability to sell labour and more.

What is class inequality?

In sociology, class analysis has most often focused on access to wealth and the distribution of resources and opportunities among the general population, and has been much less focused on the cultural and social resources that often accompany such access (Lamont 2019). For US sociologist Erik Olin Wright 'class analysis is the core of a wide-ranging agenda of research on the causes and consequences of class relations' (Wright 2000, 2; 2015) and there are different sociological traditions in the study of class. These include the Weberian concepts of class, the Marxist tradition and the stratification tradition.

Different aspects of the class structure

While sociologists have often used one out of these various three approaches, Wright noted they also all combine too. One way to see that is to acknowledge how each of the approaches is capable of revealing 'a key process that shapes a different aspect of the class structure':

- The Weberian tradition identifies 'the central mechanism that differentiates 'middle class' jobs from the broader working class by creating barriers that in one way or another restrict the supply of people for desirable employment. The key issue here is not mainly *who* is excluded, but simply the fact that there are mechanisms of exclusion that sustain the privileges of those in middle class positions' (Wright 2015, 48, emphasis in original).
- The Marxist tradition of exploitation and domination mechanisms identifies 'the fundamental class division connected to the capitalist character of the economy: the class division between capitalists and workers' (Wright 2015, 48).
- The stratification model identifies 'a key set of processes through which individuals are sorted into different positions in the class structure or marginalized from those positions altogether. Opportunity hoarding identifies exclusionary processes connected to middle class jobs. The individual attributes and life conditions approach helps specify what it is in the lives of people that explains who has access to those desirable middle class jobs and who is excluded from stable working class jobs' (Wright 2015, 48–9).

For Max Weber, class was always more than economics and wealth; it was about the unequal distribution of education, status and power in society, and how this status system connects status groups and political parties in society. However, like Marx, Weber was clear that economic class positions often provided the main mechanism by which other social positions and power were ultimately determined. That said, and as illustrated by Charles Kurzman and colleagues (2007), over time Weber's concept of status has been developed in many ways by sociologists, which readers might already be familiar with. These include Bourdieu's ideas on 'social capital' (1984, 284), Mills's concept of the 'power elite' (1956, 281), race and gender as forms of social differentiation (Robinson 2000; Brynin et al 2017) and also 'occupational status groups' (Weeden and Grusky 2005). Another way to make sense of Weber's ideas about status group formation and a multitude of social class locations is to imagine how the Indian caste system works. It has four main social categories that are further subdivided into 3,000 castes and 25,000 sub castes, with one group, 'the untouchables' or dalits, located outside the caste system completely (Khare 2006).

Weberian class analysis

In the field of class analysis associated with the work of Max Weber, Wright uses the term 'opportunity hoarding' to illustrate how in the US certain experiences, advantages and privileges can be closed off from members of other classes via exclusionary mechanisms in a process Wright describes as 'social closure'. Social closure is achieved in variety of ways, including educational credentials, private property rights and resource hoarding (Piketty 2014). In the case of education, 'high levels of education generate high income in part because of significant restrictions on the supply of highly educated people. Admissions procedures, tuition costs, risk aversion to large loans by low-income people, and a range of other factors all block access to higher education for many people, and these barriers benefit those in jobs that require higher education' (Wright 2015, 35).

Sociologist Lauren Rivera has written about this in her book *Pedigree,* documenting how elite students in the US get elite jobs (2016). The subject of how in-groups work to keep a variety of opportunities for themselves is also the subject of Charles Tilly's classic sociology text *Durable Inequality* (1999). Armstrong and Hamilton's (2015) *Paying for the Party* is a good ethnography of how US colleges through such social rituals as campus parties and return visits home, produces 'tracks' for different social classes, which then over time produce a form of unequal differentiation in the context of social networks and who gets opportunities and eventually, jobs.

In the context of private property rights, Wright illustrates how the profits of capitalist employers are reliant on their ownership of the means of production. As Wright (2015, 40–1) notes, 'The rich do things to secure their wealth that contribute to the disadvantages poor people face in the world.' According to Wright, the central distinction between the Weberian model of class and analysis, and the stratification model is: 'Opportunity-hoarding means that the economic advantages people get from being in a privileged class position are *causally connected* to the disadvantages of people excluded from those class positions' (2015, 40, emphasis in original). By this Wright means, 'the rich are rich in part *because* the poor are poor' (2015, 40, emphasis in original).

Marxist class analysis

The second tradition Wright discusses is Marxist class analysis. In this model class is understood as a relationship of 'exploitation and domination'. The central ways class is a mechanism of differentiation and difference making in this tradition is understood via who owns the 'means of production', and that those who don't own them must, to survive, provide their labour power for less than it is worth to the owners of the means of production. 'Domination' refers to the ability to control the *activities* of others. 'Exploitation' refers to the acquisition of economic benefits from the labouring activity of those who are dominated' (Wright 2015, 42). In this model, economic class contradictions between those who own the means of production and those who have to sell their labour to capitalists are also mystified by the invention of a plethora of caste-like social classes, which dilute 'class consciousness' and class solidarity between those who are exploited and those who begin to imagine others within their same economic class group as a threat. This can be seen today with false narratives about immigrants or refugees coming to steal people's livelihoods (Polletta and Callahan 2017). Instead of recognising human solidarity with each other based on mutual exploitation and oppression by capitalism and those called the bourgeoisie or elites, Marxist class analysis suggest that workers today are often turned against each other in defence of their social class, assets and location, defined in relation to government policy, problematic media narratives and everyday forms of bordering and social exclusion (Yuval-Davis et al 2018). In this sense the capitalist structure and its organisation is never challenged and instead those with relatively little capital or social power become competitors with each other rather than class allies.

Stratification tradition

In the stratification tradition people understand class as a concept in terms of their individual 'attributes and life conditions'. These personal characteristics include a wide range of elements including 'sex, age, race, religion, intelligence, education, geographical location', social connections, cultural resources, individual motivations, and more (Wright 2015, 29). We acquire such attributes in a variety of ways: some from birth, some as we grow and move through life, and some depend on our individual social situations, biographies and 'material conditions', and all are susceptible to change. These various social characteristics, attributes, and dimensions affect and shape many aspects of everyday life from how we vote and the quality of our health to explaining a variety of childrearing practices and family forms, all of which the sociologist wants to explore and understand.

Class in the stratification tradition is understood 'as a way of talking about the connection between individual attributes and these material life conditions: class identities are those economically important attributes of people that shape their opportunities and choices in a market economy and thus their material conditions of life' (Wright 2015, 30). When such individual characteristics and broader material conditions align, sociologists often cluster such groups into economic or social classes with particular social qualities, such as lower class, middle class and upper class, or other social classes tied to such factors as job, status, wealth and education. The stratification tradition provides the sociologist with important ways by which to determine clusters into social or economic classes. However,

> [w]hat is missing in this approach to class … is any serious consideration of the *inequalities in the positions themselves* that people occupy. Education shapes the kinds of jobs people get, but how should we conceptualize the nature of the jobs that people fill by virtue of their education? Why are some jobs 'better' than others? Why do some jobs confer on their incumbents a great deal of power while others do not? Rather than focusing exclusively on the process by which individuals are sorted into positions, the other two approaches to class analysis [the Marxist tradition and Weberian inspired class analysis] begin by analysing the nature of the positions themselves into which people are sorted. (Wright 2015, 34, emphasis in original)

Where do poverty and economic inequality come from?

As we have mentioned previously, some in politics and the mediascape suggest poverty and being poor is the choice of individuals and a consequence of individual idiosyncrasies and pathologies such as being lazy, addicted, not wanting to work, deviance, criminality or being a 'bad person' (Moreton-Robinson 2009, 68). The 2016 British Social Attitudes Survey conducted by sociologists in the UK illustrated a steep decline in public support for benefit claimants as compared with support in the 1980s and 1990s (NatCen Social Research 2017). Further sociological research has suggested this decline was triggered by a change in the language and rhetoric of politicians (Loopstra and Lalor 2017). Furthermore, the research illustrated how two groups are disproportionately represented among those living in poverty – disabled people and people with ill health – rather than the myth of fit yet lazy skivers.

> The social and political propensity to mark out some people as being in some way culpable or responsible for their own hardship has a long history. Explanations tend to emphasise individual behaviour, fecklessness or moral failing or – particularly in more recent times – the welfare system itself, which is deemed to encourage and support claimants into accepting welfare dependency (Murray, 1990). Morris (1994) has traced the rise and fall of sociological concern with differently labelled versions of the 'undeserving poor' over the past century and before. (Shildrick and Rucell 2015, 14)

Other explanations have focused on othering those living in poverty and blaming their situation on group level dynamics:

> Welshman has identified six variations in the terminology used to describe disadvantaged groups: the social residuum of the 1880s; the social problem group of the 1930s; the problem family of the 1950s; the culture of poverty thesis of the 1960s; the cycle of deprivation thesis of 1970s; and the underclass debates of the 1980s. More recently these ideas have morphed into more contemporary variants that point to cultures of worklessness, 'troubled families' or families who have never worked as key explanations for poverty. All these ideas have seeped into popular and policy discourse at various points in time, whilst also occupying academics who have often been keen to use empirical evidence to challenge these dominant individual, and often psychological, explanations for poverty. (Shildrick and Rucell 2015, 15)

However, as the historical and economic Austro-Hungarian sociologist Karl Polanyi wrote in *The Great Transformation*, and as the social imagination still explains, poverty and the 'market economy' are human inventions, not 'natural phenomenon' (Polanyi 1944). In sociology, 'political economy' means the politics of the economy. It is how the various resources needed to generate wealth are shared, mobilised and used. Political economy refers, then, to the human decisions taken about how and for whose benefit an economy and its profits and services should be run.

Sold as 'economic improvement' on a grand scale, the emergence of the market economy and British liberal capitalism in the late 18th and 19th centuries was accompanied by the 'Enclosure Acts', whereby the common land and small landholdings, which had been relied on by the majority of the population for their food and energy needs for hundreds of years, were taken away and privatised into large single land-holdings (Linebaugh 1976). As a result, by the early 19th century across the new industrial towns of Britain and Europe in places like Manchester a new, industrial labouring class emerged and crowded into the towns where factories, also described as 'satanic mills', would soon come to dehumanise and desolate these newly dispossessed people. As Polanyi (1944, 41) described it, 'Writers of all views and parties, conservatives and liberals, capitalists and socialists invariably referred to social conditions under the Industrial Revolution as a veritable abyss of human degradation'. Never before had society been run as an adjunct to the marketplace. Instead of the economy being embedded in social relations, social relations were now embedded in the economic system. This is most clearly seen before the emergence of market economies in Europe in how individuals rarely starved to death, but with the emergence of the market economy people were now forced to work under the penalty of starvation and filth (Linebaugh 2014). Human beings in a market economy are imagined as 'rational choice' agents, supposedly atomistic and individual, disconnected from prior forms of interconnected social organisation and solidarity. Except that rational choice individualism has been shown by political sociology, anthropology and ethnography to be a false consciousness, and an inaccurate and simplistic conception of the individual. Nonetheless, the rational choice premise and model is still mainstream in neoclassical economics and modern psychology today (Davies 2015).

> The state and its coercive powers had everything to do with the creation of what we now know as 'the market'– based as it is on institutions such as private property, national currencies, legal contracts, credit markets. All had to be created and maintained by government policy. The market was a creation of government and has always remained so. If one really reflects on the assumptions economists make about human behavior, it only makes sense that it should be so: the principle of maximization after all assumes that people will normally try to extract as much as possible from whoever they are dealing with, taking no consideration whatever of that other person's interests – but at the same time that they will never under any circumstances resort to any of the most obvious ways of extracting wealth from those towards whose fate one is indifferent, such as taking it by force. 'Market behavior' would be impossible without police. (Graeber 2016, 10)

Ideology and scholastic programming

According to sociologists, two more reasons for the successful emergence and continuance of the market economy as truth, and poverty as consequence, are ideology and education. In the 1970s Louis Althusser developed his concept of ideological state apparatuses (ISAs), a complement to his concept of 'repressive state apparatuses' we learned of in the previous chapter.

The nation-state is made up of various social institutions. These social institutions include education, religion, the family, culture, law, politics and more. Althusser saw these as state institutions or 'state apparatuses', and he explained how they work ideologically on each of us in obvious, hidden and invisible ways. These include how ideological state power operates on us in both the public and private spheres of life, and mystifies the suggestion that other forms of socioeconomic organisation other than capitalism such as a zero-growth economy, social democracy, socialism, anarchism or other alternatives are never seriously considered.

We can for the moment regard the following institutions as Ideological State Apparatuses (the order in which I have listed them has no particular significance):

- religious ISA (the system of the different churches),
- educational ISA (the system of the different public and private 'schools'),
- family ISA,
- legal ISA,
- political ISA (the political system, including the different parties),
- trade-union ISA,
- communications ISA (press, radio, television, etc.),
- cultural ISA (literature, the arts, sports, etc). (Althusser 1971, 143)

Althusser's theory of ideology asks the sociology student, why do subjects obey power? Why do people follow the law? Why hasn't there been a revolution against the social inequalities of capitalism? He answers that it is a combination of historical, social and structural forces in the relations between the state and ideological subject formation. In another concept called 'interpellation' he describes how each of us as a subject of power responds to the subject position that the state labels us with. He also describes ideology much as Marx might, as 'the ruling ideas of the ruling class imposed on the other classes' (Althusser 1971, 184–6).

Much sociological research has illustrated how poverty, growing global increases in economic migration and environmental destruction are all produced as a consequence of capitalism and a global market economy. Many sociologists have also documented how a large variety of individuals learn to adapt to the environmental realities and pressures of poverty often through techniques of resourcefulness and 'deviance', which can include many different options from making your own goods to economic redistribution via criminal activities (Gray 2006).

Sociologists have also illustrated how unemployment, low wages and a 'reserve army of surplus labour' are all characteristics of capitalist social relations too. Yet even with this knowledge, capitalism still rules everywhere, and in most societies around the world today the major way poverty and being poor has come to be interpreted is to blame poor people and to stigmatise them for it. This can play out in ways such that their spending decisions are criticised as a reason for being in poverty, or by negatively stereotyping those who are claiming social benefits or using welfare programmes to make ends meet. Or by those in positions of power blaming poor people for homelessness as though homelessness is a choice. Yet by using history and the sociological imagination it becomes clear that poverty is a human invention and its continued existence is also based on decision making involving austerity as a political choice.

Culture and hegemony

Another important way to understand ideological power in the context of the sociological imagination, but also in the context of hidden and invisible power, is to consider the work of Italian neo-Marxist Antonio Gramsci (1971). One of the questions neo-Marxism poses is: if society is so unequal and capitalism so oppressive why has society not overthrown the shackles of such oppression in revolution as Karl Marx predicted it would? For example, where is our three day week and four day weekend? For Gramsci the failure to move beyond capitalism is achieved through our consent to the general direction chosen by those with power over us, which is a process constantly 'won, reproduced and sustained' through a long-term cultural process and system he called 'hegemony'. Gramsci's translated writings do not contain a precise definition of hegemony. In *Selections from the Prison Notebooks* 'hegemony' is referred to as

> the spontaneous consent given by the great masses of the population to the general direction imposed on social life by the dominant fundamental group; this consent is historically caused by the prestige which the dominant group enjoys because of its position and function in the world of production. (Gramsci 1971, 12)

The manufacturing of consent is achieved in the 'internal' and cultural sphere of our existence, through the production of ideas, values, perceptions, prejudices, personal sentiments and beliefs, which drive certain logic and outline the parameters of agreed truth (Herman and Chomsky 2008). A good example of this process in practice is 'common-sense' itself. Tradition is another powerful means through which hegemony is accomplished. It is a deliberately selective process, far from being an inert and passive one. Tradition provides an account of time gone by which is determined to identify with and confirm the present. Tradition provides 'predisposed continuity' (Williams 1994, 600).

Hegemony is not a form of total cultural dominance whereby all alternatives are obliterated. To quote Foucault (cited in Dreyfus and Rabinow 1982, 225), 'there is no relationship of power without the means of escape or possible flight'. The field of culture is where the 'direction' imposed on social life is most contestable and subsequently most open to transformation (Rochon 2000, 9).

New sources of social inequality: contemporary celebrity

Today some sociologists like Kurzman explore and examine new sources of social inequality, which also cut across race, ethnic and gender lines but derive not from class but from status. A good example of this is the contemporary currency associated with celebrity and its interaction with social media and digital platforms. As the authors put it themselves, 'Celebrity is an omnipresent feature of contemporary society, blazing lasting impressions in the memories of all who cross its path' (Kurzman et al 2007, 347).

Their argument goes on to explain that out of the relationship between capitalism and mass media in the mid–20th century a new type of status emerged, not foreseen at the time by Weber, and has grown since into a form of global hierarchy and stratification that can be read like a caste system. This new form of high-ranking status is celebrity, wherein 'members of the high-status group … come to expect obsequious deference, exact significant financial tribute, and lay claim to legal privilege, as aristocratic and caste elites did in earlier centuries' (Kurzman et al 2007, 347). At the same time the observation is also made that this new status system, or new late 20th-century form of nobility, is 'a qualitatively different phenomenon from previous kinds of status systems. Hence, theoretical arguments that have been used to explain more traditional status systems are seen as inadequate to explain and understand the behaviours that are associated with celebrities' (Milner 2010, 379). Not all agree with this take. Milner (2010, 279) himself highlights that the differences between 'traditional and contemporary status systems have been exaggerated'.

Celebrity is of course not a new thing. Kurzman et al (2007, 352) suggest it reaches back to Alexander the Great, 'whose manipulation of publicity and global ambitions may make him "the first famous person"'. Yet it was the invention of photography, and then moving images, which took celebrity from the printed word to a whole new global level and culture that would transform the lives of some in the context of fame and celebrity in ways the printed word never could. In the 20th century with the advent of mass media under capitalism, such as cinema and television and the growth of publicists and public relations (Bernays 1928) such fame exploded in ways never seen before to produce what appeared to many as a new high-status group we today call 'celebrities'. 'Unlike earlier status groups, celebrities are a creature of capitalism: they involve the commodification of reputation' (Kurzman et al 2007, 353).

With time celebrity has come to wash over many more fields other than the films and fashion of its earlier times. By the 1980s, for example, Andy Warhol had modified his famous 1960s idiom 'In the future everyone will be famous for fifteen minutes,' to 'In fifteen minutes everyone will be famous,' to capture a sense that due to the ubiquity of media everyone had a chance to be famous for fifteen minutes (Kurzman et al 2007, 355). Yet what is qualitatively different about celebrity for Kurzman et al as a form of status is that rather than keeping people out, celebrity as a status group is constantly looking for new individuals to recruit into its high-status clique. Today in the 21st century, the internet and various forms of social media have turned celebrity as a form of status into something attainable to anyone in the minds of many, even if today it is a caste hierarchy of A-list, B-list, C-list celebrities and so on. Kurzman et al also suggest four aspects of celebrity that fit 'the general outlines of Weber's analysis' of status groups:

The formation of a high status group, not simply high-status individuals such as heroes or charismatic leaders; the usurpation of 'honor', such that lower-status groups acknowledge the superiority of high-status groups; the monopolization of economic niches, in this case the niche of fame; and the pursuit of legal privilege which celebrities have only just begun. (Kurzman et al 2007, 354)

Their argument goes on to suggest that these aspects of status give celebrities a form of interpersonal and interactional privilege over others in the society. At the same time, it is also important to note that not all sociologists agree with the idea of celebrity being a new form of status and hierarchy qualitatively different from traditional status systems, not least because 'there have long been status systems of the famous' (Milner 2010, 380). As such, celebrities as status groups within a larger status system under capitalism may appear qualitatively distinct from earlier status systems, but for Milner (2010, 385) the sociological 'theory of status relations shows that the same basic status processes are involved in traditional and contemporary systems'. Celebrity for Milner is not a new, more degraded form of status distinct from earlier times. Yes, due to transformations in society, new forms of media and technology it maybe more fluid and unstable with far more turnover than older systems; however, fame in the past can still be seen like celebrity today because fame has always 'been due to a combination of social background, performance, public relations and luck' (Milner 2010, 387)

The sociology of social inequalities

In this chapter and the previous one on power we have seen that in sociology two of the most central concerns of the sociological imagination are what holds societies together? and what drives societies apart? In answering these questions sociology departs from a certain set of basic questions on how society works, one that uses religion to provide answers, and uses secular methods instead. To answer the first question, sociological research explores and examines the history and back story behind social hierarchies, inequalities and division in society and their impacts and connections to social cohesion, social solidarity, caring for each other, mutual recognition and other forms of human cooperation and collectivism. For the second question, sociologists look at the absence of trust, lack of mutual care, social alienation and the power of structural inequalities to drive people apart. Sociologists also explore and examine these questions in line with history and how societies change over time. What drives those changes, how do foundational social divisions and inequalities at the beginning of the modernist tradition such as homophobia, sexism, racism and poverty play out and develop during modernity? And what is the role of such human-made divisions in the establishment and development of contemporary social problems like homelessness, poverty and war?

The sociological imagination works to understand the macro context of how our various societies emerged. Without such context we would simply reinforce and maintain the current system of social and economic inequalities already in the world. Not to mention that such a macro understanding also helps the sociologist to understand the micro level of everyday life –individuals and their agency – who in relation to history can be organised into various social classes based on their access to, and the general distribution of, the economic capital, social capital, cultural capital and symbolic capital they each possess. Not least, because as we saw in this chapter, 'the cognitive structures which social agents implement in their practical knowledge of the social world are internalized, "embodied" social structures' (Bourdieu 1984, 468). Which is another way of understanding social reality: not as the history of the world outside us but also the embodied history inside each of us too.

THINKING SOCIOLOGICALLY

The social world can be conceived as a multi-dimensional space that can be constructed empirically by discovering the main factors of differentiation which account for the differences observed in a given social universe, or, in other words, by discovering the powers or *forms of capital* which are or can become efficient, like aces in a game of cards, in this particular universe, that is, in the struggle (or competition) for the appropriation of scarce goods of which this universe is the site. It follows that the structure of this space is given by the distribution of the various forms of capital, that is, by the distribution of the properties which are active within the universe under study-those properties capable of conferring strength, power and consequently profit on their holder. (Bourdieu 1987, 3–4, emphasis in original)

What was Pierre Bourdieu trying to say here? What forms of capital do you have? How might those forms of capital provide you with strength and power? What capital do you not have and how can that lack of capital make you feel different from others? What might these reflections tell us about the relationship between various forms of capital and how the social world functions??

MINI PROJECT

In his article 'Is Celebrity a New Kind of Status System?' Murray Milner (2010) suggests that the differences between contemporary status systems such as celebrity and the traditional ones are not as different as other academics suggest. He demonstrates why this is the case by recruiting a theory of status relations that was initially developed to explain the Indian caste system and shows how it can explain much of the behaviour associated with celebrities and their fans.

In this case study exercise please research and answer the following questions.

1. What is a status system and what are status groups?

2. What is a caste system and how did it function in India?

3. What is the difference between fame in the past and celebrity today?

4. How can the theory of caste relations help the sociologists to see that while fame and celebrity are distinct, they are more similar than they are different?

TALKING POINTS

In this exercise you must provide examples from your everyday life about how power systems function.

1. Patriarchy

2. Austerity

3. Race science as racism

What are the individual characteristics of these systems?

Which groups are excluded or suffer obstacles that others don't in these various systems?

What can be done to transform these systems of power?

READ ON ...

Rhoda Reddock in 'Radical Caribbean Social Thought: Race, Class Identity and the Postcolonial Nation' (2014) and Cedric J. Robinson *Black Marxism: The Making of the Black Radical Tradition* (2000) both provide insights on black and brown radical sociological traditions. Eudine Barriteau in *Confronting Power, Theorizing Gender: Interdisciplinary Perspectives in the Caribbean* (2003) and of course *The Second Sex* by Simone de Beauvoir (1949) are insightful minds from different eras and locations on gender. Donna Hope 'From Browning to Cake Soap: Popular Debates on Skin Bleaching in the Jamaican Dancehall' (2011) and Margaret L. Hunter *Buying Racial Capital: Skin-Bleaching and Cosmetic Surgery in a Globalized World* (2011) provide sociological analysis of skin bleaching. Audre Lorde *Sister Outsider: Essays and Speeches* (1984b) is a classic capturing so many sociological issues in simple style that everyone should read it at least once. Lauren A. Rivera in *Pedigree: How Elite Students Get Elite Jobs* (2016) explains how opportunity hoarding and privilege intersect. *Migration, Domestic Work and Affect: A Decolonial Approach on Value and the Feminization of Labor* (2010) by Encarnación Gutiérrez-Rodríguez reveals how migrant domestic workers feel about the families they work for and who considers them to be family.

Check the companion website at https://bristoluniversitypress. co.uk/imagining-society-online-resources **for a suggested project and writing task.**

9

The social self

In this chapter, we look at the sociality of the self. This is an issue that we considered earlier (see Chapter 3), and here we explore it in further detail. As we now know, the sociological imagination is grounded in the twin assumptions that individual people's biographies and larger historical processes are intimately connected, and that individual people's personal troubles may often be usefully understood in terms of much more larger-scale social problems. The sociological imagination assumes that there is more to human life than isolated individuals engaging, cooperating, and competing with each other on their own, purely personal terms. If we agree that this is so, then it also seems reasonable to enquire in which ways and to what extent the ostensibly innermost features of human life are bound up with social forces that exist above and beyond the individual: the mind, emotions, and the notions of self and self-identity on which we draw to imagine how we exist in the world as distinct individuals. At the same time, then, it becomes important to ask how the self becomes a site of socially organised differences and inequalities, of class and race and ethnicity and sex and gender and so on as discussed in the previous chapters. Finally, it is necessary to engage with powerful arguments that deny or undermine the sociality of the self. In the early 21st century, the sociological imagination is by no means uncontested, and a range of alternative narratives, from psychology to socio-biology, have captured popular imaginings of human life. If we seek to make a case for the sociological imagination, as we have done in this book, then it is vital to understand these alternative narratives that play such powerful roles in contemporary societies. This, in general terms, is our programme for this chapter.

To an extent, this programme again reflects a Western understanding of social relationships, in the sense that it foregrounds the individual's role within wider social bonds in a way that has frequently been described as a characteristic of societies in certain parts of Europe and the Americas (Bird 1999; Armstrong 2005; Becker and Marecek 2008). It might therefore seem to be at odds with the overall agenda of a book concerned with the sociological imagination on a much broader, global and often decolonial scale. We would argue, however, that engagement with the sociality of the self is important for several reasons. First, the relationship of the Western individual self and wider social process has been central to sociological enquiry from the beginnings of the discipline (Simmel 1950; Cooley 1983; Weber 2001; Durkheim 2005). It is thus difficult to make sense of the sociological imagination without acknowledging its concern with the sociality of the self. Second, as we will explain in the following, the sociological imagination of the self may contribute in important ways to understanding socio-cultural differences between societies (MacFarlane 1978; Brindley 2010; Omobowale and Akanle 2017) as well as global social trends (Elliott and Lemert 2006; Yan 2009).

Popular psychology and the remaking of the social self

The way in which we develop our argument in this chapter is a little different from how we have written most chapters in this book. This chapter builds on our research on popular psychology (Nehring et al 2016; Nehring and Kerrigan 2018a, 2018b). In the early 21st century, popular psychology plays a very important role in defining how people experience self-identity, emotions, and their social relationships with others. Popular psychology consists of a very wide range of commercial products and services – self-help books, personal development workshops, smartphone apps, YouTube channels, newspaper and magazine advice columns, and many more – that draw on psychotherapeutic ideas to advise people on how to organise their everyday lives: how to become happy, how to become rich, how to find lasting love, how to get married, how to get divorced, and so on. The stated objective of popular psychology is to allow individuals to, in some sense, improve their individual personal lives, by revisiting and overcoming personal troubles under the guidance of professional, psychologically motivated life advice (Nehring et al 2016).

Popular psychological products are very widely consumed around the world. Table 9.1 shows the sales of self-help books in seven countries, sorted by sales values in British pounds:

In each of these seven countries, readers bought hundreds of thousands or even millions of self-help books every year and spent millions of pounds on their purchases. In part due to its very sizeable population, people in China spent more than £60,000,000 on life advice guides, and even in South Africa, the country with the lowest sales in the table, readers still bought self-help books for more than £2,000,000. If you add to this the fact that popular psychology is also consumed through many other kinds of media and events, then its cultural influence becomes easily obvious. Therefore, looking at popular psychology in contemporary societies, we can learn about both the organisation of the social self in contemporary societies and about more general features of the sociology of the self. Moreover, this chapter might be read as an – albeit very basic – example of the way in which original social research is written, as it is grounded in our own empirical fieldwork on the transnational diffusion of popular psychology. In this sense, you might find that our discussion in the following showcases sociological writing about an important contemporary social issue.

Table 9.1: Sales of self-help books in seven countries, 2014, sorted by sales values in GBP

Country	Number of copies sold	Sales value (national currency)	Sales value (£)[a]
China	16,209,486	¥ 548,363,984.9	61,695,731.99
UK	2,628,307	£ 24,938,985.89	24,938,985.89
Brazil	2,172,960	R$ 47,095,494.09	10,758,942.20
Australia	682,947	$ 15,733,358.11	8,888,569.700
USA	n/a	$ 9,847,784	7,393,650.40
India	855,026	₹ ₹ 223,685,543.86	2,513,432.0126
South Africa	251,083	R 47,362,969.60	2,463,620.10

[a] The conversion to British Pounds used currency exchange rates in September 2016 and is therefore slightly inaccurate.
Source: Beijing OpenBook (China), personal correspondence; Nielsen BookScan (all other countries), personal correspondence. Adapted from Nehring and Kerrigan (2018a, 2018b).

Social organisation of the self

If we intend to make sense of the social organisation of the self, it is important to consider processes at both the micro and the macro level of social life. By micro level, we mean small-scale social interaction: interaction between individuals in face-to-face encounters and using a variety of media, as well as the cognitive and emotional processes of mental life. In contrast, the macro level of social life refers to large-scale social patterns and processes: society's institutions, social systems, and populations. For example, students' experiences of paying tuition fees and coping with financial pressure would be a subject matter of micro-social analysis, whereas public attitudes towards higher education and the political processes that define higher-education policy are part of macro-sociology.

The social self is organised through processes at both levels. To show this, we will first look at the micro level of social life and return to our discussion of popular psychology. One of the main objectives of popular psychology is to encourage self-transformation in its readers. Drawing on themes and concepts from psychology, medicine and, sometimes, religion, popular psychology encourages its readers to systematically revisit their personal behaviour and to correct it, so as to achieve a sought-after outcome, such as happiness, love, wealth, and so forth (Hochschild 2003; Nehring et al 2016). One very prominent example of this is positive psychology. Part self-help fad and part academic field, positive psychology seeks to encourage 'positive thinking' in its consumers (Held 2004; Reveley 2013; Cabanas and Illouz 2016). In *Positive Thinking*, a self-help book published in the UK in the early 2000s, Susan Quilliam defines her subject matter as follows:

Positive thinking is about more than the thoughts that you have. It is an entire approach to life. It means focusing on the positives in any situation, rather than the negatives. It means thinking well of yourself rather than constantly putting yourself down. It means thinking well of others, and dealing with them positively. It means expecting the best from the world, and trusting it will provide. (Quilliam 2003, 6)

Note that Quilliam here describes positive thinking as 'an entire approach to life'. She asks her readers to comprehensively transform their lives by 'thinking well of yourself rather than constantly putting yourself down'. This proposal to think well of oneself can be explained through sociological notions of the self, as developed by Charles Horton Cooley (1983) and other scholars. Thus, George Herbert Mead (1863–1931), an American philosopher whom we met previously in Chapter 2 and whose work has had considerable influence on sociology all the way to the present day, argued that the self can be usefully understood in terms of a social process:

The self is not so much a substance as a process in which the conversation of gestures has been internalized within an organic form. This process does not exist for itself, but is simply a phase of the whole social organization of which the individual is a part. The organization of the social act has been imported into the organism and becomes then the mind of the individual. It still includes the attitudes of others, but now highly organized, so that they become what we call social attitudes rather than rôles of separate individuals. This process of relating one's own organism to the others in the interactions that are going on, in so far as it is imported into the conduct of the individual with the conversation of the 'I' and the 'me,' constitutes the self. (Mead 1934, 178f.)

The above is an excerpt from *Mind, Self and Society from the Standpoint of a Social Behaviorist*, a collection of his work assembled and published after his death by former students of Mead's. Its language may seem somewhat dated and difficult, but it contains observations about the social organisation of the self that are of fundamental importance to sociology at large. To begin with, note that Mead refers to a 'conversation of gestures'. By this, he means all the social interactions, verbal and non-verbal, through which people engage with each other in everyday life. Social life in this sense is an ongoing process of interaction, grounded in the exchange of such gestures – words, frowns and smiles, the movements of our limbs, and so on. Importantly, Mead (1934, 178) argues that the self forms part of and is constituted through this process of social interaction: 'The organization of the social act has been imported into the organism and becomes then the mind of the individual.' In our minds, as Mead goes on to explain in the following sentence, we organise and re-organise the observable ways in which others respond to us and the ideas we acquire from them, and they become a central part of the social self.

Mead calls this the 'me'; by this, he means the way in which we come to know ourselves through our interactions with others, their responses to us, and the organisation of social behaviour that we learn from them. In turn, Mead labels the ways in which we participate in this process of social interaction as the 'I'; by this, he refers to our very personal, idiosyncratic ways of experiencing and responding to the social world as individuals. The self, for Mead, is part of social interaction, and its organisation cannot be meaningfully analysed without accounting for the social processes of which it forms part.

Susan Quilliam (2003, 6) encourages her readers to capitalise on this sociality of the self. She argues that positive thinking is fundamental to a good life, and that, as quoted above, positive thinking 'means thinking well of yourself rather than constantly putting yourself down'. In other words, she asks her readers to selectively focus on the positive elements of their interactions with others and disregard, as much as possible, the disappointing, uncomfortable or frustrating ones. To use a rather overly simple example, to learn how to think of myself as a good lecturer and build my confidence in the classroom, I might attempt to consistently look at and think about those students who respond well to my lectures and seminar exercises, smiling and taking notes and responding to my questions instead of frowning and texting friends on their smart phones. We can, Quilliam (2003) suggests, define who we are and what our place in society is by voluntarily and consciously reorganising our minds to focus on the, in some sense, positive experiences we gain in our interactions with others.

To this end, she proposes a range of techniques that might remake the way we experience our selves. Consider the following:

Keeping a daily thought diary

To understand how your thoughts affect your moods, create a 'thought diary' in which you keep a written account of your approach to life. In a notebook, write down each thought, with the circumstances that gave rise to it. Next, think about the effect that the thought had on you and write this down too. Look back over this diary at the end of each day, to analyze whether your thoughts and feelings triggered helpful or unhelpful actions. If you reread the diary once a week, you can use the entries to trace your thought patterns, gauge how successfully you are making improvements, and spot where you need to make an extra effort. (Quilliam 2003, 11)

Quilliam here encourages her readers to engage in a continuous process of revising their selves. By keeping a diary and writing down, as she suggests, each thought, the circumstances in which it occurred, and the helpful or unhelpful actions that followed from it, Quilliam's readers may engage in a process of self-conscious reflexion about their mental life lives and modify thought processes that entail undesirable social conduct. For Quilliam, who we are, how we interact with others, and how these interactions determine our life course is open to the individual's voluntary manipulation, 'positive thinking' being the technique of choice.

The example of positive thinking allows us to revisit the notion of the social self and explore it in a little more depth. Read at face value, positive thinking, as Susan Quilliam describes it, is an individual habit of thought. Through techniques such as regular diary writing, Quilliam encourages her readers to reorganise the ways in which they experience their selves and their social relationships with others. However, positive thinking is more than just this. At the same time, it is also a cultural vocabulary (Mills 1940b; Swidler 2003). That is to say an organised set of beliefs, values and norms of conduct that is widely shared within many societies and at the transnational level. Susan Quilliam's *Positive Thinking* (2003) thus forms part of a much wider cultural pattern. Under the label 'positive psychology', positive thinking has become an academic fad, with journals and books, particularly in academic psychology, dedicated to its exploration (Miller 2008; Cabanas and Sánchez-González 2012, 2016). At the same time, positive thinking is a pervasive term in everyday life, in TV programmes, magazines, newspaper advice columns, self-help books, and so on (Nehring et al 2016). It forms part of a yet much bigger 'happiness industry' which, through mass media, consumer culture, and other avenues, is concerned with the promotion of happiness as a central cultural vocabulary for contemporary societies. Explaining just how pervasive this happiness industry has become, Will Davies points out:

> Monitoring our mood and feelings is becoming a function of our physical environment. In 2014, British Airways trialled a 'happiness blanket', which represents passenger through neural monitoring. As the passenger becomes more relaxed, the blanket turns from red to blue, indicating to the airline staff that they are being well looked after. A range of consumer technologies are now on the market for measuring and analysing well-being, from wristwatches, to smartphone, to Vessyl, a 'smart' cup which monitors your liquid intake in terms of its health effects. (Davies 2015, 10)

Davies' work points to the pervasiveness of concerns about happiness and individual wellbeing, on the part of individuals, organisations, and social institutions such as families, states, educational systems, and so forth. Indeed, both our own research (Nehring et al 2016) and that of Davies (2015) and other scholars (Shaw and Taplin 2007; Ahmed 2010; Binkley 2011b; Pérez-Álvarez 2016) suggest that the pursuit of happiness has become central to common sense in contemporary societies. Positive thinking, whether in its popular or in its academic form, constitutes an important part of this pattern, and as such it may play an important role in organising the ways in which we experience our selves in everyday life.

We will have more to say later on about the cultural and political implications of positive thinking in particular and the happiness industry at large. For the moment, what is important to understand is that our individual selves – how we experience who we are, what our place in the world is, and how we relate to other people – are deeply implicated in much broader social processes, relations and structures that develop above and beyond the control and, often, the understanding of any single individual. It is in this sense that the self may be thought of as a social process.

Scholars such as George Herbert Mead (1934), Schubert (2006) and Charles Horton Cooley (1926, 1962, 1983) have played an important part in developing this sociological understanding of the self. Their work has been foundational to the development of 'symbolic interactionism', a strand of sociological theory that has contributed in important ways to the study of the social self and everyday social interaction (Blumer 1969; Denzin 1988; Charon 2009; Knorr-Cetina 2009). There are many other, alternative, and sometimes mutually contradictory, theoretical proposals that sociologists have developed to make sense of the mutual implication of self and social process (Chalari 2017).

At the same time, it is again important to emphasise that the perspective on the social self that we have developed in this chapter draws heavily on theories grounded in Anglo-American sociology and, in turn, social life in the UK and the US. The sociocultural organisation of mental and emotional life differs considerably across societies and across historical time. Thus, for example, important strands of popular psychology in China rely on historically deeply rooted Confucian understandings of the self and interpersonal relationships, which emphasise hierarchies and the promotion of social harmony as central features of social life (Nehring et al 2016). In turn, successful self-help writers in Mexico may build on Catholic religious moral values, which have played a central role in structuring everyday life in Mexico for approximately five centuries (Nehring 2009a, 2009b). While in Trinidad and Tobago the line between religion and self-help materials blends and blurs in the writings of self-help experts and on local bookshelves, with much of the heavy morality of strict Christian teachings, in part because of colonial history and the role of religion in terms of narratives of self-improvement regionally (Nehring et al 2016). However, we do not have the space here to give a comprehensive overview of this diversity in academic theories and popular understandings of the social self. Rather, what seems important is to facilitate an at least basic understanding of the sociality of the self, and of the social and political significance of this sociality.

Self and identity

At this point in our argument, it seems useful to offer a definition of what might be meant by the social self. Definitions specify the meaning of sociological concepts in concise and clearly delineated terms, and it is for this reason that they play an important part in academic debates. At the same time, though, their specificity limits the perspectives from which we may consider a given concept or idea. As we suggested in the preceding section, sociologists have approached the social self from diverse and sometimes contradictory or even mutually exclusive perspectives. The definition we offer in the following is not meant to and cannot reflect this theoretical complexity. Therefore, the most useful way to treat it might be as a stepping stone – as a simplifying introduction that might open up your thinking about a multi-layered and difficult sociological idea.

One basic way to think about the social self, building on Athanasia Chalari's (2017, 78ff.) respective work, is as a socially structured process of thoughts and feelings, as part of which individuals come to view and judge themselves from an external point of view, much as in Charles Horton Cooley's (1983) looking-glass self or in George Herbert Mead's (1934) distinction of the 'I' and the 'me', and to experience themselves as human beings with distinct characteristics. Social processes play a fundamental role in the organisation of the self, from the use of language in our exchanges with others and our internal conversation with our selves, to processes of socialisation in institutions such as families and schools and the role which mass media play in how we experience our selves on a daily basis (Chalari 2009, 2017).

Sociological conceptualisations of the self, such as the one we have just set out, are closely bound up with another important concept: social identity. In an important book on the concept, Richard Jenkins defines social identity as follows:

> 'Identity' denotes the ways in which individuals and collectivities are distinguished in their relations with other individuals and collectivities. 'Identification' is the systematic establishment and signification, between individuals, between collectivities, and between individuals and collectivities, of relationships of similarity and difference. Taken – as they can only be – together, similarity and difference are the dynamic principles of identification, and are at the heart of the human world.' (Jenkins 2014, 18, bullet points omitted)

This definition adds a new element to our discussion in so far as it focuses on the ways in which individuals are, through social processes of identification, bound up with broader social groups, sharing similarities and experiences of such similarities. Through similarities in language, culture, place of origin, and so on, I might identify with other Germans. Given shared intellectual interests and a common way of looking at the world through the sociological imagination, I might identify with other sociologists. And so on. Conversely, however, relationships of identification may also play an important role in constituting group differences. Identifying as a German might set me apart from people of other nationalities. Even though academics from different disciplines all work on the same campus, I rarely associate with geologists, and I share at best a tenuous sense of common scholarly identity with them, as the study of rocks and the ways in which they make up our planet differs so markedly from enquiry into people and the ways in which they make up societies. And so forth.

Both concepts, the self and identity, have played an important role in sociological debates at the international level at least since the 1980s (Lasch 1984; Beck 1986; Giddens 1991; Craib 1994). In part, this growing interest in the self and identity is the outcome of developments in sociological theory. Importantly, though, it also reflects significant changes in contemporary societies themselves. This returns us to arguments that have defined sociology as an academic discipline since its earliest days in the late 18th and early 19th centuries. Since then, as we have shown in previous chapters (see Chapters 4 to 6), sociology, beginning in the Global Northwest, has been fundamentally concerned with the problem of modernity (Comte 2000; Weber 2001; Marx 2008; Simmel 2011; Durkheim 2013a). On the one hand, these changes refer to the long-term consequences of secularisation, industrialisation, the rise of capitalism, and profound political transformation, namely the end of feudalism and the rise and gradual transformation of nation- states. On the other hand, sociologists have long been interested in the de-traditionalisation of societies; that is to say, the waning binding power of institutions, practices, and moral discourses that have long played central roles in structuring societies, such as religion, monarchies and feudal economic systems (Heelas et al 1996). As part of their interest in modernity and the social transformations it entails, sociologists have long shown an interest in both the processes that tie individuals together in communities and the developments that erode the binding power of such collective ties. For example, many of Émile Durkheim's works may be read as an expression of this concern, from his study on suicide (Durkheim 2005) to his enquiry into social solidarity and the division of labour in society (Durkheim 2013a) and his research on the religious life (Durkheim 1995). Alongside the sociological study of modernity, scholars such as the early symbolic interactionists (Cooley 1962, 1983) have for more than a century pointed to the importance of analysing the self from a sociological perspective.

Therefore, it is noteworthy that the sociological study of the self and identity has attracted particular interest since the 1980s (Elliott 2013a). Some prominent sociologists have attributed this to processes of social change that have rendered social identity and, in turn, the social self, precarious. For example, individualisation theorists such as Anthony Giddens (1991, 1992), Ulrich Beck and Elisabeth Beck-Gernsheim (Beck 1992; Beck and Beck-Gernsheim 2002), and Zygmunt Bauman (2000, 2003, 2005) argue that individuals, at least in the global Northwest, have been set free from collective social bonds and obligations to an unprecedented degree. This has given them considerable freedom to fashion their lives as they choose, while simultaneously complicating personal and intimate attachments and burdening them with the need to make do on their own:

> Whatever we consider – God, nature, truth, science, technology, morality, love, marriage – modern life is turning them all into 'precarious freedoms'. All metaphysics and transcendence, all necessity and certainty are being replaced by artistry. In the most public and the most private ways we are helplessly becoming high-wire dancers in the circus tent. And many of us fall. (Beck and Beck-Gernsheim 2002, 2)

While these arguments have been controversially debated (for example, Smart 2007; Atkinson 2008; Lee 2011; Dawson 2012), they have nonetheless had a profound impact on contemporary sociology, and what was initially a topic of conversation among sociologists in the global Northwest is now much more widely debated at the international level (for example, Yan 2009; Halskov Hansen and Svarverud 2010).

Beyond theories of individualisation, psychologist Kenneth Gergen (1991, 2009) has proposed a somewhat similar, sociologically informed argument. Gergen explains that, across historical time, there has been a notable growth in the variety of interpersonal relationships in which individuals may be engaged in their daily lives. This, Gergen explains, is a result of significant social and technological changes:

> A century ago, social relationships were largely confined to the distance of an easy walk. Most were conducted in person, within small communities: family, neighbors, townspeople. Yes, the horse and carriage made longer trips possible, but even a trip of thirty miles could take all day. The railroad could speed one away, but cost and availability limited such travel. If one moved from the community, relationships were likely to end. [...] Through the technologies of the century, the number and variety of relationships in which we are engaged, potential frequency of contact, expressed intensity of relationship, and endurance through time all are steadily increasing. As this increase becomes extreme we reach a state of social saturation. (Gergen 1991, 61)

On the basis of this and related insights, Gergen develops a complex account of the development of the social self and interpersonal relationships today. In this context, one of his most important points concerns the malleability of the social self in the contemporary world: 'As belief in essential selves erodes, awareness expands of the ways in which personal identity can be created and recreated in relationships. The consciousness of construction does not strike as a thunderbolt; rather, it eats slowly and irregularly away at the edge of consciousness' (Gergen 1991, 146).

Popular psychology might be interpreted as a part of the trend that Gergen describes. Self-help guides rely on the assumption that it is both possible and desirable for individuals to refashion their sense of self and, by extension, the ways in which they relate to others. Consider, for example, the 'Fuck It' therapy, a programme of self-help workshops and advice books by John C. Parkin and Gaia Pollini, two former career professionals turned spiritual counsellors. In *F**ck It Therapy*, one of their self-help books, John Parkin (2012) argues that people tend to live in a prison, consisting of beliefs and emotions that unnecessarily restrict their freedom, such as fear, self-doubt and the habit to take life too seriously. Deciding to 'fuck it' and leave behind this prison, Parkin explains, it becomes possible to self-consciously remake one's life. For example, Parkin encourages his readers to abandon their dreary jobs and do what they truly love, making money in the process:

> The idea here, in case you haven't spotted it, is to make money (small or large amounts depending on the desired lifestyle) from doing what you love. [...] [I]t's possible to make money out of just about anything – especially with a variety of modern technologies (zippy ways to make and produce things, and zippy ways to spread the word about things and get your zippy things to zippy people all over the world). Combine the zippy technologies with some imagination and you could end up doing what you love and earning money from it very quickly. (Parkin 2012, e-book part VIII)

Parkin here argues that modern technologies make it possible for creatively minded people to commercialise practically any activities and, thus, to live creatively off the things they truly enjoy doing. This point would hardly have been plausible in, say, in pre-modern, feudal Europe, when a large part of the population was by law and custom bound to the land it farmed and thus practically unable to change its living conditions even in small ways. In the early 21st century, John Parkin's appeal to radically remake one's self and one's life rings much truer, as social boundaries of class, family, place and so forth may be much less compelling than they would have been in pre-modern times.

Of course, Parkin's arguments are still questionable from a sociological point of view – inequalities of race, ethnicity, gender, sexuality, class, and so on play a very significant role in determining individuals' life chances even today, and we would argue that the kind of self-making that Parkin encourages is mostly possible among the class of affluent, internationally mobile professionals to which he belongs (Nehring et al 2016). Nonetheless, at a time at which, following Ulrich Beck and Elisabeth Beck-Gernsheim (2002), 'precarious freedoms' are characteristic of social life to an unprecedented degree, John Parkin's proposal to 'fuck it' and radically change one's life rings may ring true at least at the level of common sense. Popular psychology makes sense to its consumers because it appeals to the new freedoms and uncertainties of the 20th and early 21st centuries.

Place of emotions

So far, we have not said much about another central dimension of contemporary popular psychology, namely its appeal to emotions. It might be argued that the success of popular psychology rests to a significant degree on the fact that promises its consumers happiness, love, security and other emotions that carry powerful positive meanings in contemporary societies. Happiness, for example, is a major subgenre among self-help guides, and a plethora of self-help books, magazines, websites, newspaper advice columns and social media groups propose how you might become a happier self. In *Be Happy*, Robert Holden proposes a meditation technique, the 'happiness circle', to help his readers achieve true happiness. He explains the purpose of this technique as follows:

> The purpose, then, of meditating on the question 'What is happiness?' is to get past the word *happiness*. It is to go beyond your learned ideas and concepts so as to enjoy a direct experience – with your whole being – of what the word *happiness* means. It's like 'happiness' is the sign on the door, and your goal is to actually walk through the door and discover for yourself what happiness really is. This is a powerful journey. Sometimes it means honoring everything you have ever learned; other times it means letting go of everything you think you know. (Holden 2009, e-book chapter 3)

In line with our argument in the preceding section, Holden here assumes that it is possible for his readers to profoundly and comprehensively transform their lives. However, notably, the focus of this transformation is an emotion – happiness, however understood.

This raises important questions. It is common sense to assume that emotions are an internal property of our selves. Emotions might be long-term states, such as the affection we feel for an intimate partner or family members over many years, or the grief we feel after a bereavement. Emotions might be short-term states, such as the boredom you might feel when reading a dreary book or the excitement you might feel when watching a thrilling film. In any case, though, it makes common sense to assume that emotions are simply a feature of who we are as individuals, and that they denote our very personal responses to situations in which we might find ourselves across our life course. However, in line with our overall argument in this chapter, we suggest that emotions are in fact socially organised.

A seminal study on the sociality of emotions is Arlie Russell Hochschild's *The Managed Heart*. Originally published in 1983 in the US, *The Managed Heart* explores how emotions come to form part of the social and economic processes of contemporary capitalism. Hochschild looks at the ways in which emotions are incorporated into the labour done by a wide range of professional groups and, most notably, flight attendants. Along the way, she sets out a range of concepts that may help us understand the sociality of emotion. For example, notably, Hochschild writes of emotion management – in simple terms, the ways in which we may consciously adjust our emotions to suit particular social situations. Hochschild argues that emotion management is not just an individual act. Rather, it is performed in response to socially defined 'feeling rules' that specify how we ought to feel in particular social encounters:

> Acts of emotion management are not simply private acts; they are used in exchanges under the guidance of feeling rules. Feeling rules are standards used in emotional conversation to determine what is rightly owed and owing in the currency of feeling. Through them, we tell what is 'due' in each relation, each role. We pay tribute to each other in the currency of the managing act. In interaction we pay, overpay, underpay, play with paying, acknowledge our dues, pretend to pay, or acknowledge what is emotionally due another person. (Hochschild 2012, 18)

So, for example, when I receive an unwanted birthday gift, I am aware of the feeling rule according to which I ought to express happiness at receiving the gift. In order to please the person who gave me the gift – particularly if I received it from someone I care about – I may adjust my emotions as much as possible to appear pleased.

However, importantly, emotion management and feeling rules are not just individual responses to specific social situations. Rather, they are patterned, often in rigorous ways, by society's institutions. Hochschild explains this complex point as follows:

> But something more operates when institutions are involved, for within institutions various elements of acting are taken away from the individual and replaced by institutional mechanisms. The locus of acting, of emotion management, moves up to the level of the institution. Many people and objects, arranged according to institutional rule and custom, together accomplish the act. Companies, prisons, schools, churches – institutions of virtually any sort – assume some of the functions of a director and alter the relation of actor to director. Officials in institutions believe they have done things right when they have established illusions that foster the desired feelings

in workers, when they have placed parameters around a worker"s emotion memories, a worker"s use of the as if. It is not that workers are allowed to see and think as they like and required only to show feeling (surface acting) in institutionally approved ways. The matter would be simpler and less alarming if it stopped there. But it doesn't. Some institutions have become very sophisticated in the techniques of deep acting; they suggest how to imagine and thus how to feel.' (Hochschild 2012, 49)

The institutional organisation of emotion management has important social and personal consequences. Notably, Hochschild suggests, it may entail a sense of alienation on the part of individuals who are obliged to publicly display certain emotions:

> Beneath the difference between physical and emotional labor there lies a similarity in the possible cost of doing the work: the worker can become estranged or alienated from an aspect of self- – either the body or the margins of the soul- – that is *used* to do the work. The factory boy's boy's arm functioned like a piece of machinery used to produce wallpaper. His employer, regarding that arm as an instrument, claimed control over its speed and motions. In this situation, what was the relation between the boy"s arm and his mind? Was his arm in any meaningful sense his *own?* (Hochschild 2012, 7)

In line with the sociology of self and self-identity, the sociology of emotions has developed into a complex sub-field of the discipline, with multiple and competing explanations of how emotions are socially patterned. Nonetheless, Hochschild's discussion of emotion management and feeling rules continues to make a particularly compelling case for the sociality of emotions. At the same time, it also draws attention to structured inequalities and forms of exploitation that are bound up with the incorporation of emotions into the market exchanges of contemporary capitalism.

The psychological turn and the politics of the self

This bring us to the final point we wish to make in this chapter. We wish to suggest that there are important political implications to the argument that the self is socially organised. Again, popular psychology serves as a case in point. On the preceding pages, we have briefly looked at a range of self-help guides that promise their consumers significant improvements to their lives, however defined. We have also pointed to the extensive consumption of popular psychological materials in contemporary societies, and we have suggested that pop psy, in turn, forms part of a yet bigger happiness industry that encourages us to consume a diverse array of products and services ostensibly meant to make us happy, as a strategy and mechanism of capital accumulation, and making money on an industrial scale.

Happiness, alongside positive thinking and other key terms of popular psychology, perhaps constitutes a highly influential cultural vocabulary in the world today. Elsewhere, we have termed this cultural vocabulary the 'psychological imagination' (Nehring et al 2016; Nehring and Kerrigan 2018b). By this we mean the ways in which psychologically and psychotherapeutically informed categories organise the ways in which we think about, feel about, and experience our selves and our relationships with others. We argue that the psychological imagination plays an increasingly dominant role in contemporary social life, from the Americas to Western Europe, informing as a 'moral grammar' how we practise our intimate relationships, how we work, or even how governments develop policies to address their citizens' wellbeing (Yang 2012; Nehring et al 2016). This is politically significant because it makes a large difference whether we consider, say, marriage in terms of a psychologically informed vocabulary of happiness, co-dependency and so forth, or whether we make sense of it in terms of socio-political categories of class, ethnicity, gender, and so on. In other words, if we come to experience our selves in terms of a purely personal, psychological vocabulary, it becomes difficult to make sense of the ways in which our selves may be a terrain for social inequalities and forms of exploitation.

At the same time, the growing influence of the psychological imagination may make it difficult for alternative, sociological arguments to be publicly recognisable. If we predominantly consider work in terms of the question whether it makes us happy or not, as the 'fuck it' therapy (Parkin 2012) does, then it may be difficult to simultaneously take stock of the social inequalities that permeate the world of work, and to use the sociological imagination to explain these inequalities. The psychological language of the self may obscure the fact that the self is also in important ways a social process.

THINKING SOCIOLOGICALLY

In this chapter, we have offered a critical perspective on positive psychology. In this exercise, we invite you to consider its origins, uses, and social and political implications for yourself. You will need to do some background research to answer this question. For this, you will be able to find a very wide variety of academic sources and non-academic publications.

1. What is positive psychology? What are its uses in contemporary societies?

2. Positive psychology may prevent its users from making sense of the ways in which our selves may be a terrain for social inequalities and forms of exploitation. Do you agree? Why (not)?

MINI PROJECT

For this exercise, you will work in groups. It will require you to conduct substantial background research. Take a look at the following questions. Then search for relevant information to answer these questions, looking at, first, academic libraries and databases and, second, other media, for example through an online search. Once you have read enough, please prepare a poster on which you display your answers. Be creative about the design of the poster, the examples you use, and the media you draw on to showcase your examples. The questions to consider are:

1. 'The socio-cultural organisation of mental and emotional life differs considerably across societies and across historical time' (Nehring et al 2016, 9). How so? Can you think of any examples that might illustrate this?

2. To what extent and in which ways is there a Chinese conception of the self? How, if at all, does it differ from the social organisation of the self in your society?

TALKING POINTS

1. **The social self** This is the key term of this chapter. What does it mean? Can you illustrate it with examples?

2. **Popular psychology** What is popular psychology? How, if at all, have you encountered it in everyday life?

3. **The psychological imagination** What did do we mean by the 'psychological imagination'? How does it differ from the sociological imagination?

4. '[I]f we come to experience our selves in terms of a purely personal, psychological vocabulary, it becomes difficult to make sense of the ways in which our selves may be a terrain for social inequalities and forms of exploitation.' [p 181]
   – What is this statement trying to say?
   – Can you think examples?
   – Do you agree? Why (not)?

5. In many countries around the world, there is increasing concern about a mental health crisis among students. Try to find more information about this issue. Is it regarded as a problem in your country? How might we use sociological arguments about the self and social change to explain this mental health crisis?

READ ON ...

There is a wide variety of introductions to the sociology of self and self-identity. Among these Athanasia Chalari's *The Sociology of the Individual* (2017), Anthony Elliott's *Concepts of the Self* (2013b) and Stephanie Lawler's *Identity: Sociological Perspectives* (2014) stand out. Anthony Elliott's *Identity Troubles* (2015) offers an important account of contemporary transformations of self-identity. For examples of locally specific changes in the organisation of the social self, see *Deep China: The Moral Life of the Person*, edited by Arthur Kleinman and colleagues (2011). On the role of psychological knowledge in contemporary societies, see Eva Illouz's *Saving the Modern Soul* (2008) and Nikolas Rose's *Our Psychiatric Future* (2018).

 **Check the companion website at** https://bristoluniversitypress. co.uk/imagining-society-online-resources **for a suggested project and writing task.**

10

Sociology in the early 21st century

In the preceding chapters, we have mainly looked at sociology as a diverse world of ideas. In this concluding chapter, we complete our portrait of sociology by looking at it instead as a form of work, and by considering how this work is structured by the organisational setting of universities, in which it most commonly takes place. We argue that sociological labour has an important political dimension, and we suggest that sociology today is facing a significant crisis that is due to important and ongoing shifts in the way that universities operate.

All this makes for an unusual conclusion to an introduction to sociology. Unless you are a professional academic yourself, you may wonder why you should take an interest in the way universities operate, or in the behind–the–scenes politics of sociological research. You may be studying for a sociology degree, with no intention at all to remain at university after you have graduated, and you may therefore feel that your connection to the academic world will be short-lived. Even so, we feel that what we have to say in this chapter is important to you.

Sociology is different from technical and vocational disciplines, such as, say, nursing or accountancy, which are primarily concerned with teaching students skills that prepare them for the world of work. While sociology does contain such skills, it is just as much about enabling students to think independently and critically about the social world, using the sociological imagination. Studying sociology is about channelling your curiosity in the social world and using your imagination to make sense of your everyday experiences. Notably, sociology is also about developing a critical mindset, coming to understand the social dimensions of major forms of difference, division and inequality. This is what the sociological imagination is all about. Here, we argue that academic sociology's capacity to promote the sociological imagination is undermined in significant ways by changes that are taking place in universities today. These changes affect you directly, and it therefore seems indicated to examine them in detail.

Sociological labour

In the preceding chapters, we largely considered sociology as a body of knowledge and also a body of knowledge that has gone through much recent decolonial and bottom-up introspection. As a body of knowledge, sociology comprises, first, concepts and theories that orient the sociological imagination towards particular dimensions of social life. For example, Émile Durkheim's 'social facts' emphasise the ways in which large-scale institutional arrangements define human life; Karl Marx's and Friedrich Engels' class struggle emphasises the conflicts produced by these arrangements; Max Weber's interpretive understanding of social action foregrounds the subjective meanings motivating individuals' actions and interactions, while Gurminder Bhambra's more 21st-century 'connected sociologies' approach builds decolonial critiques of Eurocentrism to better understand the shared sociological present, and so on (see Chapters 3 and 8). Second, as a body of knowledge, sociology draws on methodologies of empirical enquiry to observe and record social life at first-hand, and to analyse these observations, to document and explain patterns, regularities, changes, cultural meanings and so forth. Academic publications, such as articles in academic journals and books by academic publishing houses, usually refer to one or both of these two levels of sociological knowledge.

All this is essential to understand what sociology is about. However, it is equally essential to consider the institutional structures and processes through which academic sociological knowledge is produced and reproduced (Ray 2018). In other words, it is important to think about sociology as work and to analyse sociological labour from a sociological perspective.

Sociological labour tends to be invisible in academic publications, or to feature in a limited way. Publications with a primarily theoretical focus for the most part offer very few insights into the labour through which they were composed and the institutional circumstances under which their authors performed this labour. Publications that result from empirical enquiry generally do account for the labour that preceded them. However, they do this in a restrictive way, from a methodological perspective, documenting the research strategies that their authors used and certain institutional processes, such as the approval of the studies in question by universities' research ethics boards. In some more recent sociological research, there has also been a tendency for researchers to reflect critically on power relations in the context of the research process and on the personal implications of their research for their participants and themselves (Liamputtong 2010; Farrer 2013; Gerrard et al 2016). However, sociological publications that reach beyond such concerns to examine the politics of sociological labour are relatively rare (Punch 1986; Denzin and Giardina 2006; Holmwood 2010, 2011). This gap would not matter in a time in which sociology's academic identity and the norms, values, beliefs and practices organising sociological labour were largely settled and unproblematic. However, given that universities in general and sociological labour in particular are at present undergoing cataclysmic changes, it does become important to ask how sociologists go about their day-to-day work within the university system, how their work is structured by the academic environment in which they work, and what implications this may have for sociology as a discipline and as a way of imagining the world. This is particularly so in a time when, as we will show later, sociology is fading from public life and is coming under intense pressure in academic life.

To a significant degree, professional sociologists do sociology at universities. There are, of course, independent researcher centres, governmental and non-governmental organisations that recruit sociologists to contribute to their research, schools and colleges at which sociologists teach, and so on. There is also the field of public sociology that distinctly wants to catch non-academic audiences, away from students and fellow sociologists, and encourages the sociologist to take what they know and to share sociological knowledge in non-academic settings to empower those who are less powerful. Nonetheless, it is easy to conclude that the most important sociologists have been and are sociologists working at universities and that the most seminal works of sociology have been and are written at universities. Therefore, in order to understand how sociology is changing and why it might find itself in crisis, we have to take into account broader transformations that are affecting universities at large.

Big business: the remaking of social life

Over the past forty years, societies around the world have been remade in economic market terms from the top down and the bottom up. Realms of social life that once held a meaning and followed a purpose of their own – art, family life, sports, show business, religion, anything you might think of – have come to form part of capitalist market exchanges, and their meaning and purpose are now defined by the logic of business and entrepreneurship (Bröckling 2007). The much-cited marketplace of capitalism has colonised and substituted society, and an ever-expanding range of social interactions and expressions of human creativity have been reduced to an exchange of commodities in the pursuit of profit (Dardot and Laval 2013; Haiven 2014).

This process of marketisation has been discussed extensively by scholars, journalists, politicians and many others (Nussbaum 2010; Collini 2017). While the preceding paragraph depicts marketisation in rather abstract terms, its everyday expressions are easily demonstrated. For starters, let us again consider video games as an analogy. Video games have always involved financial concerns of some sort on the part of the companies producing and selling them. However, these concerns have intensified considerably in recent years. This intensification is visible in a marked shift in the language in which video games are discussed in public life, using financial terminology. One example of this is the pervasive use of the term 'franchise'. A franchise is, in the terminology of business, a licence allowing a business to operate under the trademark of another, typically more sizeable, business and use its operating procedures. Restaurant and café chains such as McDonald's, Starbucks and KFC are examples of globally prominent franchise businesses. However, the term is now also widely used to discuss video games. Consider the following opening paragraph to a recent piece on IGN, a website that publishes entertainment news:

> Sonic is back, but for real this time. Sonic Forces will let us all live out our Sonicverse fantasies, and no doubt span an incredible new cache of fan stories and custom character art. It's just what fans do. Likewise, Sonic Mania has a summer 2017 release date. But Sega has a rich catalog of similarly incredible and beloved franchises and games, which they've recently promised to dip into in the form of revivals and reboots. Here's a list of the ones we most want to see revived by Sega. (Macy 2017)

Video games are about entertainment, the artistic creativity of the programmers, coders and designers who make them and so on. The article in IGN acknowledges all this when it discussed the Sonic games, but, strikingly, it then refers to the Sega company's 'rich catalogue of similarly incredible and beloved franchises and games', shifting to financial language. Using terms like 'franchise', the everyday discussions of entertainment media like video games but also other creative cultural industry outputs like books, movies, music and much more, now all foreground the economic side of their production and consumption.

Consider football. Football's precursors have a long history dating back to medieval Europe, and the modern game as it emerged in the 19th and early 20th centuries in countries like Germany, Great Britain, Italy, Argentina or Brazil had much to do with the social identity of the urban working classes of that period (Giulianotti 1999; Tomlinson and Young 2006). Yet today's global football is in important ways a business, and football players are self-made entrepreneurs who play the game in pursuit of lucrative deals and riches (Giulianotti and Robertson 2007). The business news website Forbes has little to say about the footballing achievements of Neymar, one of the superstars of the game; instead, it offers an appraisal of his financial achievements in its list of the world's highest paid athletes:

> The Brazilian superstar's current contract has him tied to Barcelona through 2021. He has also secured his place into the next decade with his long-term commercial endorsements. The 25-year old is the only soccer player to earn more off than on the pitch, including from global sponsors Nike, Gillette, Panasonic and Beats by Dre. He was the first soccer player to have his own custom Air Jordan sneakers made by the Swoosh. (Forbes 2017)

Thus, as in the case of video games, economic considerations have become central to the world of football.

On a much larger scale still, in the early 21st century, societies may convert their entire popular culture into a commodity to be traded in the pursuit of economic gain and development. South Korea's commodification of its popular culture, from food to pop music, is a case in point (Kwon and Kim 2013; Jin and Yoon 2014). Poor in natural resources, South Korea's remarkable economic prosperity instead relies on the export of high-tech products, such as cars or smart phones, and on the marketisation of its popular culture. A business analyst at the American news service CNBC summarises this strategy as follows:

> How did a country with a relatively small population, living in an area only a little bigger than Indiana, become a popular culture giant, influencing global habits from hairstyles to fried chicken? Euromonitor's experts have studied South Korea's outsize impact on consumer goods, discovering the strategies that pushed the Asian nation to the forefront of cool and supported the sales of its consumer products. Here's how Korean FMCG (fast-moving consumer goods) companies built their brand cachet: Product placements in trendsetting Korean dramas has helped boost sales of everything from food such as fried chicken to beauty products. 'The most unique and interesting strategy for South Korea manufacturers and government is South Korea's pop-culture, from the hit song, "Gangnam Style" to the latest popular drama series, "Descendents [sic] of the Sun",' wrote Singapore-based Euromonitor International research manager Warangkana Anuwong. 'K-Pop has increased awareness regarding Korean products and lifestyles among audiences around the world. This soft approach has helped the Korean government set up companies and brands to succeed in other countries, since consumer demand is already prevalent globally. (Tan 2016)

Therefore, as a result of South Korea's economic development strategy, elements of daily life that apparently have little to do with the world of business, such as food or cosmetics or pop songs, have become part of economic transactions. The taste of a particular dish or the artistic merits of a certain song now do not matter in their own right anymore. Rather, what counts primarily in South Korea is the way in which the distinctive taste of its cuisine and the catchy music of its song may be used as instruments in the pursuit of economic gain.

As we have seen in this book the marketisation of social life is the outcome of a decisive and global shift, from the 1970s onwards, in the policies of national governments and international organisations, the language of public life, the patterns of economic activity and the common sense that guides individuals through everyday life. This shift entailed the majority of the world adopting a particular Western body of economic, political and social theories that in earlier chapters we have grouped under the label 'neoliberalism' and that play out in similar but distinct ways in societies around the world. One of the central assumptions of neoliberal theorising is the notion that the largely unrestricted operation of markets – the institutions, technical systems and social relationships through which goods and services are exchanged – is fundamental to the economic welfare of a given society, as well as to the freedom of its members. Friedrich August Hayek, an Austrian economist and one of neoliberalism's most important theorists, expressed this notion as follows:

> There is no other possibility than either the order governed by the impersonal discipline of the market or that directed by the will of a few individuals; and those who are out to destroy the first are wittingly or unwittingly helping to create the second. (Hayek 2001, 205)

Hayek here makes an important distinction between 'the impersonal discipline of the market'– that is, the economic processes that determine prices, the allocation of goods and services, the success or failure of a business, and so on – and 'the will of a few individuals' – that is, the decisions and policies of governments that may seek to control economic processes. Hayek showed a clear distaste for the latter and emphasised the need to restrict markets as little as possible.

This must be read in the context of the period in which Hayek was writing, as a warning against the catastrophic consequences of fascist and communist totalitarianism during the first half of the 20th century. However, the wariness of Hayek and other neoliberal theorists like the North American economist Milton Friedman regarding the role of government and the state in economic processes has had lasting consequences. Beginning with localised economic experiments during the military dictatorship in Chile from 1973 onwards, neoliberalism gained influence among political and economic elites and the governments of countries such as the US, China and the UK (Harvey 2007), and it has arguably retained its global dominance to date (Mirowski 2013). Neoliberalism's dominance on the battlefield of ideas has had specific consequences across all of society, such as:

- *Deregulation* An emphasis, on the part of international organisations and national governments, on the deregulation of markets; in other words, abolishment of laws and regulations that might structure, regulate or constrain market exchanges between private actors (Harvey 2007).
- *Privatisation* The privatisation of public services such as healthcare or public transport; that is, their conversion from public goods into privately owned businesses, whose prices, services and so forth are determined by concerns about profit (Cottom 2017), rather than human or citizens' rights and public welfare (Harvey 2007; Peck 2010)
- *Marketisation* In part as a consequence of privatisation, the progressive incorporation of previously unrelated institutions and social processes into

market exchanges and their instrumentalisation in the pursuit of profit in these market exchanges, as outlined earlier for video games, football and Korean popular culture (Peck 2010; Haiven 2014)

- *Entrepreneurialism* An emphasis in public life, on the part of governments, international organisations, mass media and so on, on individual self-reliance over public welfare. Individuals are encouraged to act according to the rules of the capitalist marketplace, defined by the values of individualism, competition, self-reliance and autonomous individual choice. Neoliberal public discourse portrays individuals as entrepreneurs who manage their own lives as one would manage a business. (Binkley 2011a; Nehring et al 2016)

- *Economism* Neoliberalism is not only a political and economic programme, but it also has profound cultural consequences, in that it organises the way in which we understand society and our social relationships and interactions. In other words, neoliberalism's dominance means that its foundational assumptions – individualism, competition, self-reliance and autonomous individual choice – come to be taken for granted as the basic principles of human life. They turn into common sense, and it becomes difficult to imagine society in any other way. (Dardot and Laval 2013)

Of course, the ascent of neoliberalism has not left universities untouched, and the four principles of neoliberal social life – individualism, competition, self-reliance and autonomous individual choice – very much shape academic life in the contemporary world, with important consequences for sociologists old and new.

The crisis of sociology

To explore what neoliberalism's dominance means for sociology, we concentrate on developments in British society and at British universities. In this context, we also return to our discussion of the psychological imagination and its growing influence across society. The developments we describe here operate on a global scale, and they increasingly affect sociologists worldwide. However, the British case is of particular interest because the marketisation and privatisation of British society has been particularly profound. Britain's turn to neoliberal government began at the end of the 1970s, when the Conservative Party won a general election and a government led by Margaret Thatcher rose to power. Thatcher was an enthusiastic proponent of neoliberalism. In his analysis of neoliberalism's rise to global dominance, David Harvey describes Thatcher's political programme as follows:

> In May of that year Margaret Thatcher was elected in Britain with a strong mandate to reform the economy. Under the influence of Keith Joseph, a very active and committed publicist and polemicist with strong connections to the neoliberal Institute of Economic Affairs, she

accepted that Keynesianism had to be abandoned and that monetarist 'supply-side' solutions were essential to cure the stagflation that had characterized the British economy during the 1970s. She recognized that this meant nothing short of a revolution in fiscal and social policies, and immediately signalled a fierce determination to have done with the institutions and political ways of the social democratic state that had been consolidated in Britain after 1945. This entailed confronting trade union power, attacking all forms of social solidarity that hindered competitive flexibility (such as those expressed through municipal governance, and including the power of many professionals and their associations), dismantling or rolling back the commitments of the welfare state, the privatization of public enterprises (including social housing), reducing taxes, encouraging entrepreneurial initiative, and creating a favourable business climate to induce a strong inflow of foreign investment (particularly from Japan). There was, she famously declared, 'no such thing as society, only individual men and women' – and, she subsequently added, their families. All forms of social solidarity were to be dissolved in favour of individualism, private property, personal responsibility, and family values. The ideological assault along these lines that flowed from Thatcher's rhetoric was relentless. 'Economics are the method', she said, 'but the object is to change the soul.' (Harvey 2007, 22f.)

David Harvey portrays Thatcherism as a political programme that set out to remake British society from the top down, using government policy to transform both society's institutions and individuals' everyday beliefs, values and social relationships. To cut a long story short, Thatcherism was extraordinarily successful. Institutions that were once publicly owned, such as healthcare, education, public transport, or the provision of water, electricity, postal and telephone services, have been fully or partially privatised and today operate, for the most part, as for-profit businesses. The welfare state that once provided a sizeable part of Britain's population with the means for daily survival, for example through a generous public housing programme and free public healthcare, today finds itself on the verge of collapse. At the same time, nearly forty years of neoliberal government have reorganised the prevailing common sense, and social life – football, the arts, education, immigration, video games, politics, anything – has come to be understood as a series of economic transactions. Business is everywhere, and everything is business.

Consequently, in British public life, narratives dominate that reinforce neoliberalism's core values – individualism, competition, self-reliance and autonomous individual choice. In particular, economic, psychological and neurobiological explanations of human behaviour receive widespread attention. In the economic field 'rational choice theory' – the idea that human actors always engage in transactions that they perceive will leave them better off – came to dominate how economists imagine the world, and the Hobbesian selfish human being rather than a more selfless human being or one somewhere in between, has come to hold most power in economic explanations of human behaviour.

The psychological take on human behaviour, already discussed in Chapter 9, is also often criticised for rational choice theories of human behaviour. In the main, psychology is also critiqued for omitting the larger social context and cultural relativity of various societies, to promote instead an ahistorical and psychological explanation of human behaviour. This imaginary is at times criticised for removing the relationship between socialisation and the individual, and instead being mostly focused on the individual and the development of their brain.

Both economics and psychology as taught in the academy might be described as falling back on the mystification of statistical work to give their approaches to understanding human behaviour added positivistic legitimacy, and an appearance of the natural sciences. However, both economics and psychology are critiqued for their incomplete representations of human beings as primarily competitive, self-interested individuals because both social sciences often fail to consider the larger social context within which individuals live their lives and practise their freedoms.

Furthermore, economics and psychology can be described genealogically as bedfellows of traditional 19th century liberalism and foundational supports for capitalism and contemporary neoliberalism (Davies 2015). At the same time both economics and psychology are criticised for their tendencies to ignore history and sociology in making their pronouncements on the world. Rather than a politics of the economy, or political economy as it is more traditionally called, which can tell us who gets what, when and how in society, we are left with economic and psychological imaginations of human behaviour that take neoliberal markets and capitalism as natural – two issues that are predominately sociological. Feelings, behaviours and brains to the sociologist are not adequate by themselves to imagine the world and the human beings in it, because feelings, behaviours and brains are formed in part socially (Davies 2018). Thus as this book has demonstrated, your ability to be happy for example, is not simply about you as an individual and how you feel, although that is of course important, but it also depends on your relations to the social and various forms of capital, relationships, education, family and much more that are connected to your life and the social hierarchies of modern living.

Another way of imagining the world that has similar problems to the economic and psychological ways of imagining society is neuroscience and neurobiology, which it has been suggested reduce the psychological to the biological and contain the idea that all experiences such as happiness, sadness, love and so on are simply physical occurrences in the brain. Once again, this removes the social context for why we feel how we do in our lives, and is replaced by some inner code and quantifiable data without any link to the social and society within which people live. This is then supposedly able to predict and produce knowledge about why people experience various feelings. Ironically, or perhaps at the behest of more ideological and capitalist processes, the pronouncements and voices with regard to how economists, psychologists and neurobiologists imagine the world are the loudest in the social sciences, and it would seem much louder than sociological ways of understanding society.

In this sense we are concerned with a fundamental problem, namely the fading of sociology from public view. As the public visibility of sociology declines, so does its ability to shape public debates and promote the sociological imagination as a way of imagining everyday social relationships. Today, for example, psychological arguments about mental health, emotional wellbeing and happiness are widely visible and popular, as the case study on the mindfulness fad (Chapter 3) suggested. It seems at the very least doubtful that the same could be said for sociology. Psychology, with its emphasis on individual solutions to individual life problems, fits the ethos of our neoliberal times. Sociology, with its emphasis on the collective, shared, institutional dimensions of social life, does not. Therefore, it is particularly important for sociologists to make a case for the sociological imagination and its relevance to politics, civic life and our everyday social relationships, lest sociology become a niche discipline of interest to a few scholars only.

From *Bildung* to the entrepreneurial university

The disappearance of sociology from public life is just one manifestation of its current crisis, however. In order to fully understand the waning of sociology, it is necessary to look at institutional transformations that have taken place within universities over the past forty years. In very broad terms, these transformations can be described as the remaking of universities according to the political programme of neoliberalism, in terms of their institutional objectives, their structure, and the day-to-day activities that characterise academic labour (Giroux 2015).

Contemporary universities have their historical roots in Europe. Evolving from Christian religious schools in Italy and other European societies from the 11th century onwards, early universities were dedicated to the study of theology, philosophy, law and a relatively limited number of other academic disciplines (de Ridder-Symoens 1992). From the 16th century onwards, the Western model of the university began its journey around the world through European colonial conquest; the *Universidad Nacional Mayor de San Marcos* (National University of San Marcos) in Peru was founded in 1551, making it the oldest university in the Americas and outside Europe.

Then, in the 18th and early 19th centuries, higher education came to be associated with the political and cultural programme of the Enlightenment. At a time of great political upheaval and, following the end of the Napoleonic Wars, political repression on the part of resurgent monarchic governments, a central concern for scholars came to be academic freedom. Academic freedom refers to scholars' ability to generate knowledge and disseminate it freely through teaching, academic publications and public interventions without fear of reprisal from government and academic authorities in the form of censorship, loss of employment, imprisonment and so on. Academic freedom is central to the pursuit of truth through rigorous enquiry, without 'truth' being determined by the will of powerful groups and individuals.

Alongside academic freedom, a central concern of the Enlightenment was the reconceptualisation of scholarship as the cultivation of educated and therefore autonomous and critically aware individuals. In this sense, scholarship came to be tied to the democratic civic ideal of the educated citizen able to make sense of and participate in public life on the basis of her or his education. In general terms, this ideal is expressed in Enlightenment writings such as Immanuel Kant's famous essay 'Answering the Question: What is Enlightenment?'

> Enlightenment is man's emergence from his self-imposed nonage. Nonage is the inability to use one's own understanding without another's guidance. This nonage is self-imposed if its cause lies not in lack of understanding but in indecision and lack of courage to use one's own mind without another's guidance. *Dare to know! (Sapere aude.)* 'Have the courage to use your own understanding,' is therefore the motto of the enlightenment. (Kant 1784)

Here and throughout the remainder of the essay, Kant is sharply critical of intellectual dependence. He characterises such dependence as 'self-imposed', in so far as he assumes that all human beings possess intellectual faculties that can be cultivated, in order to enable them to govern their lives autonomously.

This ideal of intellectual self-cultivation, as expressed by Kant and others, had a profound influence on universities. Notably, for example, the Prussian scholar and government official Friedrich Wilhelm von Humboldt (1767–1835) relied on it in his reforms of Prussia's education system and the establishment of the University of Berlin. Humboldt's ideal of scholarship is often referred to with the German word *Bildung*, which is most simply translated as 'education', but, in difference from the English word, it carries a double meaning, in that it refers both to the accumulation of knowledge and, in a more holistic sense, to the cultivation of educated, critically aware individuals who are able to participate actively in civic life (Sorkin 1983). Universities thus came to play a pivotal role in long-term processes of democratisation and civil society formation, both in Europe and around the world.

Today, after forty years of neoliberal university reform, it has become quaint to speak of higher education in terms of *Bildung*, and scholarship now serves entirely different purposes. Commenting on the state of British universities, sociologist John Holmwood argues that 'the only functions that are now recognised for universities – whether by policy makers or senior university leaders – are the development of human capital and the enhancement of economic growth' (Holmwood 2017). British universities, for example, have been systematically marketised and ranked, in the sense that government, higher education managers and administrators and, increasingly, academics and students now understand scholarship as a series of commercial exchanges in a highly competitive academic marketplace. On the part of students, to invest in a degree means to invest a considerable amount of money in tuition fees, in return for which a degree with good grades and good job must be expected. On the part of academics, to pursue a career in research and teaching means to compete with other academics for scarce resources by which success is determined and careers are made or broken – research grant funding, articles in prestigious journals, great student satisfaction scores in universities' internal surveys and the annual National Student Survey (NSS), high scores in the Research Excellence Framework (REF) and so on. On the part of university administrators, to run a university means much the same as managing any other business as universities compete with each other for ranks in league tables, scores in the NSS and REF, star scholars, students and grant income, and enthusiastically announce their claims to excellence and world leadership in marketing brochures and websites. On the part of governments, finally, higher education policy has meant withdrawing public funding from higher education, encouraging universities to pursue alternative sources of income – for example, from tuition fees or research grants – and promoting the view among students, lecturers and administrators that the purpose of higher education lies in its contribution to economic gain, value-added and the often unfulfilled promise of individual social mobility.

Thus, universities have been comprehensively privatised, in the sense that scholarship has ceased to be understood as a contribution to public life as intended by Humboldt, and in the sense that the achievements of scholarship – a degree certificate, an academic publication, a research grant – serve entirely private ends. A degree certificate supposedly gets students a job and a better income, an article in a prestigious journal or a big grant may land lecturers a stable job or a promotion, and administrators may use students' and lecturers' achievements to claim success in this or that audit, ranking or marketing operation.

It is in reference to all these issues that commentators have in recent years written of 'academic capitalism' and the rise of 'entrepreneurial universities' that are immersed in the world of business. Henry Etzkowitz, a leading advocate of the entrepreneurial university, describes it development as follows:

> There are three stages and phases to the development of the university as an entrepreneur, with each modality building upon the other in a usual but by no means necessary order. In an initial phase (University Entrepreneur One), the academic institution takes a strategic view of its direction and gains some ability to set its own priorities, either by raising its own resources through donations, tuition fees and grant

income or through negotiations with resource providers. […] In a second phase (University Entrepreneur Two), the academic institution takes an active role in commercializing the intellectual property arising from the activities of its faculty, staff and students. […] In a third phase (University Entrepreneur Three), the academic institution takes a proactive role in improving the efficacy of its regional innovation environment, often in collaboration with industry and government actors. (Etzkowitz 2004, 488)

In Etzkowitz's account, the intellectual and civic dimensions of scholarship do not feature. Instead, he portrays universities as motors of economic growth that strategically commercialise scholarship for their own economic benefit and that of the businesses and public institutions with which they cooperate. Elsewhere in his account, Etzkowitz is explicitly dismissive of earlier understandings of universities' role in society, and it is obvious that his entrepreneurial university is far removed from the Humboldtian ideal of *Bildung*. Etzkowitz's work arguably represents a broad trend in contemporary discourses, policies and practices of higher education. Their common feature is that they understand universities as businesses and nothing else. What happens to sociology and the production of sociological knowledge under academic capitalism? Why is this a crisis for sociology?

Sociological labour in the entrepreneurial university

Academic capitalism has direct implications for the way in which university sociologists work. The sociological imagination is closely related to the classical university's ideal of *Bildung*. *Bildung* is all about the formation of individuals who have the intellectual abilities necessary to understand and participate in civic life. In other words, it is about the cultivation of responsible citizens able to and interested in looking beyond their immediate personal concerns and engage with broader, collective, social and political concerns. Such citizens and their collectivism play a crucial role in the functioning of a democratic society. Sociology has a significant role to play in all this because it asks its students to understand individual biographies in relation to broader historical processes, and to understand individual life events in terms of larger, social–structural patterns (Mills 1959).

However, in the contemporary university and under its new pressures and concerns, sociologists are not any longer meant to critically engage with civic life or to contribute to the education of responsible citizens. As with other academics, university sociologists are required to act as entrepreneurs who contribute and act strategically in the pursuit of their own success and that of the academic business owners at which they are employed. This shift towards an entrepreneurial model of sociological labour manifests itself in several ways in everyday working life and each produces certain consequences for the production of sociological knowledge.

Top-down management

Critical sociological enquiry requires autonomy on the part of scholars, in terms of the definition of research topics, the development of research strategies to pursue these topics, and the planning of publication strategies. This autonomy constitutes a central element of what we have previously labelled as academic freedom. In contrast, contemporary British universities make extensive use of performance management, setting targets with which academics have to comply, in terms of income generated through research grants, publications in highly recognised journals, and so on.

In part, these targets are economic – academics today are often expected to recover at least the value of their own salary in research grants – and in part they are meant to contribute to their universities' prestige by adding to various rankings and league tables (Holmwood 2010). Some universities also distinguish strategically between scholars who are allowed to be 'research active' and scholars who are prevented with high teaching loads from contributing to sociological enquiry.

Finally, as part of universities' shift to top-down management, academic speech is now commonly regulated and censored through 'tone of voice policies'. Typically written by universities' marketing departments, these policies require scholars to regulate their speech in public communication, for instance by making preferred use of certain words and phrases and avoiding others. The stated purpose of these policies is to give universities a coherent and positive 'brand image', thereby contributing to their commercial success. In spite of their obvious implications for academic freedom, tone of voice policies so far seem to be enforced only rarely. However, there are reports of critical social researchers facing censure and suspension by academic managers for making public statements judged to be inappropriate. There is also the observation that in higher education such censure plays out unequally across race, class and gender (Bhopal 2015).

Audits

Audits, that is, comprehensive performance assessments on the basis of recorded evidence, play a quickly expanding role in sociologists' work lives. At British universities today, scholars are routinely asked to compile 'metrics' on their performance. These metrics typically have numeric form and can be evaluated and compared, using a statistical method of analysis. Examples of such metrics are the sociologists' annual number of publications, the impact factor of the journals they have published in (that is, a measure of these journals' prestige), the amount of money they have generated in research grants, and their ratings in student satisfaction surveys. Such audit results can have severe consequences for sociologists' careers, including even dismissal if their work is judged to be inadequate.

This has several important consequences. On the one hand, it generates pressure for sociologists to prioritise appearances, for instance by publishing a substantial number of journal articles in quick succession or by being funny and entertaining in class to do well in student satisfaction surveys. On the other hand, it means that the content of sociologists' work – the ideas they communicate in lectures and seminars and the arguments they advance in their research – matter little, in so far as they are ignored in the compilation of metrics or used simply to assign roundabout quality scores to their work, as in the NSS or the REF. In other words, sociological knowledge comes to be instrumentalised in the pursuit of metrics, and its content otherwise may matter little.

Business speak

The language we use structures the way we experience the world and interact with others. This is particularly so in sociological enquiry, which is all about generating intellectually sophisticated concepts and theories that explain social life. However, this complex language of sociology and the sociological imagination stands in contradiction to a new language of academic life that has quickly become prevalent throughout British universities. This language is used to describe administrative processes as well as research and teaching, and academic managers may place considerable emphasis on its consistent and pervasive use. The origins of this new language lie in the world of business management, and its pervasiveness might be explained by the fact that academic managers nowadays – and in difference from previous decades – are trained with management handbooks and management seminars, self-consciously seeking to emulate the world of business. Thus, heads of department have become 'line managers', a term that evokes assembly lines or lines of production in factories. Academic publications have become 'outputs', classes have become 'modules', and the term 'teaching and learning' is now the mandatory descriptor of what one does with one's students.

This language is all about thinking and speaking about academic life in standardised ways, and it has two problematic implications for sociological enquiry. On the one hand, standardisation and the rote, unthinking use of certain terms undercut sociology's efforts to look at the world sideways and question taken-for-granted assumptions that organise everyday life. It is an impossible feat for sociologists to simultaneously communicate in a highly standardised language and engage in critical enquiry in the social and cultural organisation of human life.

On the other hand, the pervasive use of business speak may shift the ways in which academics at large and sociologists in particular experience their work. If we use the term 'journal article' to think or speak about an academic publication, then we refer to a traditional mode of scholarly communication and allude to the intellectual content of our work. If instead we use the term 'output' to refer to the same publication, then we think and emphasise its contribution to our metrics and our performance assessment. In this case, the publication's contents – the sociological ideas it contains – become irrelevant, and all that matters is that we have published something or other in a high-status 'outlet' for academic research. This undercuts scholarship as a process of intellectual communication, in that it becomes insignificant whether sociologists speak to each other and what they might say; all that matters are the metrics.

The precarisation of academic labour

Stable employment is an important precondition for successful sociological labour, in that it allows sociologists to pursue their work free from concerns about contract expiry, future employment, economic security and so on. The marketisation of British universities from the 1980s onwards has entailed a pronounced decline in stable academic employment, in the form of full-time open-ended contracts, and it is now common for sociologists to teach and do research on fixed-term, hourly or even zero-hour contracts. This instability in academic employment also plays out in unequal ways across race, class and gender differences (Sian 2019)

The lack of a stable institutional affiliation limits the precariously employed sociologist's ability both to engage in long-term research and publication projects and to pursue the research funding required to conduct these projects. Moreover, it creates a hierarchy between, on the one hand, a minority of permanently employed sociologists able to concentrate on their scholarship and set agendas for our discipline and, on the other hand, a majority of sociologists looking to get by on short-term, part-time, low-paid employment contracts.

The 'student experience'

At the turn of the millennium, the term that was commonly used in the Britain for what students were doing was 'reading for a degree'. This has become somewhat obsolete, as universities now prefer to speak about the 'student experience'. The former term highlights what studying sociology – and most other degrees – is actually about, that is, spending time in the library, engaging with academic texts, and trying to understand the complex ideas they communicate. The latter term is meant to allude to students' wellbeing and enjoyment of their time at university. If 'student experience' has overtones of theme parks and nights out clubbing, this is not without reason. Universities' emphasis on the student experience has been accompanied by a shift in university funding as the British government has withdrawn substantial amounts of public money, rendering universities reliant on their income from tuition fees. Therefore, the successful marketing of degree courses and branding of universities has become an important element of academic labour. Both administrators and lecturers may now invest considerable time and effort in marketing publications and events to convince prospective students to choose their university.

This means that the relationship between universities and students, and between lecturers and students, has changed profoundly. The academic relationships of the time when people studied for a degree are now relationships between customers and customer service providers. The term 'student experience' makes this clear, as it suggests that students will gain a substantial return – lots of fun and a degree certificate on top of all that – in return for their investment in tuition fees. Universities' efforts to convince students that they are consumers has further problematic implications for sociology. Whereas a consumer is a largely passive recipient of a service – the lectures, classes and hours in the library necessary to gain a degree certificate – the study of sociology requires intellectual curiosity and an active interest in engaging with everyday social life. There is no such thing as an armchair sociologist, and it requires an active effort to look beyond common sense and develop a sociological imagination. The new consumerism of the student experience therefore contradicts the intellectual relationships that are central to the sociological imagination.

A fundamental contradiction

This chapter has sought to make the point that sociology today faces an existential crisis. Sociology is now global sociologies. There are star sociologists who hold prestigious professorships at famous universities and are highly visible in public life. Universities all around the world host sociology departments, and there are vibrant communities of students and professional academics, both at these universities and in national and international academic associations. If we accept this, it raises the question why in this chapter we have written, in rather provocative language, about the impending death of our discipline. Such arguments are highly uncommon for a book such as this. Introductions to sociology usually lay out the toolkit of concepts and methods that emerging sociologists need to become familiar with, and they rarely – if ever – engage in a critique of academic life. But this isn't your typical introduction to sociology. As we have tried to show throughout this book, making the case for sociology and the sociological imagination in the 21st century is important because its relevance for understanding and imagining the worlds around us can no longer be assumed or taken for granted.

The academic world and its relationship to public life is changing at a rapid pace. These transformations, as outlined throughout this chapter, are eroding the status of sociology, both in universities and in public life at large. While we have mainly referred to British academia in this chapter, the scale of change is worldwide. In Japan, for example, the government recently instructed public universities to close down their programmes in the humanities and social sciences, including sociology, altogether, so as to focus on more directly economically useful areas of study.

Thus, on the one hand, sociology seems to be fading from public view, and the voices of other fields of enquiry, such as economics and psychology, are heard ever more loudly. Why is sociology not being listened to, and how can we recover the role of the sociological imagination in public life? On the other hand, universities are requiring lecturers to act as academic entrepreneurs and encouraging students to act as consumers. If sociological enquiry is all about producing outputs that have the right metrics, and if modules in sociology are all about the student experience, then their content – the ideas that give our discipline its distinctive character – becomes meaningless. If all you need is the degree certificate, then it does not matter whether your module is about Émile Durkheim or the recipes for octopus pudding. If all you need is a journal article with the right metrics, then it does not matter whether you are writing on sociological theory or on the question why it rained yesterday. These are contradictions that sociologists cannot resolve without a thorough conversation about the status and purpose of their discipline. This book and the questions we have asked are meant to contribute to such a conversation. But just as sociologists have made the case for sociology in the 21st century, it will be the new sociologists of today, and the future, who will need to highlight the importance of sociology and the sociological imagination for imagining society.

THINKING SOCIOLOGICALLY

Based on your own reading of the chapter and your personal reflections, consider the impact of the features of the 'entrepreneurial university' below on the production of sociological knowledge in the academy.

1. Top-down management
2. Audit culture and ranking
3. Business speak
4. The precarisation of academic labour
5. The student experience

Finally, please elaborate on how you think academic capitalism has affected your studies of sociology.

MINI PROJECT

For this project, you will need to do some background research. Please access and read 'Academic Capitalism' by Richard Münch (2016), which is available for free here: http://oxfordre.com/politics/view/10.1093/acrefore/9780190228637.001.0001/acrefore-9780190228637-e-15#

'Academic capitalism is a unique hybrid that unites the scientific search for truth and the economic maximization of profits. It turns universities into enterprises competing for capital accumulation and businesses into knowledge producers looking for new findings that can be turned into patents and profitable commodities' (Münch 2016).

Based on your readings please develop a presentation that explains the basic features of academic capitalism. Try to explain how these features have shaped and affected the production of scientific knowledge today. What are the 'institutional conflicts' that Münch outlines in the funding of academic research by corporations? What is different about the universities today in organisational terms and quality control from previous eras?

TALKING POINTS

1. What is academic freedom? Why is it important in the production of knowledge? Why might it be important in the production of sociological knowledge, theory and concepts?

2. What was Friedrich Wilhelm von Humboldt's ideal of scholarship? What did he mean by the German word *Bildung*? How does privatisation affect the production of sociological knowledge? In your own personal life how close is your current university experience to Humboldt's ideal of scholarship?

3. In what industries can sociologists be found outside academia?

4. What sorts of jobs do they do?

5. How and why is the sociological imagination important in careers such as journalism, social work and business?

6. According to the chapter why is sociology not being listened to, and how can we recover the role of the sociological imagination in public life?

READ ON ...

For the social history behind the development of economics and psycholgy from a sociological perspective William Davies' *The Happiness Industry* (2015) is insightful. Frank Furedi tackles transformations around intellectualism in *Where Have All the Intellectuals Gone?* (2004). Tressie McMillan's Cottom's *Lower Ed: The Troubling Rise of For- Profit Colleges in the New Economy* (2017) examines how the for-profit university sector is a central mechanism for continued and growing inequality in the US today. The edited collection by Brendan Cantwell and colleagues, *Academic Capitalism in the Age of Globalization* (2014), explores the entrepreneurial university. Discrimination and experiences of racism faced by academics of colour working within UK universities is the subject of Katy Sian's *Navigating Institutional Racism in British Universities* (2019). Kalwant Bhopal's *The Experiences of Black and Minority Ethnic Academics* (2015) examines the complexities of race, gender and identity within the US and UK academic systems that continue to be directed by White middle-class values and worldviews. The new world made in the wake of neoliberal economic policies is the subject of Pierre Dardot and Christian Laval's *The New Way of the World: On Neoliberal Society* (2013). It is also central in David Harvey's *Brief History of Neoliberalism* (2007) and Max Haiven's *Cultures of Financialization: Fictitious Capital in Popular Culture and Everyday Life* (2014).

Check the companion website at https://bristoluniversitypress. co.uk/imagining-society-online-resources **for a suggested project and writing task.**

Bibliography

Adorno, T.W. 1991. *The culture industry: Selected essays on mass culture.* London/ New York: Routledge.

Agozino, B. 2003. *Counter-colonial criminology: A critique of imperialist reason.* London: Pluto Press. http://site.ebrary.com/id/10479754.

Agozino, B., Bowling, B., Ward, E. and St Bernard, G. 2009. Guns, crime and social order in the West Indies. *Criminology & Criminal Justice* 9(3): 287–305.

Agozino, O. 2011. The revolutionary sociology of C.L.R. James. *Transition* 106: 127–38.

Ahmed, S. 2010. *The promise of happiness.* Durham, NC: Duke University Press.

Ahmed, S. 2017. *Living a feminist life.* Durham, NC: Duke University Press.

Alatas, S.F. 2006. *Alternative discourses in Asian social science: Responses to Eurocentrism.* New Delhi: SAGE Publications.

Alatas, S.F. 2008 *Intellectual and structural challenges to academic dependency.* Amsterdam: SEPHIS.

Albiston, C., Brito, T. and Larson, J.E. 2002. Feminism in relation. *Wis. Women's LJ* 17:1.

Alexander, M. 2012. *The new Jim Crow: Mass incarceration in the age of colorblindness.* New York: New Press.

Althusser, L. 1971. *Lenin and philosophy, and other essays.* Transl. by Ben Brewster. New York: Monthly Review Press.

Alvesson, M. 2014. *The triumph of emptiness: Consumption, higher education, and work organization.* Oxford: Oxford University Press.

Aradau, C. and Blanke, T. 2015. The (big) data-security assemblage: knowledge and critique. *Big Data & Society* 2(2): 2053951715609066.

Armstrong, E.A. and Hamilton, L.T. 2015. *Paying for the party: How college maintains inequality.* Cambridge, MA: Harvard University Press.

Armstrong, N. 2005. *How novels think: The limits of individualism from 1719–1900.* New York: Columbia University Press.

Associated Press. 2017. Kellyanne Conway clarifies comment about false Bowling Green massacre. *The Guardian Online.* www.theguardian.com/us-news/2017/feb/03/kellyanne-conway-bowling-green-massacre-trump-travel-ban.

Atkinson, W. 2008. Not all that was solid has melted into air (or liquid): a critique of Bauman on individualization and class in liquid modernity. *Sociological Review* 56(1): 1–17.

Austin-Broos, D. 2017. *Urban life in Kingston Jamaica: The culture and class ideology of two neighborhoods.* Abingdon/New York: Routledge.

Bagley, B. 2004. Globalisation and Latin American and Caribbean organised crime. *Global Crime* 6(1): 32–53. https://doi.org/10.1080/1744057042000297963.

Baird, A. 2012. The violent gang and the construction of masculinity amongst socially excluded young men. *Safer Communities* 11(4):179–90.

Baird, A. 2018. Becoming the 'baddest': masculine trajectories of gang violence in Medellín. *Journal of Latin American Studies* 50(1): 183–210.

Baksh-Soodeen, R. 1998. Issues of difference in contemporary Caribbean feminism. *Feminist Review* 59: 74–85.

Ball, K., Haggerty, K.D. and Lyon, D. 2012. *Routledge handbook of surveillance studies.* London/New York: Routledge.

Balzacq, T. (ed.) 2011. *Securitization theory: How security problems emerge and dissolve.* Abingdon/New York: Routledge.

Barber, N.A. and Deale, C. 2014. Tapping mindfulness to shape hotel guests' sustainable behavior, *Cornell Hospitality Quarterly* 55(1): 100–14. doi: 10.1177/1938965513496315.

Barker, G. 2005. *Dying to be men: Youth, masculinity and social exclusion.* London: Routledge.

Baron-Cohen, S. 2012. *Zero degrees of empathy: A new understanding of cruelty and kindness.* London: Penguin.

Barriteau, E. 2003. *Confronting power, theorizing gender: Interdisciplinary perspectives in the Caribbean.* Kingston: University of West Indies Press.

Bauman, Z. 2000. *Liquid modernity,* Cambridge: Polity.

Bauman, Z. 2003. *Liquid love: On the frailty of human bonds,* Cambridge: Polity.

Bauman, Z. 2005. *Liquid life,* Cambridge: Polity.

Bauman, Z. and May, T. 2001. *Thinking sociologically.* Oxford: Wiley Blackwell.

Beck, U. 1986. *Risikogesellschaft: Auf dem Weg in eine andere Moderne.* Frankfurt am Main: Suhrkamp.

Beck, U. 1992. *Risk society: Towards a new modernity.* London: SAGE Publications.

Beck, U. and Beck-Gernsheim, E. 2002. *Individualization: Institutionalized individualism and its social and political consequences.* London: SAGE Publications.

Becker, D. and Marecek, J. 2008. Dreaming the American Dream: individualism and positive psychology. *Social and Personality Psychology Compass* 2(5): 767–80.

Becker, H. 1967. Whose side are we on? *Social Problems* 14(3): 239–47.

Beckles, H. 2013. *Britain's black debt: Reparations for slavery and native genocide.* Kingston: University Of West Indies Press.

Bell, J.R. 2009. *Capitalism and the dialectic: The Uno–Sekine approach to Marxian political economy.* London/New York: Pluto Press.

Berger, R.A. 1993. From text to (field) work and back again: theorizing a post(modern)-ethnography. *Anthropological Quarterly* 66: 174–86.

Bernays, E.L. 1928. Manipulating public opinion: the why and the how, *American Journal of Sociology* 33(6): 958–71.

Best, J. and Harris, S.R. (eds) 2013. *Making sense of social problems: New images, new issues*. Boulder, CO: Lynne Rienner Publishers.

Best, L. 1997. Independent thought and Caribbean freedom: thirty years later. *Caribbean Quarterly* 43(1/2):16–24.

Best, L. 2001. Race, Class and Ethnicity: A Caribbean Interpretation. Third Annual Jagan Lecture, 3 March, York University, Canada.

Bhambra, G. 2007. *Rethinking modernity: Postcolonialism and the sociological imagination*. Basingstoke: Palgrave Macmillan.

Bhambra, G.K. 2014a. Introduction: knowledge production in global context: power and coloniality. *Current Sociology* 62(4): 451–6.

Bhambra, G.K. 2014b. *Connected sociologies*, London: Bloomsbury Academic.

Bhambra, G.K. 2015. Global sociology in question. *Global Dialogue* 5(2): 8–10.

Bhambra, G.K. 2016. Postcolonial reflections on sociology. *Sociology* 50(5): 960–6. https://doi.org/10.1177/0038038516647683.

Bhambra, G.K. and de Sousa Santos, B. 2017. Introduction: global challenges for sociology. *Sociology* 51(1): 3–10.

Bhopal, K. 2015. *The experiences of black and minority ethnic academics: A comparative study of the unequal academy*. Abingdon/New York: Routledge.

Bien, T. and Bien, B. 2003. *Finding the center within: The healing way of mindfulness meditation*. Hoboken, NJ: John Wiley & Sons.

Binkley, S. 2011a. Psychological life as enterprise: social practice and the government of neo-liberal interiority. *History of the Human Sciences* 24(3): 83–102. doi: 10.1177/0952695111412877.

Binkley, S. 2011b. Happiness, positive psychology and the program of neoliberal governmentality. *Subjectivity* 4(4): 371–94. http://dx.doi.org/10.1057/sub.2011.16.

Bird, C. 1999. *The myth of liberal individualism*. Cambridge: Cambridge University Press.

Blumer, H. 1969. *Symbolic interactionism: Perspective and method*. Berkeley, CA: University of California Press.

Boffey, D. 2015. Oxford and Cambridge condemned over failure to improve state school access. *The Guardian*, 12 December. www.theguardian.com/education/2015/dec/12/oxford-cambridge-state-school-admissions-failure.

Bolin, G. and Andersson Schwarz, J. 2015. Heuristics of the algorithm: big data, user interpretation and institutional translation. *Big Data & Society* 2(2): 2053951715608406.

Bourdieu, P. 1977. *Outline of a theory of practice*. Cambridge/New York: Cambridge University Press.

Bourdieu, P. 1984. *Distinction: A social critique of the judgment of taste*. Cambridge, MA: Harvard University Press.

Bourdieu, P. 1987. What makes a social class? On the theoretical and practical existence of groups. *Berkeley Journal of Sociology* 32: 1–17. www.jstor.org/stable/41035356.

Bourdieu, P. 1999. *On television*. Paris: New Press.

Braidotti, R. 1993. Re-figuring the subject. In H. Kunnemann and H. de Vries (eds) *Enlightenments. Encounters between critical theory and contemporary French thought*. Kampen: Kok Pharos Publishing, pp. 319–41.

Brathwaite, L. 1960. Social stratification and cultural pluralism. *Annals New York Academy of Sciences* 83(5): 816–36.

Brewer, J.D. 2013. The sociological imagination and public sociology. In J. Scott and A. Nilsen (eds) *C. Wright Mills and the sociological imagination: Contemporary perspectives*. Cheltenham: Edward Elgar, pp. 219–21.

Bridges, T. and Tober, T.L. 2017. The sociological explanation for why men in America turn to gun violence. *Quartz*, 7 October. https://qz.com/1095247/the-sociological-explanation-for-why-men-in-america-turn-to-gun-violence.

Brindley, E.F. 2010. *Individualism in early China: Human agency and the self in thought and politics*. Honolulu: University of Hawai'i Press.

Bröckling, U. 2007. *Das unternehmerische Selbst: Soziologie einer Subjektivierungsform*. Frankfurt am Main: Suhrkamp.

Brynin, M., Longhi, S. and Zwysen, W. 2017. The diversification of inequality. *The British Journal of Sociology* doi: 10.1111/1468-4446.12341.

Buck-Morss, S. 2009. *Hegel, Haiti and universal history*. Pittsburgh, PA: University of Pittsburgh Press.

Bulmer, M. 1984. Introduction: problems, theories and methods in sociology – (how) do they interrelate? In M. Bulmer (ed.) *Sociological research methods: An introduction*. London: Macmillan, pp. 1–33.

Burawoy, M. 2005. For public sociology. *American Sociological Review* 70(1): 4–28.

Butler, J. 1990. *Gender trouble : Feminism and the subversion of identity*. New York: Routledge.

Cabanas, E. and Illouz, E. 2016. The making of a 'happy worker': positive psychology in neoliberal organizations. In A. Pugh (ed.) *Beyond the cubicle: Insecurity culture and the flexible self*. New York: Oxford University Press.

Cabanas, E. and Sánchez-González, J.C. 2012. The roots of positive psychology. *Papeles del Psicólogo* 33(3):172–82.

Cabanas, E. and Sánchez-González, J.C. 2016. Inverting the pyramid of needs: positive psychology's new order for labor success. *Psicothema* 28(2):107–13.

Cacioppo, J.T. and Patrick, W. 2008. *Loneliness: Human nature and the need for social connection*. London/New York: W.W. Norton & Company.

Cantwell, B., Kauppinen, I. and Slaughter, S. (eds) 2014. *Academic capitalism in the age of globalization*. Baltimore, MA: Johns Hopkins University Press.

Carlson, J. 2015. *Citizen-protectors: The everyday politics of guns in an age of decline*. New York: Oxford University Press.

Carlson, J. 2018. Why research on guns needs sociologists. And vice-versa. Understanding Gun Violence series, 6 November. https://items.ssrc.org/why-research-on-guns-needs-sociologists-and-vice-versa/.

Castells, M. 2016. A sociology of power: my intellectual journey. *Annual Review of Sociology* 42(1): 1–19. www.annualreviews.org/doi/10.1146/annurev-soc-081715-074158.

Cavarero, A. 1995. *In spite of Plato: A feminist rewriting of ancient philosophy.* New York: Routledge.

Celis, J. 2015. 'The age of school shootings': a sociological interpretation on masculinity. *Actualidades Investigativas en Educación* 15(1): 520–41.

Césaire, A. 1955. *Discours Sur Le Colonialisme.* Paris: Presence Africaine.

Chakrabarti, S. and Patnaik, U. 2017. *Agrarian and other histories: Essays for Binay Bhushan Chaudhuri.* New Delhi: Tulika Books. https://books.google.co.in/books?id=TvnstAEACAAJ.

Chalari, A. 2009. *Approaches to the individual: The relationship between internal and external conversation.* New York/Basingstoke: Palgrave Macmillan.

Chalari, A. 2017. *The sociology of the individual: Relating self and society.* London: SAGE Publications.

Charon, J.M. 1998. *The meaning of sociology.* New Jersey: Prentice Hall.

Charon, J.M. 2009. *Symbolic interactionism: An introduction, an interpretation, an integration.* New York: Pearson.

Chrisman, J.A., Chambers, C.J. and Lichtenstein, S.J. 2008. Qigong as a mindfulness practice for counseling students: a qualitative study. *Journal of Humanistic Psychology* 49(2): 236–57. doi: 10.1177/0022167808327750.

Christman, J.P. 2002. *Social and political philosophy: A contemporary introduction.* London/New York: Routledge. www.loc.gov/catdir/toc/fy043/2002069912.html.

Clough, P.T. 2000. *Autoaffection : Unconscious thought in the age of teletechnology.* Minneapolis, MN: University of Minnesota Press.

Collini, S. 2017. *Speaking of universities.* London: Verso.

Comte, A. 2000. *The positive philosophy of Auguste Comte.* Transl. by H. Martineau, Ontario: Batoche Books.

Connell, R. 2007. *Southern theory: Social science and the global dynamics of knowledge.* Cambridge: Polity.

Connell, R. 2014. The sociology of gender in Southern perspective. *Current Sociology* 62(4): 550–67.

Conway, D. 1997. Pursuing an appropriate development model for Caribbean small islands: can past experience help subvert the neo-liberal agenda? Paper presented at the Latin American Studies Association, XX International Congress, Guadalajara, Mexico, 17–19 April.

Cooley, C.H. 1926. The roots of social knowledge. *American Journal of Sociology* 32(1): 59–79.

Cooley, C.H. 1962. *Social organization: A study of the larger mind*. New York: Schocken Books.

Cooley, C.H. 1983. *Human nature and the social order*. New Brunswick: Transaction Publishers.

Cooper, A.J. 1988. *A Voice from the South*. New York: Oxford University Press.

Cottom, T.M. 2017. *Lower ed: The troubling rise of for-profit colleges in the new economy*. New York: New Press.

Cottom, T.M. 2019. *Thick: And other essays*. Narrated by Tressie McMillan Cottom. Audible. Audiobook.

Craib, I. 1994. *The importance of disappointment*. Abingdon: Routledge.

Creese, G., McLaren, A.T. and Pulkingham, J. 2009. Rethinking Burawoy: Reflections from Canadian feminist sociology. *The Canadian Journal of Sociology / Cahiers Canadiens de Sociologie* 34(3): 601–22.

Crichlow, W. 2015. Critical race theory: a strategy for framing discussions around social justice and democratic education. Paper presented at the Higher Education in Transformation Conference, Dublin, 31 May–1 April.

Dandaneau, S.P. 2009. Sisyphus had it easy: Reflections of two decades of teaching the sociological imagination. *Teaching Sociology* 37(1): 8–19. http://tso.sagepub.com/cgi/doi/10.1177/0092055X0903700102.

Daniels, J., Gregory, K. and McMillan Cottom, T. 2017. *Digital sociologies*. Bristol: Policy Press.

Dardot, P. and Laval, C. 2013. *The new way of the world: On neoliberal society*. London: Verso.

Davies, W. 2014. A bibliographic review of neoliberalism. *Theory, Culture & Society* [commentary], 7 March. http://theoryculturesociety.org/william-davies-a-bibliographic-review-of-neoliberalism.

Davies, W. 2015. *The happiness industry: How the government and big business sold us well-being*. London: Verso.

Davies, W. 2018. *Nervous states: How feeling took over the world*. London: Jonathan Cape.

Davis, A.Y. 1983. *Women, race & class*. New York: Vintage Books.

Davison, G. 2004. *Car wars: How the car won our hearts and conquered our cities*. Crows Nest, Australia: Allen & Unwin.

Dawson, M. 2012. Reviewing the critique of individualization: the disembedded and embedded theses. *Acta Sociologica* 55(4): 305–19. http://asj.sagepub.com/content/55/4/305.abstract.

de Beauvoir, S. 1949. *The second sex*. Harmondsworth: Penguin Books.

de Ridder-Symoens, H. (ed.) 1992. *A history of the university in Europe*. Cambridge: Cambridge University Press.

de Sousa Santos, B. 2002. The processes of globalisation. *REČ* 68.14: 67–131. http://www.fabrikaknjiga.co.rs/rec-68-14/

de Sousa Santos, B. 2006. Globalizations. *Theory, Culture & Society* 23(2–3): 393–9.

de Sousa Santos, B. 2012. Public sphere and epistemologies of the South. *Africa Development* 37(1): 43–67.

Dean, J. 2016. 'Submitting love?' A sensory sociology of Southbourne. *Qualitative Inquiry* 22(3): 162–8.

Decker, S.H. and Van Winkle, B. 1996. *Life in the gang: Family, friends, and violence.* Cambridge: Cambridge University Press.

Deleuze, G. and Guattari, F. 1977. *Anti-Oedipus: Capitalism and schizophrenia.* New York: Viking Press.

Denzin, N.K. 1988. *Symbolic interactionism and cultural studies: The politics of interaction.* Malden, MA: Blackwell Publishing.

Denzin, N.K. and Giardina, M.D. (eds) 2006. *Qualitative inquiry and the conservative challenge: Confronting methodological fundamentalism.* New York: Routledge.

Deosaran, R. 2016. *Inequality crime & education in Trinidad and Tobago: Removing the masks.* Trinidad: Ian Randle Publishing

Dépelteau, F. (ed.) 2018. *The Palgrave handbook of relational sociology.* New York/ Basingstoke: Palgrave Macmillan.

Diderot, D. and D'Alembert, J. le R. 1954. *The encyclopédie of Diderot and d'Alembert: Selected articles.* Edited by J. Lough. Cambridge: Cambridge University Press.

Doucet, A. 2018. Shorelines, seashells, and seeds: feminist epistemologies, ecological thinking, and relational ontologies. In F. Dépelteau (ed.) *The Palgrave handbook of relational sociology.* New York/Basingstoke: Palgrave Macmillan, pp. 375–91.

Doucet, A. and Mauthner, N.S. 2006. Feminist methodologies and epistemology. In *Handbook of 21st century sociology*, Thousand Oaks, CA: SAGE Publications, pp. 36–45.

Dreyfus, H.L. and Rabinow, P. 1982. *Michel Foucault: Beyond structuralism and hermeneutics.* Brighton: Harvester Press.

Du Bois, W.E.B. 2007. *The souls of black folk.* Oxford: Oxford University Press.

Dunlap, R.E. 2013. Climate change skepticism and denial: An introduction. *American Behavioral Scientist* 57(6): 691–8.

Durkheim, E. 1995. *The elementary forms of religious life.* New York: Free Press.

Durkheim, E. 2005. *Suicide: A study in sociology.* London/New York: Routledge.

Durkheim, E. 2013a. *The division of labour in society.* New York/Basingstoke: Palgrave Macmillan.

Durkheim, E. 2013b. *The rules of sociological method.* Edited by S. Lukes. New York/Basingstoke: Palgrave Macmillan.

Eldridge, J.E.T. 1983. *C. Wright Mills.* Chichester/London: Ellis Horwood/ Tavistock Publications.

Elliott, A. (ed.) 2013a. *Routledge handbook of identity studies.* Abingdon: Routledge.

Elliott, A. 2013b *Concepts of the self.* Cambridge: Polity.

Elliott, A. 2015. *Identity troubles.* Abingdon: Routledge.

Elliott, A. and Lemert, C. 2006. *The new individualism: The emotional costs of globalization*. London: Routledge.

Elliott, A. and Turner, B. 2012. *On society*. Cambridge: Polity.

Elliott, M.A. 2007. Human rights and the triumph of the individual in world culture. *Cultural Sociology* 1(3): 343–63.

Engels, F. 2009. *The condition of the working class in England*. Oxford: Oxford University Press.

Engels, F. 2010. *The origin of the family, private property and the state*. London: Penguin.

Enloe, C. 2017. *The big push: Exposing and challenging the persistence of patriarchy*. Oakland, CA: University of California Press.

Epp, C.R., Maynard-Moody, S. and Haider-Markel, D.P. 2014. *Pulled over: How police stops define race and citizenship*. Chicago, IL: University of Chicago Press.

Escobar, A. 2004. Beyond the third world: imperial globality, global coloniality and anti-globalisation social movements. *Third World Quarterly* 25(1): 207–30.

Espeland, W.N. and Sauder, M. 2016. *Engines of anxiety: Academic rankings, reputation, and accountability*. New York: Russell Sage Foundation.

Etzkowitz, H. 2004. The evolution of the entrepreneurial university. *International Journal of Technology and Globalisation* 1(1): 64–77. doi:http://dx.doi.org/10.1504/IJTG.2004.004551.

Evans, B. and Giroux, H.A. 2015. *Disposable futures: The seduction of violence in the age of spectacle*. San Francisco, CA: City Lights Books.

Evans, K. and Buhle, P. 2015. *Red Rosa: A graphic biography of Rosa Luxemburg*. London: Verso.

Everytown for Gun Safety Support Fund. 2018. Gunfire on school grounds in the United States. https://everytownresearch.org/gunfire-in-school/#13201

Eze, E.C. 2008. *Race and the Enlightenment: A reader*. Cambridge, MA/Oxford: Blackwell.

Fanon, F. 1965. *The wretched of the Earth*. New York: Grove Press.

Fanon, F. 2008. *Black skin, white masks*. London: Pluto Press.

Farmer, P. 2004. An anthropology of structural violence. *Current Anthropology* 45(3): 305–25.

Farrer, J. 2013. Good stories: Chinese women's international love stories as cosmopolitan sexual politics. *Sexualities* 16(1–2): 12–29. doi: 10.1177/1363460712465568.

Fei, X. 1992. *From the soil: The foundations of Chinese society*. Berkeley, CA: University of California Press.

Forbes. 2017. Neymar. www.forbes.com/profile/neymar/.

Foster, J.B. and R.W. McChesney. 2014. Surveillance capitalism: monopoly-finance capital, the military-industrial complex, and the digital age. *Monthly Review* 66(3): 1–31. https://search.proquest.com/docview/1543483454?accountid=45039.

Foucault, M. 1977. *Discipline and punish: The birth of the prison*. London: Penguin.

Foucault, M. 1990. *The history of sexuality: An introduction*. London: Penguin Books.

Frank, A.G. 1971. The development of underdevelopment. In R.I. Rhodes (ed.) *Imperialism and underdevelopment: A reader*. New York: Monthly Review Press.

Freeman, C. 2000. *High tech and high heels in the global economy: Women, work, and pink collar identities in the Caribbean*. Durham, NC/London: Duke University Press.

Friedrichs, D. 1997. Responding to the challenge of white collar crime as a social problem: implications for Caribbean states. *Caribbean Journal of Criminology and Social Psychology* 2(2): 84–99.

Fuentes, A. 2014. Things to know when talking about race and genetics. *Psychology Today*, 13 May. www.psychologytoday.com/gb/blog/busting-myths-about-human-nature/201405/things-know-when-talking-about-race-and-genetics.

Fulcher, J. and Scott, J. 2011. *Sociology*. New York: Oxford University Press.

Furedi, F. 2004. *Where have all the intellectuals gone?* London: Continuum.

Furedi, F. 2014. *What's happened to the university? A sociological exploration of its infantilisation*. London: Routledge.

Gangadharan, S.P. 2017. The downside of digital inclusion: expectations and experiences of privacy and surveillance among marginal internet users. *New Media & Society* 19(4): 597–615.

Gardner, A.W. 1971. *A history of Jamaica*. London: Frank Cass and Company.

Garry, A. and Pearsall, M. 2010. *Women, knowledge, and reality: Explorations in feminist philosophy*. New York/London: Routledge.

Gaudio, R.P. 2003. Coffeetalk: Starbucks™ and the commercialization of casual conversation. *Language in Society* 32(5): 659–91.

Gergen, K.J. 1991. *The saturated self: Dilemmas of identity in contemporary life*. New York: Basic Books.

Gergen, K.J. 2009. *Relational being: Beyond self and community*. Oxford: Oxford University Press.

Gerrard, J., Rudolph, S. and Sriprakash, A. 2016. The politics of post-qualitative inquiry: history and power. *Qualitative Inquiry* 23(5): 384–94. https://doi.org/10.1177/1077800416672694

Gerth, H.H. and Mills, C.W. (eds) 1946. *From Max Weber: Essays in sociology*. New York: Oxford University Press.

Gerth, H.H. and Mills, C.W. 1953. *Character and social structure: The psychology of social institutions*. New York: Harcourt, Brace and Company.

Giddens, A. 1970. Marx, Weber, and the development of capitalism. *Sociology* 4(3): 289–310. http://soc.sagepub.com/cgi/doi/10.1177/003803857000400301.

Giddens, A. 1984. *The constitution of society*. Berkeley, CA: University of California Press.

Giddens, A. 1991. *Modernity and self-identity: Self and society in the late modern age*. Cambridge: Polity.

Giddens, A. 1992. *The transformation of intimacy*. Cambridge: Polity.

Gilman, C.P. 1998. *Women and economics: A study of the economic relation between men and women.* Berkeley, CA: University of California Press.

Gilman, C.P. 2002. *The dress of women: A critical introduction to the symbolism and sociology of clothing.* Westport, CT: Greenwood Press. doi: 10.2307/3089949.

Gilman, CP. 2004. *Social ethics: Sociology and the future of society.* Westport, CT and London: Praeger Publishers.

Gilman, C.P. 2009. *The yellow wallpaper and selected writings.* London: Little, Brown Book Group.

Giroux, H.A. 2014. The swindle of democracy in the neoliberal university and the responsibility of intellectuals. *Democratic Theory* 1(1): 9–37. doi: 10.3167/dt.2014.010102.

Giroux, H.A. 2010. Rethinking education as the practice of freedom: Paulo Freire and the promise of critical pedagogy. *Policy Futures in Education* 8(6): 715–21.

Giroux, H.A. 2015. Democracy in crisis, the specter of authoritarianism, and the future of higher education. *Journal of Critical Scholarship on Higher Education and Student Affairs* 1(1): 101–13.

Girvan, N.P. 1967. *The Caribbean bauxite industry.* Institute of Social and Economic Research, University of the West Indies, Jamaica.

Girvan, N. 1971. *Foreign capital and economic underdevelopment in Jamaica.* Institute of Social and Economic Research, University of the West Indies.

Girvan, N. 2017. *Corporate imperialism: Conflict and expropriation: Transnational corporations and economic nationalism in the third world.* Abingdon: Routledge.

Giulianotti, R. 1999. *Football: A sociology of the global game.* Cambridge: Polity.

Giulianotti, R. and Robertson, R. 2007. Recovering the social: globalization, football and transnationalism. *Global Networks* 7(2): 166–86. doi: 10.1111/j.1471-0374.2007.00163.x.

Goffman, E. 1990. *The presentation of self in everyday life.* London: Penguin.

Gordon, L. 2018. Black issues in philosophy: the African decolonial thought of Oyèrónké Oyěwùmí. [Blog] APA, 23 March. https://blog.apaonline.org/2018/03/23/black-issues-in-philosophy-the-african-decolonial-thought-of-oyeronke-oyewumi/.

Goswami, M. 2013. 'Provincializing' sociology: the case of a premature postcolonial sociologist. In J. Go (series ed.) *Postcolonial sociology, political power and social theory*, Vol. 24. Bingley: Emerald Group Publishing, pp. 145–75.

Gouldner, A.W. 1968. The sociologist as partisan: sociology and the welfare state. *The American Sociologist* 3(2): 103–16.

Graeber, D. 2016. *Toward an anthropological theory of value: The false coin of our own dreams.* New York/Basingstoke: Palgrave Macmillan.

Graeber, D. and Sahlins, M. 2017. *On kings.* Chicago, IL: HAU Books/University of Chicago Press.

Graham, H. 2009. *Understanding health inequalities.* Maidenhead: Open University Press/McGraw-Hill Education.

Gramsci, A. 1971. *Selections from the prison notebooks*. Edited by Q. Hoare and G. Nowell Smith. London: Lawrence and Wishart.

Gravlee, C.C. 2009. How race becomes biology: embodiment of social inequality. *American Journal of Physical Anthropology* 139(1): 47–57.

Gray, O. 2006. *Demeaned but empowered: The social power of the urban poor in Jamaica*. Kingston: University of the West Indies Press.

The Guardian. 2010. Does your social class decide if you go to university? Get the full list of colleges. 28 September [datablog]. www.theguardian.com/news/datablog/2010/sep/28/social-class-university-data.

Gutiérrez-Rodríguez, E. 2010. *Migration, domestic work and affect: A decolonial approach on value and the feminization of labor*. New York: Routledge.

Haiven, M. 2014. *Cultures of financialization: Fictitious capital in popular culture and everyday life*. New York/Basingstoke: Palgrave Macmillan.

Halberstam, J. 2005. *In a queer time and place: Transgender bodies, subcultural lives*. New York/London: New York University Press.

Halford, S. and Savage, M. 2017. Speaking sociologically with big data: symphonic social science and the future for big data research. *Sociology* 51(6):1132–48.

Halskov Hansen, M. and Svarverud, R. (eds) 2010. *iChina: The rise of the individual in modern Chinese society*. Copenhagen: NIAS Press.

Harding, S. 2003. Introduction: standpoint theory as a site of political, philosophic, and scientific debate. In S.G. Harding (ed.) *The feminist standpoint theory reader: Intellectual and political controversies*. London/New York: Routledge

Harvey, D. 2007. *A brief history of neoliberalism*. New York: Oxford University Press.

Haugaard, M. 2012. Power and truth. *European Journal of Social Theory* 15(1): 73–92. http://journals.sagepub.com/doi/10.1177/1368431011423591.

Haugaard, M. 2018. Justification and the four dimensions of power. *Journal of Political Power* 11(1): 93–114. www.tandfonline.com/doi/full/10.1080/2158379X.2018.1433759.

Hayden, T. 2006. *Radical nomad: C. Wright Mills and his times*. Boulder, CA: Paradigm.

Hayek, F.A. 2001. *The road to serfdom*. London/New York: Routledge. doi: 10.1177/000271624221900157.

Hearn, J. 2012. *Theorizing power*. Basingstoke: Palgrave Macmillan.

Hearn, J. and Morgan, D.H.J. 2014. *Men, masculinities and social theory (RLE Social Theory)*. London/New York: Routledge.

Heath-Kelly, C. 2013. Counter-terrorism and the counterfactual: producing the 'radicalisation' discourse and the UK PREVENT strategy. *The British Journal of Politics & International Relations* 15(3): 394–415.

Heelas, P., Lash, S. and Morris, P. (eds) 1996. *Detraditionalization*. Oxford: Wiley Blackwell.

Heidegren, C.-G. 2002. Anthropology, social theory, and politics: Axel Honneth's theory of recognition. *Inquiry* 45(4): 433–46.

Held, B.S. 2004. The negative side of positive psychology. *Journal of Humanistic Psychology* 44(1): 9–46.

Hendrix, C.S. and Salehyan, I. 2012. Climate change, rainfall, and social conflict in Africa. *Journal of Peace Research* 49(1): 35–50.

Herman, E.S. and Chomsky, N. 2008. *Manufacturing consent: The political economy of the mass media.* New York: Pantheon Books.

Highsaw, R.B. 1957. Review of: *The power elite. The Journal of Politics* 19(1): 144–6.

Hill Collins, P. 1990. *Black feminist thought: Knowledge, consciousness, and the politics of empowerment.* Boston, MA: Unwin Hyman.

Hochschild, A.R. 2003. *The commercialization of intimate life: Notes from home and work.* Berkeley, CA: University of California Press.

Hochschild, A.R. 2012. *The managed heart: The commercialization of human feeling.* Berkeley, CA: University of California Press.

Holden, R. 2009. *Be happy: Release the power of happiness in YOU.* [Kindle edn] Carlsbad, CA: Hay House.

Holmwood, J. 2010. Sociology's misfortune: Disciplines, interdisciplinarity and the impact of audit culture. *British Journal of Sociology* 61(4): 639–58. doi: 10.1111/j.1468-4446.2010.01332.x.

Holmwood, J. 2011. The impact of 'impact' on UK social science. *Methodological Innovation Online* 6(1): 13–17. doi: 10.4256/mio.2010.0025.

Holmwood, J. 2017. *Requiem for the public university, campaign for the public university.* https://publicuniversity.org.uk/2017/05/02/requiem-for-the-public-university.

Holmwood, J. and Scott, J. (eds) 2014. *The Palgrave handbook of sociology in Britain.* Basingstoke: Palgrave Macmillan.

hooks, b. 1981. *Ain't I a woman: Black women and feminism.* Boston: South End Press.

hooks, b. 1984. *Feminist theory: From margin to center.* New York: South End Press.

Hoop, K. 2009. Students' lived experiences as text in teaching the sociological imagination. *Teaching Sociology* 37(1): 47–60. http://tso.sagepub.com/content/37/1/47.short.

Hope, D. 2011. From Browning to cake soap: popular debates on skin bleaching in the Jamaican dancehall. *Journal of Pan African Studies* 4(4): 165–94.

Horowitz, I.L. 1983. *C. Wright Mills: An American Utopian.* New York: Free Press.

Horst, H., Miller, D., Austin-Broos, D., Bauer, E., Carrier, J.G., Chevannes, B., Hinrichs, L., Khan, A., Olwig, K.F. and Slater, D. 2005. From kinship to link-up: cell phones and social networking in Jamaica. *Current Anthropology* 46(5): 755–78.

Hosein, G. and Outar, L. 2016. *Indo-Caribbean feminist thought: Genealogies, theories, enactments.* New York: Palgrave Macmillan.

Hunter, M.L. 2011. Buying racial capital: skin-bleaching and cosmetic surgery in a globalized world. *Journal of Pan African Studies* 4(4): 142–64.

Illouz, E. 2008. *Saving the modern soul: Therapy, emotions, and the culture of self-help.* Berkeley, CA: University of California Press.

Illouz, E. 2019. Is self-worth crucial for the reproduction of inequality? A response to Michele Lamont's lecture. *The British Journal of Sociology* 70(3): 739–46.

Jaffe, R. 2009. 'They ain't gonna see us fall': affect, popular culture, and criminal governance in urban Jamaica. Paper presented at the annual meeting of the American Anthropological Association, Philadelphia, 4 December.

Jaffe, R. 2013. The hybrid state: crime and citizenship in urban Jamaica. *American Ethnologist* 40(4): 734–48.

Jaffe, S. 2018. The collective power of #MeToo. *Dissent* 65(2): 80–87.

James, C.L.R. 1963. *The Black Jacobins: Toussaint L'Ouverture and the San Domingo revolution: The C.L.R. James Reader.* New York: Vintage Books.

Jameson, F. 1991. *Postmodernism, or, the cultural logic of late capitalism.* Durham, NC: Duke University Press.

Jenkins, R. 2014. *Social identity.* Abingdon: Routledge.

Jin, D.Y. and Yoon, K. 2014. The social mediascape of transnational Korean pop culture: Hallyu 2.0 as spreadable media practice. *New Media & Society* 18(7): 1277–92. doi: 10.1177/1461444814554895.

Jones, H., Gunaratnam, Y., Bhattacharyya, G., Davies, W., Dhaliwal, S., Forkert, K., Jackson, E. and Saltus, R. 2017. *Go home? The politics of immigration controversies.* Oxford University Press.

Kabat-Zinn, J. 2005. *Coming to our senses: Healing ourselves and the world through mindfulness.* New York: Hyperion.

Kahn, J. et al. 2018. How not to talk about race and genetics. BuzzFeed Opinion [open letter]. www.buzzfeed.com/bfopinion/race-genetics-david-reich.

Kamugisha, A. 2007. The coloniality of citizenship in the contemporary anglophone Caribbean. *Race & Class* 49(2): 20–40.

Kant, I. 1784. What is Enlightenment? www.columbia.edu/acis/ets/CCREAD/etscc/kant.html.

Keeley, B. 2015. *Income inequality: The gap between rich and poor.* OECD Insights. Paris: OECD. https://doi.org/10.1787/9789264246010-en.

Kerrigan, D., Jamadar, P., Elahie, E. and Sinanan, T. 2017. Securing equality for all in the administration of justice: the evidence and recommendations. Paper presented at the Caribbean Judicial Dialogue, 30 November–1 December, Trinidad and Tobago.

Khan, S.R. 2012. *Privilege: The making of an adolescent elite at St Paul's School.* Princeton University Press.

Khare, R.S. 2006. *Caste, hierarchy, and individualism: Indian critiques of Louis Dumont's contributions.* New Delhi: Oxford University Press.

Kimmel, M. 2013. *Angry white men: American masculinity at the end of an era.* New York: Nation Books.

Kleinman, A., Yan, Y., Jun, J., Lee, W., Zhang, E., Tianshu, P., Fei, W. and Jinhua G. (eds) 2011. *Deep China: The moral life of the person.* London/Berkeley, CA: University of California Press.

Knorr-Cetina, K. 2009. The synthetic situation: interactionism for a global world. *Symbolic Interaction* 32(1): 61–87.

Kolb, W.L. 1960. Review of: *The Sociological Imagination. American Sociological Review* 25(6): 966–9.

Kurzman, C., Anderson, C., Key, C., Lee, Y.O., Moloney, M., Silver, A. and Van Ryn, M.W. 2007. Celebrity status. *Sociological Theory* 25(4): 347–67.

Kwon, S.H. and Kim, J. 2013. From censorship to active support: the Korean state and Korea's cultural industries. *The Economic and Labour Relations Review* 24(4) 517–32. doi: 10.1177/1035304613508873.

Lambevski, S.A. 2004. Movement and desire: on the need to fluidify academic discourse on sexuality. *GLQ: A Journal of Lesbian and Gay Studies* 10(2): 304–8.

Lamont, M. 2019. From 'having' to 'being': self-worth and the current crisis of American society. *The British Journal of Sociology* 70(3): 660–707.

Lander, E. 2000. La Colonialidad Del Saber: Eurocentrismo y Ciencias Sociales. *Perspectivas Latinoamericanas*. Buenos Aires: CLACSO.

Lankford, A. 2015. Mass shooters in the USA, 1966–2010: differences between attackers who live and die. *Justice Quarterly* 32: 360–79.

Lasch, C. 1984. *The minimal self: Psychic survival in troubled times*. New York/London: W.W. Norton & Company.

Lasswell, H.D. 1936. *Politics: Who gets what, when, how*. New York/London: Whittlesey House McGraw-Hill Book Co.

Latour, B. 2002. *War of the worlds: What about peace?* Chicago, IL: Prickly Paradigm Press.

Latour, B. 2004. Whose cosmos, which cosmopolitics? Comments on the peace terms of Ulrich Beck. *Common Knowledge* 10(3) 450–62.

Lawler, S. 2014. *Identity: Sociological Perspectives*. Cambridge: Polity.

Lee, R.L. 2008. In search of second modernity: reinterpreting reflexive modernization in the context of multiple modernities. *Social Science Information* 47(1): 55–69.

Lee, R.L.M. 2011. Modernity, solidity and agency: liquidity reconsidered. *Sociology* 45(4): 650–64. http://soc.sagepub.com/content/45/4/650%5Cnhttp://soc.sagepub.com/content/45/4/650.full.pdf.

Lengermann, P.M. and Niebrugge, G. 1998. *The women founders: Sociology and social theory, 1830–1930*. New York: McGraw-Hill.

Lenin, V.I. 1917. *Imperialism, the highest stage of capitalism*. Petrograd: Zhizn i Znaniye (Life and Knowledge) Publishers.

Lewis, W.A. 1950. Industrialisation of the British West Indies. *Caribbean Economic Review* 12(May): 1–34.

Liamputtong, P. 2010. *Performing qualitative cross-cultural research*. Cambridge: Cambridge University Press.

Linebaugh, P. 1976. Karl Marx, the theft of wood, and working-class composition: a contribution to the current debate. *Crime and Social Justice* 6: 5–16.

Linebaugh, P. 2014. *Stop, thief! The commons, enclosures and resistance*. Oakland, CA: PM Press.

Locke, J. 2003. *Two treatises of government and a letter concerning toleration*. Edited by I. Shapiro. New Haven/London: Yale University Press.

Loopstra, R. and Lalor, D. 2017. Financial insecurity, food insecurity, and disability: the profile of people receiving emergency food assistance from the Trussell Trust Foodbank Network in Britain. https://trusselltrust.org/wp-content/uploads/sites/2/2017/06/OU_Report_final_01_08_online.pdf

Lorde, A. 1983. There is no hierarchy of oppressions. *Bulletin: Homophobia and Education*, 14(3/4): 9.

Lorde, A. 1984a. The transformation of silence into language and action. In *Sister outsider: Essays and Speeches*. Trumansburg, NY: Crossing Press, pp 40–4.

Lorde, A. 1984b. *Sister outsider: Essays and speeches*. Trumansburg, NY: Crossing Press.

Lowe, S. 2016. A cross to bear: President Nixon's tactical war on drugs policy implemented to destroy the black race. SSRN: https://ssrn.com/abstract=2769997

Lucas Jr, G.R. 2009. *Anthropologists in arms: The ethics of military anthropology*. Plymouth: Altamira Press.

Lugones, M. 2016. The coloniality of gender. In W. Harcourt (ed.) *The Palgrave handbook of gender and development*. New York/Basingstoke: Palgrave Macmillan, pp. 13–33.

Lukes, S. 1990. *Power: A radical view*. New York/Basingstoke: Palgrave Macmillan.

Lupton, D. 2016. Digital companion species and eating data: implications for theorising digital data–human assemblages. *Big Data & Society* 3(1): 205395171561994.

Lyon, D. 2007. *Surveillance studies: An overview*. Cambridge: Polity.

MacFarlane, A. 1978. *The origins of English individualism: The family, property and social transition*. New York: Cambridge University Press.

Macy, S. 2017. 13 Sega franchises we want brought back. IGN Entertainment, 4 August. www.ign.com/articles/2017/08/02/13-sega-franchises-we-want-brought-back.

Madsen, O.J. 2018. *The psychologisation of society: On the unfolding of the therapeutic in Norway*. Abingdon/New York: Routledge.

Mama, A. 2002. Editorial. *Feminist Africa Intellectual Politics* (1):1–8.

Mann, M. 1986. *The sources of social power. Volume I: A history of power from the beginning to 1760 AD*. New York/London: Cambridge University Press.

Mann, M. 2006. The sources of social power revisited: a response to criticism. In J. Hall and R. Schroeder (eds) *An anatomy of power: The social theory of Michael Mann*. Cambridge: Cambridge University Press, pp. 343–96.

Mann, M. 2012. *The sources of social power: Volume 3, global empires and revolution, 1890–1945*. New York: Cambridge University Press.

Manza, J. 2011. Political sociology. In *Oxford bibliographies: Sociology*. https://www. oxfordbibliographies.com/browse?module_0=obo-9780199756384

Marchi, R. 2012. With Facebook, blogs, and fake news, teens reject journalistic 'objectivity'. *Journal of Communication Inquiry* 36(3): 246–62.

Martin, E. 1991. The egg and the sperm: how science has constructed a romance based on stereotypical male–female roles. *Signs: Journal of Women in Culture and Society* 16(3): 485–501.

Marvasti, A.B. 2004. *Qualitative research in sociology: An introduction*. London: SAGE Publications.

Marx, K. 2008. *Capital: An abridged edition*. Oxford: Oxford University Press..

Marx, K. and Engels, F. 1988. *Economic and philosophic manuscripts of 1844 and the communist manifesto*. New York: Prometheus Books.

Marx, K. and Engels, F. 1998. *The German ideology: Includes theses on Feuerbach*. New York: Prometheus Books.

Mascia-Lees, F.E., Sharpe, P. and Cohen, C.B. 1989. The postmodernist turn in anthropology: cautions from a feminist perspective. *Signs: Journal of Women in Culture and Society* 15(1): 7–33.

May, V.M. 2007. *Anna Julia Cooper, visionary black feminist: A critical introduction*. Abingdon: Taylor & Francis.

May, V. 2013. *Connecting self to society: Belonging in a changing world*. Basingstoke: Palgrave Macmillan.

Mayors Against Illegal Guns. 2013. Analysis of recent mass shootings (January 2009–September 2013). http://libcloud.s3. amazonaws.com/9/56/4/1242/1/analysis-of-recent-mass-shootings.pdf.

McFarland, D.A. and McFarland, H.R. 2015. Big data and the danger of being precisely inaccurate. *Big Data & Society* 2(2): 2053951715602495.

Mead, G.H. 1934. *Mind, self and society from the standpoint of a social behaviorist*. Edited by C.W. Morris. Chicago, IL/London: University of Chicago Press.

Meeks, B. and Girvan, N. (eds) 2010. *Caribbean reasonings: The thought of new world, the quest for decolonisation*. Jamaica: Ian Randle Publishers.

Mendes, K., Ringrose, J. and Keller, J. 2018. # MeToo and the promise and pitfalls of challenging rape culture through digital feminist activism. *European Journal of Women's Studies* 25(2): 236–46.

Mignolo, W.D. 2011a. Geopolitics of sensing and knowing: on (de)coloniality, border thinking and epistemic disobedience. *Postcolonial Studies* 14(3): 273–83.

Mignolo, W.D. 2011b. *The Darker Side of Western Modernity: Global Futures, Decolonial Options*. Durham, NC: Duke University Press

Mignolo, W.D. 2014. Spirit out of bounds returns to the East: the closing of the social sciences and the opening of independent thoughts. *Current Sociology* 62(4): 584–602.

Milanovic, B. 2011. *The haves and the have-nots: A brief and idiosyncratic history of global inequality*. New York: Basic Books.

Milanovic, B. 2016. *Global inequality: A new approach for the age of globalization.* Cambridge, MA: Belknap Press.

Miller, A. 2008. A critique of positive psychology – or the new science of happiness. *Journal of Philosophy of Education* 42: 591–608.

Miller, V., VeneKlasen, L., Reilly, M. and Clark, C. 2006. *Making change happen (3): Power. Concepts for revisioning power for justice, equality and peace.* Washington, DC: Just Associates.

Mills, C.W. 1939. Language, logic and culture. *American Sociological Review* 4(5): 670–80.

Mills, C.W. 1940a. Methodological consequences of the sociology of knowledge. *American Journal of Sociology* 46(3): 316–30.

Mills, C.W. 1940b. Situated actions and vocabularies of motive. *American Sociological Review* 5(6): 904–13.

Mills, C.W. 1943. The professional ideology of social pathologists. *American Journal of Sociology* 49(2): 165–80.

Mills, C.W. 1945. The powerless people: the social role of the intellectual. *Bulletin of the American Association of University Professors* 31(2): 231–43.

Mills, C.W. 1946. The middle classes in middle-sized cities: the stratification and political position of small business and white collar strata. *American Sociological Review* 11(5), 520–9.

Mills, C.W. 1948. *The new men of power: America's labor leaders.* New York: Harcourt, Brace and Company.

Mills, C.W. 1951. *White collar: The American middle classes.* New York: Oxford University Press.

Mills, C.W. 1953. Two styles of research in current social studies. *Philosophy of Science* 20(4): 266–75.

Mills, C.W. 1956. *The power elite.* New York: Oxford University Press.

Mills, C.W. 1958. *The causes of World War Three.* New York: Simon and Schuster.

Mills, C.W. 1958. The structure of power in American society. *British Journal of Sociology* 9(1): 29–41.

Mills, C.W. 1959. *The sociological imagination.* London: Oxford University Press.

Mills, C.W. 1960. *Images of man: The classic tradition in sociological thinking,* New York: George Braziller.

Mills, C.W. 1960. *Listen, Yankee: The revolution in Cuba.* New York: McGraw-Hill.

Mills, C.W. 1962. *The Marxists.* New York: Dell Publishing.

Mills, C.W. 1963. *Sociology and pragmatism: The higher learning in America.* Edited by I.L. Horowitz. New York: Oxford University Press.

Mills, C.W. 1999. *The racial contract.* Ithaca, NY/London: Cornell University Press.

Mills, C.W. 2008. Racial liberalism. *PMLA* 123(5): 1380–97. www.jstor.org/stable/25501942.

Mills, C.W., Senior, C. and Goldsen, R.K. 1950. *The Puerto Rican journey: New York's newest migrants.* New York: Harper & Bros.

Milner, M. 2010. Is celebrity a new kind of status system? *Society* 47(5): 379–87.

Mindfulness for Students. 2017. Mindfulness courses at UK universities. http://mindfulnessforstudents.co.uk/mindfulness-courses-at-uk-universities/.

Mirowski, P. 2013. *Never let a serious crisis go to waste: How neoliberalism survived the financial meltdown*. London: Verso.

Misztal, B. 2000. The sociological imagination. *Journal of Sociology* 37(1): 104–5.

Mjøset, L. 2013. The fate of the sociological imagination: Mills, social science and contemporary sociology. In J. Scott and A. Nilsen (eds) *C. Wright Mills and the sociological imagination: Contemporary perspectives*. Cheltenham: Edward Elgar, pp. 57–87.

Mohammed, P. 1994. Nuancing the feminist discourse in the Caribbean. *Social and Economic Studies* 41(2): 135–67.

Mohanty, C.T., Russo, A. and Torres, L. 1991. *Third world women and the politics of feminism*. Bloomington, IN: Indiana University Press.

Moreton-Robinson, A. 2009. Imagining the good indigenous citizen: race war and the pathology of patriarchal white sovereignty. *Cultural Studies Review* 15(2): 61.

Morgan, P. (2014) *The terror and the time: Banal violence and trauma in Caribbean discourse*. Kingston: University of the West Indies Press.

Münch, R. 2016. Academic capitalism. *Oxford Research Encyclopedia of Politics*. Online publication date: May. DOI: 10.1093/acrefore/9780190228637.013.15

Mützel, S. 2015. Facing big data: making sociology relevant. *Big Data & Society* 2(2): 2053951715599179.

Nash, K. 2001. The 'cultural turn' in social theory: towards a theory of cultural politics. *Sociology* 35(1): 77–92.

NatCen Social Research. 2017. *British Social Attitudes Survey: The 34th report* [data collection]. UK Data Service. http://doi.org/10.5255/UKDA-SN-8252-1.

Nehring, D. 2009a. Cultural models of intimate life in contemporary urban Mexico: a review of self-help texts. *Delaware Review of Latin American Studies* 10(2).

Nehring, D. 2009b. Modernity with limits: the narrative construction of intimate relationships, sex and social change in Carlos Cuauhtemoc Sanchez's *Juventud en extasis*. *Sexualities* 12(1): 33–59.

Nehring, D. and Kerrigan, D. 2018a. *Therapeutic worlds: Popular psychology and the socio-cultural organisation of intimate life*. Basingstoke: Routledge.

Nehring, D. and Kerrigan, D. 2018b. Thin selves: Popular psychology and the transnational moral grammar of self-identity. *Consumption Markets & Culture*: 1–23.

Nehring, D., Alvarado, E., Hendriks, E.C. and Kerrigan, D. 2016. *Transnational popular psychology and the global self-help industry: The politics of contemporary social change*. Basingstoke: Palgrave Macmillan.

Newman, J. 2013. Spaces of power: feminism, neoliberalism and gendered labor. *Social Politics* 20(2): 200–21.

Nisbet, R. 1976. *Sociology as an art form*. New York: Oxford University Press.

Nussbaum, M. 2010. *Not for profit: Why democracy needs the humanities*. Princeton: Princeton University Press.

O'Donnell, J., Chávez Chávez, R. and Pruyn, M. 2004. Situating the discourse of social justice in these times. In J. O'Donnell, R. Chávez Chávez and M. Pruyn (eds) *Social justice in these times*. Charlotte, NC: Information Age Publishing, pp. 3–15.

O'Neil, C. 2017. *Weapons of math destruction: How big data increases inequality and threatens democracy*. London: Penguin Books.

Oakley, A. 1974. *The sociology of housework*. New York: Pantheon Books/Random House.

Offer, J. 2010. *Herbert Spencer and social theory*. Basingstoke: Palgrave Macmillan.

Omobowale, A.O. and Akanle, O. 2017. Asuwada epistemology and globalised sociology: challenges of the South. *Sociology* 51(1): 43–59.

ONS (Office for National Statistics) 2019. Crime in England and Wales: year ending March 2019. www.ons.gov.uk/peoplepopulationandcommunity/crimeandjustice/bulletins/crimeinenglandandwales/yearendingmarch2019

Oxaal, I. 1968. *Black intellectuals come to power: The rise of Creole nationalism in Trinidad and Tobago*. Cambridge, MA: Schenkman Publishing Company.

Oxaal, I. 1971. *Race and revolutionary consciousness: A documentary interpretation of the 1970 black power revolt in Trinidad*. Cambridge, MA/London: Schenkman Books.

Pager, D. and Shepherd, H. 2008. The sociology of discrimination: racial discrimination in employment, housing, credit, and consumer markets. *Annual Review of Sociology* 34: 181–209.

Pantucci, R. 2011. A typology of lone wolves: preliminary analysis of lone Islamist terrorists. *Developments in Radicalisation and Political Violence* (March). London: ICSR.

Parkin, J.C. 2012. *F**k it therapy: The profane way to profound happiness*. [ePdf] London: Hay House.

Parsons, T. 1939. The professions and social structure. *Social Forces* 17(4): 457–67.

Parsons, T. 1957. The distribution of power in American society. *World Politics* 10(1): 123–43.

Pascale, R., Sternin, J. and Sternin, M. 2010. *The power of positive deviance: How unlikely innovators solve the world's toughest problems*. Boston, MA: Harvard Business Press.

Peck, J. 2010. *Constructions of neoliberal reason*. Oxford: Oxford University Press.

Pérez-Álvarez, M. 2016. The science of happiness: as felicitous as it is fallacious. *Journal of Theoretical and Philosophical Psychology* 36(1): 1–19.

Phelps, J. 2018. Trump calls for raising minimum age to buy all guns to 21. ABC News, 28 February. http://abcnews.go.com/Politics/president-trump-vows-care-bump-stocks-executive-action/story?id=53421961.

Pieterse, J.N. 2016. New modernities: what's new? In E.G Rodríguez, M. Boatcǎ and S. Costa (eds) *Decolonizing European sociology*. New York: Routledge, pp. 99–116.

Piketty, T. 2014. *Capital in the twenty-first century*. Cambridge, MA: Belknap Press.

Pink, S., Ruckenstein, M., Willim, R. and Duque, M. 2018. Broken data: conceptualising data in an emerging world. *Big Data & Society* 5(1): 2053951717753228.

Platt, J. 1998. *A brief history of the ISA: 1948–1997*. Madrid: International Sociological Association/ISA.

Plummer, K. 2016. *Sociology: The basics*. Abingdon: Routledge.

Polanyi, K. 1944. *The great transformation: The political and economic origins of our time*. Boston, MA: Beacon Press.

Polletta, F. and Callahan, J. 2017. Deep stories, nostalgia narratives, and fake news: storytelling in the Trump era. *American Journal of Cultural Sociology* 5(3): 392–408. doi: 10.1057/s41290-017-0037-7.

Powell, C. and Dépelteau, F. (eds) 2013. *Conceptualizing relational sociology: Ontological and theoretical issues*. New York: Palgrave Macmillan.

Prashad, V. 2007. *The darker nations: A people's history of the third world*. London: New Press.

Punch, M. 1986. *The politics and ethics of fieldwork: Muddy boots and grubby hands*. London: SAGE Publications.

Quijano, A. 2000. Coloniality of power, Eurocentrism, and Latin America. *Nepantla: Views from South* 1(3): 533–80.

Quilliam, S. 2003. *Positive thinking*. London: Dorling Kindersley.

Ray, V.E. 2018a. Reproducing inequality in sociology. *Sociological Forum* 34(1): 236–44

Ray, V. 2018b. Why critique inequality in our disciplines? [Blog] Inside Higher Ed, 16 March. www.insidehighered.com/advice/2018/03/16/assessing-inequality-sociology-opinion.

Reddock, R. 1990a. The Caribbean feminist tradition. *Women Speak!* 26/27: 12–17.

Reddock, R. 1990b. Feminism, nationalism and the early women's movement in the English-speaking Caribbean (with special reference to Jamaica and Trinidad and Tobago), in S.R. Cudjoe (ed.) *Caribbean Women Writers: Essays from the First International Conference*. Wellesley: Calaloux Publications, pp. 61-81

Reddock, R. 2014. Radical Caribbean social thought: race, class identity and the postcolonial nation. *Current Sociology* 62(4): 493–511, doi:10.1177/0011392114524507.

Redshaw, S. 2013. Feminist preludes to relational sociology. In C. Powell and F. Dépelteau (eds) *Conceptualizing relational sociology: Ontological and theoretical issues*. New York: Palgrave Macmillan, pp. 13–26.

Reveley, J. 2013. Enhancing the educational subject: cognitive capitalism, positive psychology and well-being training in schools. *Policy Futures in Education* 11(5): 538–48.

Rhys-Taylor, A. 2013. The essences of multiculture: a sensory exploration of an inner-city street market. *Identities* 20(4): 393–406.

Rimke, H. 2010. Remembering the sociological imagination: transdisciplinarity, the genealogical method, and epistemological politics. *International Journal of Interdisciplinary Social Sciences* 5(1): 239–54.

Ritzer, G. 2004. *The globalization of nothing.* London: SAGE Publications.

Rivera, L.A. 2016. *Pedigree: How elite students get elite jobs.* Princeton University Press.

Robertson, R. 1997. Glocalization: time-space and homogeneity-heterogeneity. In M. Featherstone, S. Lash and R. Robertson (eds) *Global modernities.* London: SAGE Publications, pp. 25–44.

Robinson, C.J. 2000. *Black Marxism: The making of the black radical tradition.* Chapel Hill, NC: University of North Carolina Press.

Rochon, T.R. 2000. *Culture moves: Ideas, activism, and changing values.* Princeton University Press.

Rodney, W. 1972. *How Europe underdeveloped Africa.* London/Tanzania: Bogle-L'Ouverture Publications.

Rolfe, J.C. (ed.) 1979. *Suetonius.* London: William Heinemann Ltd.

Rose, H. 1983. Hand, brain, and heart: a feminist epistemology for the natural sciences. *Signs: Journal of Women in Culture and Society* 9(1): 73–90.

Rose, N. 2018. *Our psychiatric future.* Cambridge: Polity.

Rostow, W.W. 1960. *The stages of economic growth.* Cambridge University Press.

Said, E.W. 1993. *Culture and imperialism.* New York: Knopf.

Salandy, T. 2018. Development as ideology: coloniality and epistemic violence in the global south. [preprint] 10.13140/RG.2.2.12539.82727.

Sanda, A.M. 1988. In defence of indigenisation in sociological theories. *International Sociology* 3(2): 189–99.

Santucci, A.A. 2010. *Antonio Gramsci.* New York: Monthly Review Press.

Sassen, S. 2014. *Expulsions: Brutality and complexity in the global economy.* Cambridge, MA: Belknap Press.

Schubert, H.-J. 2006. The foundation of pragmatic sociology: Charles Horton Cooley and George Herbert Mead. *Journal of Classical Sociology* 6(1): 51–74.

Schultz, B. and Sheffer, M.L. (eds) 2015. *Sport and religion in the twenty-first century.* Lanham: Lexington Books.

Scott, J. and Bromley, R.J. 2013. *Envisioning sociology: Victor Branford, Patrick Geddes, and the quest for social reconstruction.* Albany, NY: State University of New York Press.

Scott, J. and Nilsen, A. (eds) 2013. *C. Wright Mills and the sociological imagination: Contemporary perspectives.* Cheltenham: Edward Elgar.

Scott, J.C. 2014. *Two cheers for anarchism: Six easy pieces on autonomy, dignity, and meaningful work and play.* Princeton University Press.

Sedgwick, E.K. 1990. *Epistemology of the closet.* Berkeley, CA: University of California Press.

Seepersad, R. 2016. *Crime and violence in Trinidad and Tobago*. IDB Series on Crime and Violence in the Caribbean. IDB Technical Note 1062. Washington: Inter-American Development Bank.

Seepersad, R. and Wortley, S. 2017. Ethnicity and crime victimisation in Trinidad and Tobago. In K.J. Joosen and C.A. Bailey (eds) *Caribbean Crime and Criminal Justice Impacts of Post-Colonialism and Gender*. London/New York: Routledge.

Shaw, I. and Taplin, S. 2007. Happiness and mental health policy: a sociological critique. *Journal of Mental Health* 16(3): 359–73.

Shaw, R. 2015. Big data and reality. *Big Data & Society* 2(2): 2053951715608877.

Shildrick, T. and Rucell, J. 2015. *Sociological perspectives on poverty*. York: Joseph Rowntree Foundation.

Shils, E. 1961. Professor Mills on the calling of sociology. *World Politics* 13(4): 600–21.

Sian, K.P. 2019. *Navigating institutional racism in British universities*. Cham, Switzerland: Palgrave Macmillan.

Simmel, G. 1950. *The sociology of Georg Simmel*. Edited and transl. by K.H. Wolff. Glencoe, IL: Free Press.

Simmel, G. 2011. *The philosophy of money*. London: Routledge.

Slobodian, Q. 2018. *Globalists: The end of empire and the birth of neoliberalism*. Cambridge, MA: Harvard University Press

Smart, C. 2007. *Personal life: New directions in sociological thinking*. Cambridge: Polity.

Smith, A. 1999. *An inquiry into the nature and causes of the wealth of nations*. London: Penguin. doi: 10.2307/2221259.

Smith, D. 1987. *The everyday world as problematic: A feminist sociology*. Toronto: University of Toronto Press.

Smith, G.J.D. 2018. Data doxa: the affective consequences of data practices. *Big Data & Society* 5(1): 2053951717751551.

Smith, M. 2007. Glocalization. In *The Blackwell Encyclopedia of Sociology*. Oxford: John Wiley & Sons. http://doi.wiley.com/10.1002/9781405165518.wbeosg060

Sorkin, D. 1983. Wilhelm Von Humboldt: the theory and practice of self-formation (Bildung), 1791–1810. *Journal of the History of Ideas* 44(1): 55–73.

Spencer, H. 2017. *First principles*. [POD] CreateSpace Independent Publishing Platform.

Springer, S., Birch, K. and MacLeavy, J. 2016. *Handbook of neoliberalism*. New York/London: Routledge.

Steinmetz, G. 2005. Return to empire: the new US imperialism in comparative historical perspective. *Sociological Theory* 23(4): 339–67.

Steinmetz, G. 2007. American sociology before and after World War II: the (temporary) settling of a disciplinary field. In C. Calhoun (ed.) *Sociology in America: A History*. Chicago, IL: University of Chicago Press, pp. 314–66.

Steinmetz, G. 2013a. A child of empire: British sociology and colonialism, 1940s–1960s. *Journal of the History of the Behavioral Sciences* 49(4): 353–78.

Steinmetz, G. 2013b. Major contributions to sociological theory and research on empire, 1830s–present. In G. Steinmetz (ed.) *Sociology and empire: The imperial entanglements of a discipline*. Durham, NC: Duke University Press, p. 632.

Steinmetz, G. 2014. Defensive anthropology, *Postcolonial Studies* 17(4): 436–50. doi: 10.1080/13688790.2014.963928.

Stone, C. (1980) *Clientelism and democracy in Jamaica*. New Brunswick: Transaction Books.

Storrs, D. 2009. Teaching Mills in Tokyo: developing a sociological imagination through storytelling. *Teaching Sociology* 37(1): 31–46. http://tso.sagepub. com/cgi/content/abstract/37/1/31%5Cnhttp://tso.sagepub.com/cgi/ doi/10.1177/0092055X0903700104.

Summers, J.H. (ed.) 2008. *The politics of truth: Selected writings of C. Wright Smith*. Oxford: Oxford University Press.

Sussman, R.W. 2014. *The myth of race: The troubling persistence of an unscientific idea*. Cambridge, MA: Harvard University Press.

Swain, H. 2016. Mindfulness: the craze sweeping through schools is now at a university near you. *The Guardian*, 26 January, www.theguardian.com/ education/2016/jan/26/mindfulness-craze-schools-university-near-you- cambridge.

Swidler, A. 2003. *Talk of love: How culture matters*. Chicago, IL: University of Chicago Press.

Tan, H. 2016. From K-Pop to fried chicken: how South Korea became a trendsetter. CNBC, 9 June. www.cnbc.com/2016/06/09/from-k-pop-to-fried- chicken-how-south-korea-became-a-trendsetter-in-china-and-beyond.html.

Tett, Gillian. 2015. *The silo effect: Why putting everything in its place isn't such a bright idea*. London: Little, Brown

Thomas, D.A. 2006. Demeaned but empowered: the social power of the urban poor in Jamaica. *Social and Economic Studies* 55(1-2): 191–205. http://repository. upenn.edu/anthro_papers/58.

Thompson, E.P. 1960. *Out of apathy: Essays*. London: Stevens.

Thompson, E.P. 1967. Time, work–discipline, and industrial capitalism. *Past and Present* 38(1): 56–97.

Tilley, L. 2017. Resisting piratic method by doing research otherwise. *Sociology* 51(1): 27–42. https://doi.org/10.1177/0038038516656992.

Tilly, C. 1999. *Durable inequality*. Berkeley, CA: University of California Press.

Tomaskovic-Devey, D. 2011. The politics and practice of sociology in the courts. *Sociological Methods & Research* 40 (4): 621–34.

Tomlinson, A. and Young, C. (eds) 2006. *German football: History, culture, society*. Abingdon: Routledge.

Townsend, D. 2009. *No other life: Gangs, guns and governance in Trinidad and Tobago*. Geneva, Switzerland: Small Arms Survey.

Treas, J. and Tai, T. 2016. Gender inequality in housework across 20 European nations: lessons from gender stratification theories. *Sex Roles* 74(11–12): 495–511.

Treviño, A. Javier. 2011. *The social thought of C. Wright Mills.* Thousand Oaks, CA: Pine Forge Press.

Turner, J. 2003. *The structure of sociological theory.* 7th edn. Wadsworth Thomson Learning USA.

UNDP. 2016. *Human development report 2016: Trinidad and Tobago.* http://hdr. undp.org/sites/all/themes/hdr_theme/country-notes/es/TTO.pdf

University of Aberdeen. 2017. MSc Studies in Mindfulness. www.abdn.ac.uk/ education/degrees-programmes/studies-in-mindfulness-pgcertpgdipmsc-407. php.

University of Bangor. 2017a. The 8-week mindfulness course. www.bangor. ac.uk/mindfulness/8weekcourse.php.en.

University of Bangor. 2017b. Welcome to the Centre for Mindfulness Practice and Research. www.bangor.ac.uk/mindfulness/.

UNODC (United Nations Office on Drugs and Crime). 2014. *Global study on homicide 2013.* Vienna: United Nations Publications. https://data.unodc.org/

Varley-Winter, O. and Shah, H. 2016. The opportunities and ethics of big data: practical priorities for a national council of data ethics. *Philosophical Transactions of the Royal Society A: Mathematical, Physical and Engineering Sciences* 374.

VeneKlasen, L. and Miller, V. 2002. Power and empowerment. *PLA Notes* 43: 39–41.

VeneKlasen, L., Miller, V., Budlender, D. and Clark, C. (eds) 2002. *A new weave of power, people & politics: The action guide for advocacy and citizen participation.* Oklahoma City: World Neighbors.

Venn, C. 2009. Neoliberal political economy, biopolitics and colonialism: a transcolonial genealogy of inequality. *Theory, Culture & Society* 26(6): 206–33.

Vidich, A.J. 1954. Review of Gerth, H. and Mills, C. *Character and social structure. Man*, 185 (August): 124–5.

Virilio, P. 1997. *Open sky.* London: Verso.

Virilio, P. 2000. *Polar inertia.* London: SAGE Publications.

Wagley, C. 1965. On the concept of social race in the Americas, in D.B. Heath and R.N. Adams (eds) *Contemporary cultures and societies of Latin America.* New York: Random House, pp. 531–45.

Wajcman, J. 2015. *Pressed for time: The acceleration of life in digital capitalism.* Chicago, IL/London: University of Chicago Press.

Walker, A. 1983. *In search of our mothers' garden: Womanist prose by Alice Walker.* San Diego/New York/London: Harcourt Brace Jovanovich.

Wardle, H. and Obermuller, L. 2019. 'Windrush generation' and 'hostile environment': symbols and lived experiences in Caribbean migration to the UK. *Migration and Society* 2(1): 81–9.

Watson, H.A. (ed.) 2015. *Globalization, sovereignty and citizenship in the Caribbean*. Mona: University of the West Indies Press.

Watts, R. 2017. *Public universities, managerialism and the value of higher education*. New York/Basingstoke: Palgrave Macmillan.

Weale, S. 2016. Privately educated elite continues to take top jobs, finds survey. *The Guardian2*, 24 February. www.theguardian.com/education/2016/feb/24/privately-educated-elite-continues-to-take-top-jobs-finds-survey.

Weber, M. 1949. *The methodology of the social sciences*. Glencoe, IL: Free Press.

Weber, M. 1965. *Politics as a vocation*. Philadelphia, PA: Fortress Press.

Weber, M. 1968. *The religion of China*. Glencoe, IL: Free Press.

Weber, M. 1978. *Economy and society: An outline of interpretive sociology*. Berkeley, CA: University of California Press.

Weber, M. 1994. *Weber: Political writings* (Cambridge Texts in the History of Political Thought). Edited by P. Lassman and R. Speirs. Cambridge: Cambridge University Press. doi: 10.1017/CBO9781107415324.004.

Weber, M. 2001. *The Protestant ethic and the spirit of capitalism*. London: Routledge.

Weeden, K.A. and Grusky, D.B. 2005. The case for a new class map. *American Journal of Sociology* 111(1): 141–212.

Weick, K.E. and Putnam, T. 2006. Organizing for mindfulness: Eastern wisdom and Western knowledge. *Journal of Management Inquiry* 15(3): 275–287. doi: 10.1177/1056492606291202.

Welz, G. 2008. Multiple modernities – the transnationalization of cultures. In F. Schulze-Engler and S. Helff (eds) *Transcultural English Studies: Theories, Fictions, Realities*. Cross Cultures 102/ASNEL Papers 12. Amsterdam/New York: Rodopi, pp. 37–57.

Whitehead, N.L. 2009. Ethnography, torture and the human terrain/terror systems. *Fast Capitalism* 5(2).

Wilkinson, I. 2012. With and beyond Mills: social suffering and the sociological imagination. *Cultural Studies–Critical Methodologies* 12(3): 182–191.

Wilkinson, I. and Kleinman, A. 2016. *A passion for society: How we think about human suffering*. Berkeley, CA: University of California Press.

Williams, C.L. 1992. The glass escalator: hidden advantages for men in the 'female' professions. *Social Problems* 39(3): 253–77.

Williams, C.L. 2013. The glass escalator, revisited: gender inequality in neoliberal times, SWS feminist lecturer. *Gender & Society* 27(5): 609–29.

Williams, E. 1994. *Capitalism and slavery*. Chapel Hill, NC: University of North Carolina Press.

Williams, J. 2012. *Consuming higher education: Why learning can't be bought*. London: Bloomsbury Academic.

Williams, M. and Penman, D. 2011. *Mindfulness: A practical guide to finding peace in a frantic world*. London: Piatkus.

Wimberley, R.C. 2008. Sociology with a Southern face: why are we sociologists and what are we doing about it in the South? *Social Forces* 86(3): 881–909. https://doi.org/10.1353/sof.0.0020.

Wingfield, A.H. 2009. Racializing the glass escalator: reconsidering men's experiences with women's work. *Gender & Society* 23(1): 5–26.

Wodak, R. 2015. *The politics of fear: What right-wing populist discourses mean.* London: SAGE Publications.

Wolff, R.D. 2016. *Capitalism's crisis deepens: Essays on the global economic meltdown 2010-2014.* Chicago, IL: Haymarket Books.

Wolff, R.D. 2018. Capitalism as obstacle to equality and democracy: the US story. *CounterPunch*, 23 February. www.counterpunch.org/2018/02/23/capitalism-as-obstacle-to-equality-and-democracy-the-us-story/

Wright, E.O. 2000. *Class counts:Student edition.* Cambridge: Cambridge University Press.

Wright, E.O. 2015. *Understanding class.* London: Verso Books. Ebook collection (EBSCOhost) http://search.ebscohost.com/login.aspx?direct=true&scope=site&db=nlebk&db=nlabk&AN=891072.

Yan, Y. 2009. *The individualization of Chinese society.* Oxford: Berg.

Yang, J. 2012. *Song wennuan*, 'sending warmth': unemployment, new urban poverty, and the affective state in China. *Ethnography* 14(1): 104–25.

Young, I.M. 2008. Structural injustice and the politics of difference. In G. Craig, T. Burchardt and D. Gordon (eds) *Social justice and public policy: Seeking fairness in diverse societies.* Bristol: Policy Press.

Young, M. and Woodiwiss, M. 2019. Organised crime and security threats in Caribbean Small Island Developing States: a critical analysis of US assumptions and policies. *The European Review of Organised Crime* 5(1): 85–117.

Yuval-Davis, N., Wemyss, G. and Cassidy, K. 2018. Everyday bordering, belonging and the reorientation of British immigration legislation. *Sociology* 52(2): 228–44.

Zuboff, S. 2015. Big Other: surveillance capitalism and the prospects of an information civilization. *Journal of Information Technology* 30(1): 75–89.

Zuboff, S. 2019. *The age of surveillance capitalism: The fight for a human future at the new frontier of power.* London: Profile Books.

Index

Note: Page locators in *italic* refer to tables.